"Barry and Emily McCarthy continue to produce high-quality, highly relevant, and extremely readable books that can be enjoyed by professional and lay readers alike. In their most recent collaboration, they address the complexities of male sexuality. Male sexuality is often misunderstood as being simple, straightforward, and unsophisticated. The authors quickly debunk that myth and recognize that male sexuality is every bit as complex and nuanced as female sexuality. With beautifully presented case studies, as well as thoughtfully designed behavioral exercises, the McCarthys have given us a book that will not only make men better men, but also make them better relationship partners. I am certain to recommend this book to many, many of my patients."

— *Daniel N. Watter, Ed.D., past president, The Society for*
Sex Therapy and Research (SSTAR)

"*Contemporary Male Sexuality* is well written and with very clear and direct messages which are easy to understand. This will be a very valuable contribution to a new model of male sexuality from two of the most preeminent and prolific authors in the history of sex therapy."

— *Pedro Nobre, professor of psychology, Porto University, Portugal;*
president of the World Association for Sexual Health

"I am pleased to have the opportunity to endorse this insightful and timely book by Barry and Emily McCarthy. In an era of changing sex roles and sexual polemics, the McCarthys offer a clear perspective and guidepost for couples. They emphasize that male and female sexuality are both complex and that both sexes are more similar than dissimilar. The goal should be empower both members in a relationship to develop their mutual manner of sharing intimacy and to celebrate their uniqueness as individuals and as a couple. This is the fifteenth book co-authored by the McCarthys and written for the general public. In my opinion, this text is their best."

—*R. Taylor Segraves, MD, editor,* Journal of Sex and Marital Therapy

"This timely book belongs on every mental health professional's shelf, as it adds important knowledge and perspective, yet is written in a style accessible to the general public. Emily and Barry McCarthy identify the dangers of toxic male behavior and attitudes, yet sensitively express how male sexuality is more complex and nuanced than portrayed in the media; emphasizing that males do not belong on a pedestal nor should they be shamed. The McCarthys offer both a solution and a pathway to it, utilizing their models of female-male sexual equity and Good Enough Sex (GES), that promote acceptance and valuing male and couple sexuality."

— *Michael A. Perelman, PhD, co-director, Human Sexuality*
Program and clinical professor emeritus of psychology in
psychiatry, Weill Cornell Medicine, NewYork-Presbyterian

"The dynamic duo of Barry and Emily McCarthy have written another blockbuster presenting their vision for transforming the manner in which men, women and couples think about and engage in lovemaking. While this volume focuses on men's sexuality, be they young or old, gay, straight or unconventional, it goes beyond the man and stresses the importance of the partner and the relationship. There are chapters on sexual desire, erection, ejaculatory disorders, sexual orientation, compulsive sexual behaviors, fetishes and affairs describing the McCarthys' unique vision on these distressing issues and varied solutions as to how they might be resolved.

Mythbusters, Barry and Emily McCarthy rip apart the destructive influence on boys and men regarding traditional sex roles and sexual expectations in the Western world and how these destructive influences lead to sexual and relationship dysfunction. Each chapter is filled with scientific information on the development of sexual and relationship problems, alternative solutions to these difficulties as well as case illustrations and recommended exercises for men to gain a deeper understanding of the issues. This is definitely a book I would use with patients in my clinical practice to augment our therapy sessions."

— *Stanley E. Althof, PhD, executive director, Center for Marital and Sexual Health of South Florida; professor emeritus, Case Western Reserve University School of Medicine*

CONTEMPORARY MALE SEXUALITY

This accessible guide confronts myths and pressures surrounding men and sex, promoting a positive and healthy model of male sexuality that replaces traditional expectations.

The chapters in this book engage with cultural assumptions about male sexuality, from harmful early messaging, to the importance of enjoying intimacy, pleasure, and eroticism over the age of 60. The authors challenge the effects of toxic masculinity and traditional gendered roles in sex, celebrating sexual diversity, confronting double standards, and empowering men and couples to develop an equitable sexual bond. Case studies and psychosexual skill exercises are integrated throughout to make each concept personal and concrete, and incorporate the Good Enough Sex (GES) model to promote an authentic sexual self throughout the lifespan.

With a focus on mutual consent and pleasure, *Contemporary Male Sexuality* offers a new model of male sexuality that helps men and couples achieve a satisfying, secure, and sexual bond, replacing damaging expectations with healthy sexual values.

Barry McCarthy and **Emily McCarthy** are a writing team. Barry is a professor emeritus of psychology, a diplomate in clinical psychology, a diplomate in sex therapy, and a certified couple therapist. He has authored 120 professional articles, 33 book chapters, and 22 books. In addition, Barry has presented 450 professional workshops nationally and internationally. He received the Masters and Johnson award for lifetime contributions to the sex therapy field. Emily McCarthy received a B.S. degree in speech communication. Her writing and wisdom provides a balanced, humanistic perspective to issues of male and couple sexuality. This is their fifteenth co-authored book.

CONTEMPORARY MALE SEXUALITY

Confronting Myths and Promoting Change

Barry McCarthy and Emily McCarthy

Routledge
Taylor & Francis Group

NEW YORK AND LONDON

First published 2021
by Routledge
52 Vanderbilt Avenue, New York, NY 10017

and by Routledge
2 Park Square, Milton Park, Abingdon, Oxon, OX14 4RN

Routledge is an imprint of the Taylor & Francis Group, an informa business

Library of Congress Cataloging-in-Publication Data
A catalog record for this title has been requested

ISBN: 978-0-367-42721-4 (hbk)
ISBN: 978-0-367-42720-7 (pbk)
ISBN: 978-0-367-85460-7 (ebk)

Typeset in Perpetua
by codeMantra

CONTENTS

1

MEN ARE NOT SIMPLE

Promoting Male and Couple Sexuality

One of the best-selling books in the history of "pop psych" was "Men are from Mars, Women are from Venus", including spin-off books such as "Mars and Venus in the Bedroom". These simplistic, humorous books were based on the mistaken assumption that relationally and sexually, men and women are entirely different species. The individual male sex performance model was glorified as the natural way to be sexual-easy arousal, totally predictable intercourse, and reliable orgasms. Men were simple sexually, while women were emotionally and sexually complex. The challenge for women was to catch up to the sexually superior man. Female sexuality was inferior.

This book presents a very different model of male and couple sexuality. Psychologically, relationally, and sexually, there are many more similarities than differences between men and women, especially those in a married or partnered relationship (Hyde, 2005). Both men and women are complex, not simple. This is especially true sexually. A key for healthy sexuality is to accept the individual responsibility/intimate sexual team model. Each person is responsible for your sexuality. It is not the man's responsibility to give the woman desire or an orgasm. Nor is it her responsibility to convince him to value intimacy and pleasuring. Each partner affirms the value of the new sexual mantra —desire/pleasure/eroticism/satisfaction (Foley, Kope, & Sugrue, 2012). Male, female, and couple sexuality are complex with large individual, couple, cultural, and value differences. Sexually, one size never fits all. Value your individual and couple uniqueness.

Understanding and accepting the complexity of male sexuality are healthier than putting men on a sexual pedestal or demonizing men. In the media, on the internet, and in bookstores, male sexuality is viewed as simple, predictable, and one-dimensional. Sadly, the focus is on destructive male sexual behavior – child sexual abuse, rape, affairs, sexual harassment, inability to express emotions, relational ignorance, and sexual entitlement. Our culture engages in male blaming and shaming.

In this book, we explore the strengths and vulnerabilities of men and male sexuality. We carefully assess the psychological, bio-medical, and social/relational factors that promote and support sexuality as well as confront destructive male sexuality. Knowledge is power. We provide information and guidelines so that you can make "wise" sexual decisions (wise means it works emotionally and practically, in the short and long terms). You deserve for sex to have a 15–20% positive role in your life and relationship. Rather than the "war between the sexes", we provide a positive and realistic approach to male sexuality which empowers and motivates both partners to make wise decisions. Male sexuality is more complex and nuanced than portrayed in the media. Males do not belong on a pedestal nor should they be shamed. Understanding male sexuality from the perspective of psychological, bio-medical, and social/relational factors is valuable for you and your relationship. This book is addressed to men, women, couples, and clinicians. We focus on mainstream heterosexual married and partnered men. In addition, we honor diversity and non-traditional values in sexuality and relationships.

In a previous book, "Finding Your Sexual Voice: Celebrating Female Sexuality" (McCarthy & McCarthy, 2019a), we strongly argued that female sexuality is first-class, not inferior to male sexuality. Female sexuality is more variable, flexible, complex, and individualistic. Sexuality is healthy when men and women are intimate and erotic allies. Treat your partner in a respectful and trusting manner. This is much more than socially desirable words. It entails changing attitudes, behavior, emotions, and accepting new values about gender and sexuality.

We emphasize the importance of recognizing vulnerabilities and challenges in order to achieve female-male sexual equity. Each gender has vulnerabilities which can subvert or even poison sexuality. Rather than blaming men and feeling oppressed by male sexuality, the woman's challenge is to strengthen her sexual voice (especially her power to veto sexual scenarios which are aversive) and replace these with healthy sexual attitudes, behavior, and emotions. Healthy sexual attitudes and values promote psychological, relational, and sexual well-being.

Vulnerabilities for men are different than vulnerabilities for women. A major vulnerability is the difficulty giving up the individual perfect sex performance demand and replacing it with variable, flexible, pleasure-oriented couple sexuality. Although gender vulnerabilities are different, the challenges for healthy couple sexuality are similar. Affirm that desire/pleasure/eroticism/satisfaction is the essence of couple sexuality. Understanding the complexity of male sexuality promotes being an intimate sexual team. Be clear what you value sexually. Create a respectful, trusting, emotional commitment. As well, confront and change components of male sexuality which are oppressive and unacceptable.

We explore healthy and unhealthy components of male sexuality to increase awareness and understanding so you're in a position to make wise personal, relational, and sexual decisions. You deserve a healthy sexual relationship.

It is crucial to challenge the belief that love and sex are magical, so when you find your "soul mate", all you need is loving communication. Inherent in the romantic love/soul mate model is the mistaken notion that sex is the man's domain with the woman following his sexual lead. The myth "As long as you are in love everything will be fine" has caused untold damage to relationships throughout generations and cultures.

On the other extreme, confront the cynicism that results from labeling men as sexual predators. Barry remembers a professional workshop where a female participant yelled "All men are rapists. Given the opportunity all men will rape". Cynicism about men and male sexuality causes women to be hypervigilant and defensive. This is not in anyone's best interest. Certainly, there are men whose sexual attitudes and behavior are toxic (we will confront this in Chapter 3), but they are in the minority. The great majority of men want a healthy emotional and sexual relationship. There is solid scientific evidence that men benefit from a respectful, trusting, intimate marriage even more than women (Stanley, Rhoades, & Whitton, 2010). Single, divorced, or widowed men are more vulnerable to emotional distress and physical illness than married men. Culturally, men are not supposed to value women or an intimate relationship, doing so only for sex. Like so much in our culture, this is based on simplistic myths not genuine scientific understanding about men, women, couples, and sexuality.

The Myth of Male Sexuality

A core male learning is that sex function is easy, predictable, in his control, and most important "autonomous". As an adolescent and young adult, he has spontaneous erections, intercourse, and orgasm, needing nothing from his partner. This is the basis for the assumption that male sexuality is stronger and better than female sexuality. Most males experience first orgasm between ages 10 and 14 with either nocturnal emission or masturbation. Very few males experience their first orgasm during partner sex. First orgasm during partner sex occurs between ages 15 and 21 with manual, oral, intercourse, or rubbing stimulation. Most males begin intercourse as premature ejaculators (intercourse lasting less than two minutes and not feeling in control of when you ejaculate). Autonomous sex function is idealized, especially in porn videos. In porn, he always has a firm erection and needs nothing from the woman. This simplistic view of male sexuality is almost totally wrong. Male sexuality is complex, with large individual, couple, cultural, and value differences. Men are intimidated by the simplistic performance model. An example is that 80% of men believe that their penis is smaller than average. This makes no statistical or logical sense, but demonstrates the tyranny of sex demands and expectations. The message is clear – you need to perform perfectly; otherwise, you're a "sexual loser". Fear of not being "man enough", not having enough partners, and not being as sexually skilled as other men dominates male culture. The pressure is to perform perfectly, needing to give your partner an orgasm the "right way" with a large penis and hard-driving intercourse. Sex is about performance to impress your partner as well as male peers.

Men are notorious sexual braggarts and liars. You are not supposed to have questions or anxieties.

It is no wonder that it is so challenging to have a genuine sexual dialogue between a man and a woman. Adolescent and young adult men and women learn such different sexual languages, feel such different pressures, and have such different vulnerabilities.

Healthy Male, Female, and Couple Sexuality

This book is for men, women, and couples to learn the language of desire/pleasure/eroticism/satisfaction and be intimate and erotic allies. This is a challenge for men, women, couples, and the culture. Yet, it is a very worthwhile challenge. Sexuality can have a positive 15–20% role in your life and relationship. Understanding the strengths and vulnerabilities of male sexuality is important in accepting yourself. Female sexuality has many more similarities than differences from male sexuality. The important concept is that female sexuality is more variable, flexible, complex, individualistic, and, most important, first-class, not inferior. This understanding is the foundation for the female-male sexual equity model (McCarthy & McCarthy, 2019b). It is the basis of a new, healthy dialogue about sexuality. This opens you and your partner to be intimate and erotic friends rather than the traditional war between the sexes. It allows you to have genuine conversations about the roles, meanings, and outcomes of sexuality rather than a destructive, adversarial argument where male sexuality is either on a pedestal or demonized. It provides an opportunity to be allies, not adversaries.

Sexually one size never fits all. Men, women, and couples are complex and unique. The information and guidelines we present are based on scientific data and clinically relevant perspectives (Metz, Epstein, & McCarthy, 2017). We strongly believe in these guidelines scientifically, clinically, and try to apply them in our lives. We believe in individual differences and honoring each person's unique sexual voice, relationship, and sexual reality. It is your responsibility to implement these guidelines into your life and relationship. There are couples who choose to stay with the traditional double standard and are comfortable with the woman being in a subservient role. However, the great majority of women embrace the challenge of "finding your sexual voice" as a first-class woman. Healthy sexuality is a one-two combination of personal responsibility and being an intimate sexual team. The female-male sexual equity model promotes this, while the traditional double standard subverts it. The essence of a healthy marriage (life partnership) is a respectful, trusting, emotional commitment. The paradox is that sex dysfunction, conflict, and especially avoidance can destroy a relationship, but good sex cannot save a bad relationship. The 15–20% function of healthy sexuality is to energize your bond and reinforce feelings of desire and desirability.

Special Issues for Men

This book focuses on understanding male sexuality. We want to increase psychological, relational, and sexual understanding of the complexity of men and male sexuality. Although it should be read by men, you are not the sole audience. This is written for men, women, couples, and clinicians. The simplistic theme regarding male sexuality focused on strength with a sex test of erection and intercourse. This must be challenged. The mistaken belief is that male sexuality is superior because it is autonomous. A "real man" is able to experience desire, erection, intercourse, and orgasm without needing anything from the woman. The extreme is that "A real man can have sex with any woman, any place, and any time". Spontaneous erection, a large penis, totally predictable intercourse, and orgasm are in his control.

The great majority of men have been exposed to porn and use porn images to accompany masturbation. In porn videos, the man always has a firm erection and needs no additional stimulation. The message of porn is male dominant/female submissive. The crazier the scenario and the crazier the woman, the more erotic it is. He always ejaculates whether on her body, or more typically, on her face. She is portrayed as lusting for dramatic sex whether double penetration (vaginal and anal) or turned-on by pain and aggression. Erotic sex is male dominant/female out of control.

These scenarios intimidate men, not empower you. The message is that sex is a competition, and in order to not fall behind, you need to perform perfectly to impress your partner and male peers. She is not an intimate partner; she is someone to perform for, impress with your large erection, a strong sex drive, and a dominance scenario. In the individual performance model, there is no space for sharing intimacy or pleasure.

These sex images are pervasive and destructive. They are not challenged by men for fear of being labeled a "wimp" or" not man enough". Sex myths dominate men, couples, and the culture. This is the basis for the male-female double standard and sets up the power struggles of intercourse or nothing.

In describing myths and misinformation, our intention is not to minimize problems or explain them away. The male performance model of sex and the degradation of female sexuality must be confronted. Demonizing and shaming men and male sexuality are not in your best interest as a couple. Awareness regarding myths and destructive elements of male sexual socialization does not mean accepting them. Just the opposite. You can replace these with a genuine understanding of male sexuality, female sexuality, and couple sexuality. Confront the myth that male sexuality is superior. Confront the myth that sex is an individual performance test. Confront the myth that an erect penis is the measure of male sexuality. As an intimate sexual team, build healthy sexual attitudes, behaviors, emotions, and values. You do not change for the woman; you change for yourself and your relationship.

Special Issues for Women

This book is also for women. She makes wise decisions about her sexuality. Understanding the complexity of men and male sexuality is a solid foundation for couple decision-making. A healthy relationship promotes psychological well-being, including intimacy and sexuality. Being in a satisfying, secure, and sexual relationship is a major factor for both physical and psychological well-being. A healthy marriage meets needs for intimacy and security better than any other relationship (Doherty, 2013). People in a healthy relationship report high levels of psychological well-being. Interestingly, women get more out of a healthy relationship than men. Sadly, men do not value their marriage as much as they should. However, both in terms of physical and mental health, men need marriage more than women.

A dissatisfying or destructive marriage has more impact on women than men. Men tolerate mediocre or dissatisfying marriages better than women. A major cause of depression (which has considerably higher rates for women) is a mediocre, dissatisfying, or destructive relationship. We are pro-marriage, but are not anti-divorce. We advocate for a satisfying, secure, and sexual marriage (life partnership). Satisfying is the major factor. Satisfying does not mean romantic love and idealization. Satisfying means accepting your feelings, life experiences, and values. It means knowing and accepting your spouse with his strengths and vulnerabilities. A healthy relationship makes you a healthier woman.

A healthy relationship is non-perfectionistic – you are not perfect, your spouse is not perfect, and your marriage is not perfect. The core of respect is accepting yourself and your spouse with strengths and vulnerabilities. It is the opposite of the romantic love belief that "if you love me, you will change for me". The scientific reality is that only 30% of marital problems are resolvable, the majority are modifiable, and even in the most loving marriages, 10–20% of problems are not changeable (Gottman & Silver, 2015). You love and respect your spouse for who he really is. A favorite example is that before we married, Barry told Emily that he had a perceptual-motor learning disorder (she remembers that conversation but feels that he did not make clear how severe it was). As the world has become more technological and on-line, Barry's disability has become more problematic. I regret it, but am not ashamed of my disability. I am grateful that Emily loves and respects me in spite of this chronic problem.

Respect, Trust, and Intimacy

Respect is based on genuine understanding and acceptance, the opposite of idealistic romantic love. If you do not respect yourself, your partner, and your bond, no amount of great sex will save your relationship. The best sex integrates intimacy and eroticism. It is possible to have good sex with a partner you don't respect or even like. Throughout cultures and generations, people have been harmed by the belief that love and sex was the sign of a healthy relationship and the major reason to marry. The paradox is that sex problems can destroy a loving marriage, but good sex cannot save a bad marriage.

The second core factor in marriage is trust. Trust does not mean you won't be disappointed or hurt by your spouse. Trust means your spouse would not intentionally do something to harm you emotionally or sexually. Trust involves believing that she acts in your best interest and wants you to thrive personally, relationally, and sexually. Believing that love means "Never having to say you're sorry" is self-defeating. In a respectful, trusting, marriage, you say you're sorry at least once a month. The core trust issue is the belief that your spouse will act in your best interest. Hurt or disappointment was not intentional or meant to harm you. You trust your spouse "has your back".

Many women trust their partner emotionally, but not sexually. When you are aroused and erect, she fears your sexual wants override her emotional needs. Sexual pressure is a major cause of low desire. Unless she has the power to say no to sex she doesn't have the freedom to embrace desire/pleasure/eroticism/satisfaction. She can learn to trust you sexually. It is a one-two process of trusting her sexual voice, including her power to veto a sexual scenario and trusting you to be her intimate and erotic friend. Her sexual feelings and preferences are as important as yours. She trusts you will honor her veto. A healthy relationship involves emotional and sexual trust.

Emotional intimacy and sexual intimacy are different dimensions, but both are crucial.

Emotional intimacy is an integral component of your respect, trust, and intimacy bond. She feels emotionally open and confident. Emotional intimacy reinforces a secure attachment. Emotional intimacy is different than "romantic love" or a "perfect relationship". She is herself in this relationship. She feels accepted and loved by you. She is accepted with her vulnerabilities and accepts your vulnerabilities. She loves you for who you really are not a "perfect romantic image".

Sexual intimacy is particularly challenging. Sexual intimacy involves integrating intimacy and eroticism. Many women value emotional intimacy. She experiences a split between intimacy and eroticism. In his clinical work, Barry has heard "I love my spouse, but am no longer in love with him" hundreds if not thousands of times. She has "de-eroticized" you and your relationship. The challenge for both men and women is to integrate intimacy and eroticism into your relationship. Finding her "erotic voice" is a challenge. Eroticism is as important for her as for you. Challenge the traditional gender split of eroticism being the man's domain while intimacy is the woman's domain. In a healthy relationship, both partners value integrated eroticism. Each partner has a different vulnerability and different challenge. Your relationship is stronger when both of you are fully functional sexual people.

The Challenge of Couple Sexuality

You are responsible for your sexuality. Yet, at its essence, understanding sexuality is a team effort. Turn toward each other as intimate and erotic allies. Sexually you win or lose as a team. The female-male sexual equity model is much superior to the traditional double standard. As adults in an intimate relationship, there are many more psychological, relational, sexual, and value similarities than differences. This is especially true with the aging of your relationship. Recognizing these similarities helps you be successful individually and as a couple. Being aware personally, relationally, and sexually facilitates making wise decisions. Knowledge is power. Implement your understandings so that you can enjoy a healthy life, relationship, and sexuality. A core understanding is that your emotional and sexual relationship is based on a positive influence process. Your relationship brings out healthy parts of you. You deserve sexuality to have a positive, integral role in your life.

Who We Are and the Format of This Book

Barry and Emily McCarthy are a husband-wife writing team; this is our 15th co-authored book. When we married in 1966, the male-female double standard was dominant. We were the first in our families to graduate college, and were committed to living our lives in a healthier manner than our backgrounds. We wanted to create a life we would be proud of personally and relationally. However, we assumed there would be major differences sexually. We challenged this assumption and committed to creating a satisfying, secure, and sexual marriage. We are not clones of each other. We approach our sexual bond as equitable partners who affirm desire/pleasure/eroticism/satisfaction.

Writing this book has been a challenge. We are pro-male, pro-female, pro-couple, and pro-sexuality. We promote the 15–20% role of sexuality for individual and couple well-being whether you are 26, 46, or 76. This book has value for men, women, couples, clinicians, and the culture. We confront the harmful effects of the double standard which emphasizes male-female differences and splits intimacy and eroticism. Scientifically, clinically, and personally we advocate for the female-male sexual equity model.

We respect each other's contributions to the writing of this book. Emily's background is in speech communication and her writing and wisdom provides a balanced, humanistic perspective. Barry's background is a professor of psychology and a clinical psychologist with a specialty in sex and couple therapy. This book is grounded in scientific and clinically validated psychological, bio-medical, and social/relational information. We empower and motivate you to embrace sexuality. In his clinical practice of 42 years, Barry addressed chronic psychological, relational, and sexual problems. If the couple had the motivation and skills to prevent sexual problems or dealt with them in the acute phase, their lives would have been much better. Prevention is the best, cheapest, and most efficacious way to address sexual issues.

We present scientifically and clinically validated sexual information, and provide personally relevant guidelines, psychosexual skill exercises, and case studies (we use composite cases with details altered to protect confidentiality) to make concepts personal and concrete. This is not meant to be read as a textbook. Each chapter is self-contained. Start with chapters which are personally relevant. The material can be read for information and concepts but is best used as an interactive learning medium. Share this book with your spouse/partner. Talking and sharing (especially the psychosexual skill exercises) make concepts personal and meaningful. Implement relevant strategies, skills, and coping techniques so that sexuality has a positive role in your life and relationship.

Healthy Sexuality

Be your "authentic sexual self". We affirm sexuality whether you are married, partnered, divorced, single, or widowed. Our message is relevant whether you are 30, 50, or 80. We emphasize traditional heterosexual married couples, but these learnings are applicable to partnered and gay couples as well as single, divorced, or widowed individuals. This book is meant to be inclusive and respectful of diversity and individual differences. Rather than use "he" or "she", we utilize "you" when possible. We also alternate use of "married" or "partnered".

This is a book of ideas, guidelines, and exercises. It is not a "do it yourself therapy" book. The more information, understanding, and resources, the more likely you will make wise relational and sexual decisions. The psychosexual skill exercises help you assess and change sexual attitudes, behaviors, and feelings. Seeking sex, couple, or individual therapy is a wise decision. Appendix A provides information and guidelines on how to choose a sex therapist, couple therapist, or individual therapist.

Let us begin our journey to healthy male and couple sexuality.

2

THE SEXUAL WAR BETWEEN
MEN AND WOMEN
Changing the Dialogue

The cultural theme is that because men and women are so different, it is natural to always be at war, especially about sex. Whether arguments at a bar, on a talk show, or at academic conferences, the theme of a war between the genders is widely accepted. This is especially true when arguing about differences in sexual behavior, feelings, and values. Sex is the man's domain, not a shared domain. The double standard is the basis for the war between the sexes.

This chapter confronts sexual war myths and introduces a new, healthy dialogue about sexual roles, meanings, and values. It is based on the female-male sexual equity model. Rather than a war, sexuality is a couple process of sharing intimacy, pleasuring, and eroticism. Men and women are intimate and erotic allies, not enemies. Television sit-coms and talk shows are filled with stories of the sex war. Although funny and entertaining, it is not healthy for men, women, couples, or our culture. Replace it with a dialogue featuring a respectful, trusting, equitable model of female-male relationships and sexuality. End the sex war and replace it with an equitable female-male sexual team model (McCarthy & McCarthy, 2019b).

Sadly, same-gender friends reinforce the war. There are a myriad of stories and jokes about the opposite sex. People have overlearned these and hate to give them up. These narratives are unhealthy, but fit like an "old shoe". It is easy to maintain destructive behaviors and values. The media, internet, and friends reinforce self-defeating beliefs. There is no freedom or wisdom in the sex war, just overlearned habits with destructive themes. It would be funny if it didn't do such damage to men, women, couples, and the culture. Even well-educated, thoughtful men fall into the traditional double standard trap. It's simple and easy, but scientifically wrong and personally destructive. "Pop psych" and "pop sex" books, articles, and blogs reinforce the sexual war. This is especially true of male peer groups and sexually oriented materials. In female groups and on-line sites, there is significant male-blaming and shaming. How long will it take to end the sex wars? The dialogue about female-male sexual equity is strongly supported by scientific data and clinically relevant individual and couple experiences. In contrast, there is little empirical support for the double standard (Baumeister, 2000). There is a plethora of clinical data and case studies which point out the negative impacts of the double standard. The double standard negates the sexual growth of men and women.

People worry about sexual change because they fear that it will lead to confusion and chaos. The female-male sexual equity model provides a road map and guidelines for change. Identify your "authentic sexual self" from which you create an intimate sexual relationship. Men have the freedom to break away from rigid gender roles and stereotypes. Engage sexually rather than be controlled by anxieties and shame. A common fear is that sexual awareness and openness will lead to scary revelations and destabilize the person and relationship. This, like most fears, is irrational. People can become comfortable with who they are sexually and value an intimate sexual relationship. It is normal to have sexual feelings and preferences that are different than your partner's. You are not sexual clones. In the great majority of cases, differences can be integrated into your couple sexual style. In fact, differences spice up and enhance couple sexuality. Sexuality need not be feared nor be subverted by shame. Sexuality is about energizing you and your bond.

When there are personal or relational issues which interfere with being your authentic sexual self, we urge you to consult a therapist. A self-help book is not an adequate resource to deal with these complex issues. Appendix A provides guidelines for choosing a sex, couple, or individual therapist. Seeking therapy is a sign of good judgment, not weakness. You deserve sexuality to have a positive role in your life and relationship.

A New Sexual Dialogue

Female-male sexual equity sounds easy and straight-forward; it's anything but. Creating a new psychological, relational, and sexual dialogue is challenging. Meeting this challenge is worthwhile to enhance relational and sexual satisfaction.

The easier part is confronting the double standard. It is fun challenging myths and emphasizing freedom from oppressive demands and expectations. However, you can't stop there. Engage with your partner to develop a strategy for ending the war between the sexes. The core of the dialogue is to treat each other as respectful and trusting partners who share emotional and sexual intimacy. It's easy to say, "Stop the war", but when there are differences or conflicts, people fall into old attitudes and habits. Resist this. Healthy relationships are based on a positive influence process. The dialogue about female-male sexual equity and being intimate and erotic allies is based on a positive influence process.

Set aside time to talk about your perspective on desire/pleasure/eroticism/ satisfaction. A crucial conversation involves accepting responsive sexual desire as healthy, not inferior to spontaneous desire. In fact, we argue (discussed in detail in Chapter 9) that responsive sexual desire is a key for the man and couple with aging. Sexuality is not a "zero sum game". Accept similarities and honor differences. This empowers the man, woman, and couple.

First, focus on shared meanings and values. For example, the benefit of a relationship where you are intimate and erotic friends. Then address differences like spontaneous vs. responsive desire. Don't make it a "right-wrong" argument, but a discussion where you accept differences while being aware that with aging, these differences lessen. An example is that after age 50, responsive sexual desire becomes the norm for both men and women.

An example of the new dialogue is a discussion of masturbation and erotic fantasies. Acknowledge that the majority of men and women (married or partnered) occasionally masturbate, especially when the partner is not available or interested. The majority of both genders utilize erotic fantasies and materials. By its nature, erotic fantasies are not "socially desirable". What makes the fantasy erotic is that it's different than real-life sexuality. It is normal to have "abnormal" erotic fantasies.

Sexuality, including erotic differences, can be openly discussed. Start with common ground and then explore differences. Some males (less than 15%) and some females (less than 3%) masturbate in a compulsive manner, misusing porn or other erotic materials. Rather than demonizing male sexuality or shaming him, discuss the healthy and unhealthy uses of masturbation and fantasy. This can be a difficult dialogue, but need not be adversarial, and certainly not turn into a war.

A healthy dialogue affirms your shared humanity. The war between the sexes sacrifices respect for yourself and your partner. Dialogue as respectful friends who embrace similarities and honor differences. An example involves relational sex (a spouse, partner, lover) vs. non-relational sex (hook-up, anonymous). In the war, the message is that men have sex wherever they can, while women can only have sex with an intimate partner. Is that the basis of your relationship? Simplistic myths fire the war between the sexes.

There are major differences in the meaning of intimate partner sex in contrast to high opportunity-low involvement sex. This is also true for women. Rigid gender roles rob you of humanity and complexity. By its nature, sexuality is complex with a range of roles, meanings, and outcomes. Your dialogue needs to be personally meaningful. Focus on your relational and sexual values.

Let's examine another contentious issue in the war between the sexes – contraception and children. Traditionally, contraception was the woman's domain. If she became pregnant, it was her decision whether to have the child. The man had a minimal, if any, role. In the new dialogue, contraception, abortion, childbirth, children, and parenting involve both partners. In the great majority of cases, it is the woman who is responsible for contraception. From a bio-medical perspective, the most effective contraceptives are for women (iuds, injections, birth control pills). The exception is sterilization – vasectomy is just as effective as tubal ligation and with less risks. However, the majority of sterilizations are performed on women.

The science is clear; the best situation is when both partners agree on effective contraception. When a child is planned and wanted, both partners are involved in the birth process and parenting. Achieving this requires a major change in the dialogue and the roles of men and women. A daunting but worthwhile challenge.

It is normal for men and women to have differences and disagreements on important issues. Contrary to war talk that all women want children and men don't care, there are more similarities than differences between genders. Some women are not interested in children. Some men feel being a father is the most important thing in their lives.

A crucial dialogue involves the role of sexuality in your lives. Sex differences are a core conflict in the war between men and women. Simplistic myths and misunderstandings dominate. There are biological differences – pregnancy, accessibility of the penis, nocturnal emissions, vulnerability to STI/HIV. However, the underlying mechanisms for sexual desire and response are similar. There are clear differences in adolescent and young adulthood sexual socialization, but greater similarities in adulthood, especially with married and partnered couples. With aging, psychological and relational similarities increase.

When you reject the double standard and embrace female-male sexual equity, the dialogue promotes acceptance and encourages development of your couple sexual style. Ideally, both partners have the freedom to initiate sensual, playful, erotic, and intercourse scenarios. Both have the power to say no to sex and their veto is honored. The foundation for the dialogue is pleasure and consent. Sex is not a shameful force which negates a person or subverts a relationship. Sex is a small, integral part of life and your relationship. Sex energizes your bond and promotes feelings of desire and desirability. This reinforces healthy sexuality for you and your relationship.

Aliza and Marshall

Aliza 29 and Marshall 32 were socially active. Both played in sports teams, were involved with community projects, had large extended families, and were part of a religious community. They enjoyed hanging out and joking with friends. A frequent source of jokes were sex roles and the foibles of the opposite sex. They had a foot in both camps – they knew and shared all the stereotypes from the double standard. On the other hand, they were aware and well-educated. They worked with colleagues of the opposite sex and had friendships with both genders. Aliza was particularly supportive of transgender people and advocated for gender fluidity.

What appealed to Marshall about the double standard were expectations that men worked harder, made more money, were freer to travel, and were not sexually harassed. He had empathy for Aliza when she told him of friends who had been hassled or mistreated, but his attitude was this was the way of the world. Aliza saw Marshall as a good man, but felt that he indulged in male sport and drinking habits and took advantage of male privilege.

They became engaged after three years. The clash of the double standard vs. the female-male equity model became apparent as they talked about the wedding. In following the traditional male role, Marshall felt that wedding planning was Aliza's domain, not his role. His input was the music and alcohol – the rest was up to her. Arguments about the size of the wedding and who to invite were stressful.

The most disruptive issue was Aliza's wedding dress. She had a friend who made an elegant white dress which Marshall's mother and aunts objected to since, like most of their friends, Aliza and Marshall were cohabitating. Aliza turned to Marshall for support, but he wanted to avoid being in the middle of the controversy. He saw this as a silly woman's argument. Aliza felt abandoned by Marshall, especially that her sexuality was not validated. Marshall did not understand the emotional significance of Aliza's right to be sexual and to wear a white dress for her wedding. Aliza wanted to be treated as a first-class person, not subjected to the judgments of the double standard. This was a couple issue, not just Aliza's. Marshall needed to be her intimate ally, not avoid the conflict. Did Marshall "walk the walk" or hide behind the traditional male role?

Would this marriage begin by affirming the female-male sexual equity model or start under a cloud of misunderstanding and blaming caused by double standard judgments?

Sadly, the advice from male friends was for Marshall to not get caught in the conflict. A sign of a healthy relationship is working together to deal with differences and conflicts. Could Marshall go against the male tradition and show Aliza that "I have your back"? Aliza wanted Marshall to support her choice of a white wedding dress. He didn't need to attack his mother and aunts, but did need to clearly state his love and support of Aliza and affirm being a sexual couple. This reinforces female-male equity where sexuality is honored rather than the double standard of blaming and shaming women.

In a healthy marriage, you are proud of yourself, each other, and being a sexual couple. You don't need to fight others or be "holier than thou". You do need to affirm respect, trust, and intimacy. Starting with the female-male equity model provided Aliza and Marshall a solid foundation for a satisfying, secure, and sexual marriage.

Navigating the Details of Female-Male
Sexual Equity

The female-male equity model presents challenges and opportunities. Like other worthwhile changes, it requires awareness, thought, and dialogue to make a genuine difference.

Sexual issues can be the most challenging. The rules of the double standard are very easy to understand. Sex initiation is the man's domain, sex frequency is most important, sex = intercourse, and eroticism is the driving force. The female-male sexual equity model has a very different approach with a set of complex guidelines (not rules). Guidelines require awareness and communication – sexuality is not simple. A crucial guideline is that couple sexuality is about sharing pleasure, not counting intercourse events. Either partner can initiate a sexual encounter. Either partner can say no without feeling blamed or guilty. In the double standard, the woman is the sexual gatekeeper. She feels pressured to not say no too frequently. In the equity model, the man learns to feel comfortable saying no. This gives him flexibility, but means challenging the tradition that men never say no to sex. Men take this as a joke – not a healthy response. It does not reduce your masculinity to accept that for whatever reason you do not want to be sexual at a specific time or situation. You have a right to say no to sex whether at 20, 40, or 60. Freedom to use your no is key to enjoying sexuality in your 60s, 70s, and 80s. Embrace desire/pleasure/eroticism/satisfaction throughout your life. Let your partner be your intimate and erotic ally.

Even more important than the power to say no is your ability to stay physically and emotionally connected rather than turning away. In an equitable relationship, willingness to turn toward your partner is crucial. An example is when you initiate intercourse and your partner says no, rather than turning away with you feeling rejected and she feeling punished for saying no, turn toward each other. She could suggest cuddling, going for a walk, asking whether you would like a back rub or body massage, offering to pleasure you to orgasm, make a pot of coffee, or say she wants to be sexual the next day or two. There are a number of ways to feel connected; it isn't intercourse or nothing. The positive message is I love you, value you, prioritize our relationship, and recognize that there are many ways of being together.

Power struggles about intercourse initiation and frequency reinforce the war between men and women. Breaking this struggle requires two changes. First, redefine sexuality to include sensual, playful, and erotic scenarios in addition to intercourse. Second, intercourse is a shared domain rather than the man's domain. A key is to transition to intercourse at high levels of erotic flow and utilize multiple stimulation before and during intercourse.

Exercise – Implementing the Female-Male Dialogue

It is easy to say, "End the sexual war". It is challenging to establish and maintain communication as intimate and erotic friends. Each partner agrees to stop at least one and up to three defensive or angry behaviors. Examples include the woman stop saying, "Men are control freaks", "An erect penis has no conscience", or "Sex has to be his way". A behavioral example is insisting that only man-on-top intercourse is acceptable. Examples of destructive male comments include "Why can't you have a real orgasm during intercourse", or "Sex takes too long and too much work to give you an orgasm", or "You have too many excuses for saying no". A behavioral example is refusing to do multiple stimulation during intercourse. Rigid beliefs and communication patterns reinforce the war and undermine being a sexual team.

The challenge is to establish a new dialogue about female-male equity and being sexual team. The dialogue must be genuine in creating new attitudes, behaviors, emotions, and values. This is not a politically correct exercise. A genuine dialogue recognizes personal strengths and vulnerabilities. Don't be idealistic and overemphasize love and sexual ecstasy. Make a realistic commitment to trust your partner and act in a respectful and intimate manner.

Genuine respect involves knowing your partner for who he is, not an idealistic image. She accepting you with strengths and vulnerabilities is a sign of genuine love and respect. Our culture focuses on extremes – "the perfect man" or the "dysfunctional man". Love is not blind; love involves an emotional commitment to a real person and real relationship. Acceptance of your partner makes self-acceptance easier.

Trust is an example of the importance of a genuine dialogue. The romantic love, idealized extreme is "Love means never having to say you're sorry". The cynical extreme is "You can never trust a man, especially sexually". A genuine dialogue focuses on the theme of intentionality. You trust your partner would not intentionally do something to harm or undercut you, especially with friends, relatives, and children. Trust doesn't mean that you won't be disappointed, angry, or frustrated with your partner. Trust includes being able to say you are sorry – even if not intentional you hurt your partner. Perfectionism on one extreme and cynicism on the other extreme undercut your relationship.

Emotional and sexual intimacy are different but related. In the war, men believed that sexual intimacy was key while women elevated emotional intimacy.

In the new dialogue, you speak as intimate and erotic friends. Explore similarities and differences based on personal attitudes and feelings, not cultural stereotypes. What are shared emotional needs? How important is feeling close? Feeling accepted? Feeling understood? What is true for you, regardless of cultural expectations? Be who you are, not governed by fears of partner judgment.

Sexual intimacy is a complex, challenging dimension. How do you feel about sensual, playful, and erotic touch? Are these genuine ways of sharing sexuality or is intercourse the definition of sex? Do you prefer mutual, synchronous sexual experiences? Be clear and specific about your attitudes, emotions, and values regarding asynchronous sexuality. What makes an asynchronous sexual encounter healthy for you? What makes it unhealthy? This can be the most difficult component of your sexual intimacy dialogue.

Be honest – how important is sexual intimacy in your relationship? Does it have a 15–20% role or do sex problems and concerns stress you and undermine your relationship? If the latter, do you blame yourself, your partner, or your relationship? Are you motivated to change yourself and your relationship? What do you need to do and/or request your partner do to implement female-male sexual equity?

What have you learned from this exercise? Are you ready and able to end the war between men and women? Are you able to dialogue about issues based on sexual equity? Can you be intimate and erotic friends who are open to changing sexual attitudes, behaviors, emotions, and values? Can you honor differences? Does sexuality have a positive role for you individually and as a couple?

From Theory to Implementation

Throughout this book, we emphasize the importance of confronting male sex myths and creating a new dialogue about male, female, and couple sexuality based on a scientific foundation and personally relevant guidelines (Metz, Epstein, & McCarthy, 2017). Reading and discussion is of value, but the real change occurs when you implement the equity model. Barry remembers a client who was shocked when his very traditional father told him how much he admired that he treated his wife as an equitable partner, was affectionate with her in public, and changed the baby's diapers. The father had not done any of those things, but was proud that his son did. Both spouses worked and they lived on one salary – saving for their daughter's college and starting a retirement fund. They did not talk about their sexual equity bond with anyone else, but did dialogue with each other. Sex was more predictable for him, but he accepted her desire and orgasm pattern as right for her. Implementing the sexual equity model early in the marriage made it easier to maintain a variable, flexible couple sexual style with aging.

The real measure of the new dialogue occurs when dealing with sexual differences, especially desire discrepancies. Rather than the belief that more sex is better, the focus of the equity model is sharing pleasure as an intimate sexual team. This is more important than intercourse frequency. The woman's acceptance of her sexual voice as first class makes the couple sexual dialogue meaningful. Intimacy, pleasuring, and eroticism bring you together rather than splitting you. Accepting that you are not clones of each other facilitates couple sexuality. Intimacy, pleasuring, and eroticism are a shared experience.

Summary

The traditional gender war is destructive for men, women, couples, and the culture. It has caused pain for people across generations and cultures. The rules of the war are simplistic and easy to follow, but totally wrong. The war is the basis for the male-female double standard which burdens couple sexuality. With the aging of the man, the double standard causes loss of erectile confidence, resulting in stopping sex. When couples stop being sexual, especially after age 50, it is almost always the man's choice because he cannot meet the performance demands of the double standard.

Stopping the war between men and women is necessary, but not sufficient. Replace it with a genuine dialogue based on the female-male sexual equity model. A respectful, trusting, and emotionally intimate relationship promotes well-being. Establish and maintain an equitable relationship which integrates intimacy, pleasuring, and eroticism. Be intimate and erotic friends. Sexuality energizes your bond and reinforces feelings of desire and desirability.

3

CONFRONTING CONTEMPORARY MALE SEXUALITY

Breaking the Abusive Cycle

The theme of this book is to promote healthy male and couple sexuality. This chapter focuses on the necessity of confronting toxic male sexuality, especially child sexual abuse, rape, and incest (the big three "poisons"). In addition, it is crucial to confront sexual harassment, intimating and shaming women, sexual coercion, sexual entitlement, use of prostitutes or massage parlors, compulsive use of porn and cyber sex, and using sex as a weapon to impress male peers. Toxic sexuality involves destructive attitudes, behaviors, emotions, and values.

Confronting does not mean "shaming". Shaming makes the toxic behavior worse by reinforcing negative feelings about being a man. This tears at sexual self-esteem and makes you more likely to repeat toxic behavior. It is necessary to confront sexual attitudes, behaviors, and values which harm women and poison relationships. Eliminating sexual poisons is crucial but is not enough. Adopt an understanding of couple sexuality which affirms intimacy, pleasure, and eroticism in the context of a respectful, trusting, and emotionally equitable relationship.

Toxic sexuality is not integral to being a man. The majority of men do not indulge in toxic sexuality. However, toxic attitudes are part of traditional male sexual socialization. Toxic sexuality impacts a significant number of men, not a small minority. Issues of toxic sexuality need to be exposed and confronted not just to protect women, but to change men and the culture. Exploration of healthy and toxic sexual attitudes, behaviors, emotions, and values is crucial.

The core sexual values are pleasure and consent. Sexuality is about giving and receiving pleasure-oriented touching. It is not about individual sex performance, nor proving yourself. Sexuality is voluntary, not coerced, pressured, or demanded. Without consent, sex is toxic. These values need to be reinforced in the culture. This is true for men as well as women. Pleasure and consent are not prime topics for men, especially in peer groups. This needs to change.

The double standard assumes that sex is the man's domain. The belief is that "pure" women cannot be sexually abused or raped. Destructive or traumatic sexual experiences are blamed on women (being provocatively dressed, putting herself in harm's way, choosing the wrong man, enjoying being a sex object, being promiscuous, leading men on, and a large range of rationalizations). Let us be clear, the responsibility for toxic behavior lies with the man, not the woman.

The Big Three Toxic Behaviors – Child Sexual Abuse, Rape, and Incest

Almost all agree that child sexual abuse, rape, and incest are destructive. Unfortunately, this is an example that sexuality involves more than objective, scientific information. Child sexual abuse is the most common toxic sexual behavior. The best estimate is that by age 18, 35–40% of females have had an abusive sexual experience. The mistaken assumptions are that child sexual abuse involves a stranger, force, and intercourse. In reality, abuse incidents involve a man the child knows. Most do not involve physical force. In fact, half of abusive incidents do not involve touching (voyeurism, exhibitionism, harassment). The most common sexual abuse incidents do not involve intercourse, but rather manual or oral stimulation.

The core of child sexual abuse is that the man's (or adolescent male) sexual wants override the child's emotional needs. Female children are much more likely to be sexually abused than male children. Sadly, male children and adolescents are unlikely to disclose abuse to anyone; instead, you feel shameful. Victimized males experience more hands-on abuse. Although female adolescents and adults do perpetrate abuse, the great majority of abuse of male children is perpetrated by men or male adolescents.

Rape or attempted rape is quite common, especially between ages 15 and 25 (although 1- and 71-year-olds are raped). In addition to intercourse, rape can involve manual, oral, or anal sex. Coercion and sexual pressure are common as well as forced penetration. Acquaintance rape is much more common than stranger rape. Date/acquaintance rape is the double standard taken to its illogical extreme. The man says, "Sex was consensual, she said yes to kissing and touching, and that turned me on". The destructive rationale is that an erect penis has no conscience. Women who say no to intercourse are labeled "cock teasers" and blamed for the rape. Often, alcohol or drugs are involved. Rape is a toxic sexual behavior which cannot be justified but is viewed as "natural" in the heat of sexual arousal. The adage "rape is a crime of power, not sex" is widely accepted, but has little empirical support (Daigle, Evier, & Cullen, 2008). Males who would not beat up a woman even if drunk will commit rape, especially when drinking. Rape is driven by both sex and coercion/force. Like other toxic sexual behaviors, rape is never justified or acceptable.

Incest is the third toxic sexual behavior. Most writing about incest involves father-daughter or step-father-stepdaughter incidents. The reality is that the majority of incest involves cousins, in-laws, uncles, siblings, and live-in boyfriends. The reason that father-daughter is highlighted is that it is such a violation of trust and a shameful secret. She has a right to feel safe in her home – psychologically, physically, and sexually. Incest is surrounded by stigma and silence. Incest is a shameful secret that needs to be confronted, processed, and stopped.

Dealing with a History of Sexual Trauma

Negative sexual experiences are very common and very challenging. In addition to the big three traumas, there are a range of experiences, including dealing with an STI, an unwanted pregnancy, being sexually harassed or humiliated, sexual guilt, sex dysfunction, caught masturbating, being sexually manipulated. Over 90% of 25-year-old men and women identify at least one negative sexual experience. This is a sad reality but makes it clear that you are not alone. Destructive sexual incidents happen to good people.

The message is clear that toxic sexual behavior needs to be confronted and stopped. It cannot be explained away, tolerated, or worked around. Toxic male sexuality is not just harmful to women, children, and families; it is harmful to men and the culture. The assumption that male sexuality is superior and that the double standard is the norm is the underlying rationale for toxic sexuality.

The essence of healthy sexuality is consent and pleasure – the opposite of toxic sexuality. Men and women as intimate and erotic friends are negated by toxic sexuality. The mantra of desire/pleasure/eroticism/satisfaction has no role in toxic sexuality. Once toxic sexuality has been eliminated, it is necessary to build healthy male and couple sexuality. We usually advocate for a "both-and" approach to change, but with toxic sexuality, you have to stop the "poison" before addressing healthy sexuality.

Male Peer Influence

A major source for creating and maintaining toxic sexuality is the influence of male peers. There is nothing inherently toxic in men or male sexuality. Toxic sexuality involves a learned set of attitudes and behaviors which is reinforced by peers as well as the media and culture.

A core poison is male sexual privilege. Barry remembers as a child hearing, "If she's old enough to bleed she's old enough to butcher". At the time, he did not understand what that meant, but the laughter of male peers meant that it must be okay. Barry grew up with the double standard and the message that "A real man never says no to sex". Sex was a source of jokes at the expense of women. Adolescent and young adult men are exposed to hundreds of examples of toxic male sexuality which are seldom challenged. In addition, the pervasive messages in porn celebrate toxic sexuality. Most men accept porn for what it is – an erotic fantasy dimension to promote masturbation. However, it is too easy to fall into the trap of accepting a porn narrative as normal male sexuality. Porn reinforces toxic male sexual behavior.

In adolescent and young adult male sexual socialization, there is no mention of female-male sexual equity, consent, pleasuring, or integrating intimacy and eroticism. The messages are that masculinity and sexuality are closely linked, that men never say no to sex, and it is your role to convince or seduce the woman to have sex. These messages are fertile ground to develop toxic attitudes and values. Male authority figures – fathers, uncles, teachers, older brothers, and ministers – do not present a clear message which confronts toxic sexuality. Nor do they offer a clear message in support of healthy sexual attitudes, behaviors, emotions, and values. The usual message is don't get a woman pregnant or contract an STI or HIV. Few males receive an explicit message that sexual coercion is wrong. The destructive learning is that there are "good girls" and "bad girls". The implicit message is bad girls get what they deserve.

These crazy-making learnings do not justify toxic male sexuality nor does it change the need to confront and stop destructive behavior. Rather than demonizing the man and male sexuality, focus on increasing awareness of toxic sexuality and your responsibility to break this poisonous pattern. Recognize the harm this causes to women. It is easier to change individual and couple sexual attitudes and behavior, especially in the context of an intimate relationship. It is crucial to confront and change cultural norms from tolerating toxic sexuality to a realization that this is poisonous and must be stopped. The hardest issue involves male peer groups. It takes courage to confront toxic male sexuality. Peers are likely to counterattack or make a joke of it and you. Confronting toxic sexuality is a task for the individual man, the couple, the family, and the culture.

Intimate Partner Violence and Toxic Sexuality

Intimate partner violence is a common problem. The traditional belief was that violence always involved a male perpetrator and female victim. His agenda was control and dominance. Although this is true of some men, the more common pattern is an interactive couple process which signifies being emotionally out of control (Stosny, 2017). Part of the pattern is sex to "make-up" or "compensate". This misuse of sex reinforces intimate partner violence. You need to confront and stop intimate partner violence. A strategy is a clear agreement that there is no affectionate or sexual touching for 72 hours after a partner violence incident. It is crucial to break the association between partner violence and sexuality. Toxic sexuality needs to be confronted in all its forms.

Confronting the Man, Not Shaming the Man

Toxic sexuality is destructive for the woman, couple, family, and culture. In addition, it is emotionally and physically unhealthy for the man. It leaves you isolated and vulnerable to rejection and legal and social consequences.

Confronting the man involves two themes. First, you need to take responsibility for the hurt/harm inflicted on others. Don't deny or minimize. What you did caused damage. Your sexual wants are met at the expense of the emotional needs of others. This is harmful and cannot be justified. Second, you are better than this toxic sexual behavior. Sex is bringing out the worst in you. Toxic male sexuality meets short-term sexual wants at the expense of long-term psychological and relational well-being. Toxic sexuality is destructive for you and the people in your life. The three to ten seconds of orgasm is not worth the reality of hurting others. Toxic attitudes and behaviors cannot be accepted. This sexual pattern brings out the worst in you.

What is the difference between confronting and shaming? Confrontation motivates you to change. Shaming reinforces that you are bad, sex is bad, and makes it almost certain that toxic sexuality will continue. Shame is destructive. Shame makes you feel bad about yourself as a person (rather than confronting the destructive behavior) and keeps you stuck in the cycle. Confrontation, regret, and guilt motivate change. Shame keeps you stuck in toxic attitudes, behaviors, and emotions.

Shaming the man feels good at the time, but serves to reinforce the self-defeating pattern. Shame undercuts motivation for change. Shame is the most destructive of human emotions, leaving you clinging to toxic sexuality.

It is your responsibility to confront and change your sexual attitudes, behavior, emotions, and values. The more you feel shame or are shamed by others, the less able you are to change.

Brad

Twenty-nine-year-old Brad would not have identified himself as a sexually toxic man. His narrative was that he is a regular guy who likes sex and women. He was proud of his masculinity and felt accepted by male peers. Brad bragged that he had a strong sex drive and needed at least one orgasm a day. Brad had a girlfriend of two years, but was negative toward her, especially when talking with friends. Although she earned more money, Brad said she was not as smart as he and had to work too much. He labeled her "sexually slow" and complained she gave "bad head". Brad was the dominant partner, and she clung to him. When asked if he was in a relationship, Brad said no.

The social/sexual scenario he found most erotic was going to bars with friends and "hooking-up". Brad bragged that he had a large penis which made women want to "suck him off". Just before orgasm, he pulled her hair so she would insert more deeply. About once a month after midnight and drinking heavily, Brad would "accidently" urinate on the woman who had just given him a "blow job". This was highly erotic scenario for Brad.

Brad never asked a woman's age, but was particularly attracted to very young women. He later learned that some were younger than 16. Brad found "breaking the cherry" erotically charged. For Brad, sex was about illicitness and dominance. He believed that this was the way male sexuality should be.

Brad's friends knew women who became pregnant and said the friend was the father. Brad claimed that he and others had sex with this "promiscuous" woman and anyone could be the father.

Although Brad claimed to have many sex partners, the truth is that most of his orgasms involved masturbation to porn videos. Brad resonated with the porn themes of domination, sexually crazy women, pain as a turn-on for women, the eroticism of double penetration, and ejaculating on the woman's face. Porn themes reinforce toxic male sexuality. Brad did not differentiate erotic fantasy from real-life couple sexuality.

His toxic sexual pattern continued for years before he was arrested for a forced sexual incident at a bar with an underage woman. Brad claimed to all who would listen that he was innocent. His expensive attorney made him stop talking. Although some continued their friendship, most peers avoided Brad. The arrest and investigation was reported in the newspaper and on the internet. The girlfriend's peer group and her parents convinced her to end contact with Brad. He was feeling increasingly isolated and besieged.

The attorney counseled Brad to accept a plea bargain to a lesser charge which allowed him to avoid being placed on the sex offender registry. Brad was sentenced to two years probation, community service, and court-ordered group therapy for at least six months. In the individual session before the group therapy began, the male therapist used the term "toxic male sexuality" to describe Brad's sexual pattern. This was the first time Brad has been confronted with this concept.

The group consisted of male-female co-therapists and six men. Three of the group members had served jail time for sexual offenses. Listening to their stories was sobering for Brad, especially the legal consequences and impact on their lives.

When Brad described his sexual history and the sexual incident with the underage woman, a veteran group member bluntly told Brad that he was "full of b.s.". Brad minimized the incident and "sugar-coated" his history. The male co-therapist focused on Brad not taking responsibility for toxic sexual attitudes and behavior. The female co-therapist said that for a smart man, Brad was oblivious to the damage he had caused women throughout his life. Brad was shaken by these confrontations. If the therapy were not court-mandated, he would have dropped out.

Brad admired one group member, a man in his 50s who had turned around not just his sexual life, but also his career and relational life. This man spoke of the impact of toxic sexuality, including being sexually humiliated and made fun of by peers. He described the process of increasing awareness of the impact of toxic attitudes, behaviors, and emotions. The major breakthrough involved confronting his destructive sexual values. He'd only had sex with women he thought were over 18, so he felt that this was a private matter. He realized that he had been coercive, manipulative, and harassed women. He'd used drugs and alcohol to make it easier to dominate. In retrospect, he realized that he had "hurt-harmed" over 30 women.

The group member told Brad that change was a 1–2 process. First, Brad needed to take responsibility for toxic sexual behavior and commit to getting the "poisons" out of his life. Second, to learn and implement healthy sexual attitudes, behaviors, emotions, and values. A major component of the group member's change process was establishing an intimate relationship with a divorced woman in her forties. He told her the sexual history and his commitment to an equitable, pleasure-oriented sexual relationship. She had the power to veto a sexual scenario, and he would honor her veto.

The group member's story was motivating. Brad's toxic approach to sexuality had a number of life consequences. Brad had dropped out of college and was working in unstable, marginal jobs. Part of his life change process was entering a three-year electrician apprenticeship program. The issue was not his intellectual capability, but motivation to finish the apprenticeship and take pride in his new career. It was crucial to ensure that toxic behavior and sexual shame do not subvert his life plans.

Brad hoped that a new sexual relationship would save him. The therapists and group members told him that at this time he was not healthy enough to establish an intimate relationship. He needed to focus on breaking the toxic sexual pattern. This surprised Brad and left him unsure of how to proceed, especially regarding sexual expression. He needed to stay away from partner sex because it would reinforce the toxic pattern. Intellectually, this made sense, but emotionally, it was very hard to accept. The therapists and group members encouraged Brad to work on himself psychologically, to change values and attitudes toward women, and to adopt a new understanding of sexuality generally, and couple sexuality specifically.

What could Brad do sexually in the present? The logical next step involved masturbation and erotic fantasies. There is no shame regarding masturbation. Masturbation is a normal, healthy behavior for adolescents, young adults, and adults.

Brad accepted that masturbation was normal, but realized that his pattern of masturbation was compulsive. The first issue was sexual motivation. Brad had masturbated for negative reasons – anxiety, depression, isolation, embarrassment, boredom, anger. Brad needed to masturbate with positive motivation because he felt sexual. He would not masturbate for negative reasons. This provided a crucial insight. So much of Brad's sexual behavior was driven by negative motivation, especially feeling he wasn't "man enough".

There was a lot of hard work ahead for Brad, but toxic sexuality no longer controlled him. Brad was looking forward to a healthy relationship. He wanted desire/pleasure/eroticism/satisfaction to have a positive role in his life.

Being a Proud Sexual Man

Toxic male sexuality poisons your self-esteem and relationship. Even if toxic sexuality has not had negative life or social repercussions, it undermines respect for yourself. You cannot be a proud man if your attitudes and behavior cause damage to others. Men who engage in toxic sexual behavior deny its destructiveness. However, at some level, they realize it's harmful. They joke and rationalize with other men or in "one-up" bar conversations. They do not try to justify toxic sexual behavior, especially child sexual abuse and incest. These are "shameful secrets".

The best self-help resources, including this book, are not enough to confront and change toxic sexuality. You need therapeutic help, whether group therapy, individual therapy, or a therapy group focused on out of control sexual behavior. There is no shame in seeking professional help. The shame is living a life of toxic sexuality which harms you and others. You cannot establish genuine pride in being a man until you have confronted and ended toxic sexuality (McCarthy & Metz, 2008).

Exercise – Confronting Toxic Male Sexuality

Almost all the psychosexual skill exercises in this book involve couples, but this exercise is for the man alone. Engage in this exercise in an honest manner. Your partner makes it clear that she cannot be in a relationship with you if you maintain toxic sexual attitudes, behaviors, and values.

Confronting toxic sexuality is daunting, but worthwhile. You can do this exercise with a trusted friend, therapist, counselor, or minister, although some men do it on their own.

Begin with a comprehensive assessment of your negative/toxic sexual learnings from family, peers, neighborhood, media, and porn. Be honest about toxic learnings and sexual experiences.

Many men were sexually abused by an adult man or older adolescent. Typically, this is not disclosed, much less processed. This exercise provides the opportunity to break the shameful silence. Write a letter to yourself about your experience. How old were you, how old was the man (or adolescent), what happened sexually, were you coerced or threatened, how did you feel about the experience at the time, were you manipulated and told it was your fault? How did you understand your sexual response? A common sexual abuse experience involves being fellated to orgasm. Abuse can also involve giving and receiving manual and/or anal stimulation. The boy/adolescent says how could it be abuse because you were aroused and orgasmic. It was abusive/toxic because the older male met his sexual wants at your emotional expense. It was a shameful secret which could not be discussed or processed, yet controlled your sexual self-esteem.

Just as important as your personal sexual history is your history of engaging in destructive sexual behavior with others. Sexual harassment and sexual coercion are the most frequent toxic sexual behaviors. When was the first time you engaged in sexual harassment or pressured a woman sexually? Was it just you or a group of males? Did the woman say no verbally or physically? Did you stop when she said no or did you ignore it and pressure her? Did this involve manual, oral, anal, rubbing, or intercourse sex? Did it include shaming or blaming the woman?

What was the most physically violent sexual activity you ever engaged in? How did you justify it at the time? Was it just you or were others involved? Have you ever been involved in a physical incident which required the woman to seek treatment at an emergency room or doctor's office?

Has anyone ever accused you of child sexual abuse, rape, or incest? What happened and what was the outcome? Have you ever had a woman say you harassed her, coerced her, or were emotionally or sexually abusive? Do not be defensive or counterattack; carefully examine your experiences and emotions. Identify what was harmful. An important adage is you can learn from the past, but you cannot change the past. Confront your past so you eliminate toxic attitudes, behaviors, emotions, and values. Your power for change is in the present and future.

When you have completed this exercise, turn toward the woman in your life and ask her support in ensuring that you remain free of toxic sexuality. You can build a healthy sexual relationship.

Summary

This was a difficult chapter to write and a difficult chapter to read. Yet, it is necessary to confront toxic sexuality. You cannot be a healthy man in a healthy relationship if toxic sexual attitudes, behaviors, emotions, and values remain in your life.

Sadly, much in traditional sexual socialization and in our culture (subtlety and not so subtlety) reinforce toxic male sexuality. The woman's role is not to rescue you or force you to change. Her role is to be clear that toxic and destructive sexual attitudes, behaviors, and values are not acceptable. Toxic sexuality cannot be explained away or tolerated. Assume responsibility for change – she cannot do it for you. You have the ability to be a good man emotionally, relationally, and sexually. She will support your growth. Change so that sexuality has a positive 15–20% role in your life and relationship.

4

FEMALE-MALE SEXUAL EQUITY

Confronting the Double Standard

Throughout the world, even in 2020, the great majority of people grow up with the traditional male-female double standard. The double standard holds that men and women are very different psychologically, relationally, and especially sexually. Sex is the man's domain. Men are sexually superior with the male model of desire, arousal, intercourse, and orgasm natural and best. The negative consequences of sex – unwanted pregnancy, STIs, failed relationships, sexual trauma, rape, sexual harassment, and child sexual abuse – are problems for women, not men. A positive thing about the double standard is that the rules are simple and clear, although almost totally wrong. The rigidity of the double standard is particularly harmful for younger women and older men, subverting sexual pleasure and satisfaction. Rather than bringing out the best in people, it keeps men and women stuck in rigid roles which lead to conflict and low satisfaction. The couples are trapped in the "intercourse or nothing" power struggle. When it's intercourse or nothing, the result is usually nothing. You feel rejected and she feels pressured, if not coerced. The key to healthy sexuality is consent and pleasure. The double standard does not promote either consent or pleasure.

Female-male sexual equity is the new, healthy model. You are intimate and erotic friends. The equity model affirms that the essence of couple sexuality is giving and receiving pleasure-oriented touching (McCarthy & McCarthy, 2019a). You give up sexual dominance and control, but gain much more than you lose. You experience genuine sharing of pleasure and eroticism with her as your intimate ally. The double standard keeps the woman in the passive role as a second-class sexual citizen who struggles to keep up. The double standard is based on you being an autonomous sex functioner who has totally predictable erections. Each sexual encounter must end in intercourse and orgasm. You need nothing from her except to show up. This works for men in their teens, 20s and 30s (although not a healthy learning), but becomes more difficult with aging, especially after 50. The double standard sets the stage for you to develop erectile dysfunction (ED). When you have a sensitizing experience (lose your erection and cannot perform intercourse) whether at 25, 45, or 65, you do not return to autonomous function. The double standard does not provide a role for her to help you regain erectile comfort and confidence. You do not have the space to reach out for sexual help nor engage her in sharing pleasure and eroticism. She is not in a position to support you. In contrast, the female-male equity model promotes being intimate and erotic friends. This is particularly valuable for couples in their 50s, 60s, 70s, and 80s. Implementing the sexual equity model in your 20s is an example of primary prevention. Being a sexually equitable couple before you need to promotes good feelings and good sex. Usually, the woman is open to sexual equity. When men talk to peers about sex, there is a strong impulse to brag and "one-up" each other.

It is a challenge to give up the double standard and accept female-male sexual equity. You need to do more than accept – embrace sexual equity. Her enthusiasm for sharing sexuality allows you to join in affirming sexual equity.

When men speak to other men about sex, there is a lack of honesty and a strong tendency to brag and exaggerate. This reinforces clinging to traditional male power and the double standard. Men fear being labeled a "wimp", "not man enough", or "weak". You struggle to win the approval of male peers and maintain the dominant sex role. The double standard treats sex as a competitive sport. The female-male equity model emphasizes sexuality as a team sport. This is not accepted by male peers, but is healthy for you and your intimate relationship.

Embracing the female-male sexual equity approach is good for the man, couple, and culture. This affirms psychological, relational, and sexual similarities. Similarities are more common than differences, especially in a married or partnered relationship. The equity model serves as the basis for a respectful, trusting, and emotionally committed relationship. Sexuality has a 15–20% role of energizing your bond and reinforcing feelings of desire and desirability.

Exercise – Confronting the Double Standard and Replacing It with the Female-Male Sexual Equity Model

This is a crucial exercise. You go first – describe what you learned growing up about masculinity and sexuality generally and the double standard specifically. Be honest and specific, not defensive nor give a "politically correct" narrative. Discuss what you learned from peers, family, religion, the media, and teachers. Although you might feel embarrassed, when and how did you first use porn and what was your reaction to porn videos and themes? Did porn strengthen your belief in the double standard? What other factors reinforced the double standard?

Were there people or learnings which challenged the double standard or at least caused you to question it? Was there personal, family, educational, religious, or relational support for the female-male equity model? In male peer groups, there is no support for sexual equity. There is more support among female peer groups. There is often a generational split with older people justifying the double standard even if they do not advocate it. Younger people are open to exploring this issue, especially college-educated women and men.

There is nothing "natural" about the double standard. It is a rigid cultural legacy whose time has passed. Have you heard objections to the double standard from the media, peers, minister, or family members? What do you think about this? Have you heard support for the female-male equity model? Don't be surprised if you did not hear anything (or even thought about it). If you heard about the equity model, what was your reaction?

Next, examine your present attitudes, behaviors, emotions, and values about the double standard vs. female-male sexual equity. Be honest, not say what you think your partner wants to hear. Most men have not given this much thought. If there is a discussion, it is likely to be abstract rather than a personally relevant discussion. In this exercise, we want you to dialogue about the double standard vs. female-male sexual equity as a personally relevant issue.

Now it is the woman's turn to disclose her learnings from the double standard. What were the assumptions you grew up with — whether from family, religion, school, peers, media? Was the double standard assumed or was it challenged? What were the advantages of the double standard? Did the double standard cause problems in your emotional and sexual development? Women learn that they are very different than men — the message is that she is inferior. A hidden message is that men are stronger physically, emotionally, and sexually. The world is a dangerous place for women. Is that what you learned, even if sub-consciously? Growing up, what was the best thing about being a female and what was the worst thing? Are women strong or weak? What were your sexual learnings from childhood and adolescence? A core component of the double standard, especially for adolescents and young adults, are differences in sexual socialization. Men are encouraged to be sexual to reinforce masculinity — to "sow their wild oats". Women are cautioned to not become pregnant, contract an STI, be labeled a "slut", or let sex undermine her life. Did double standard learnings hurt your psychological, relational, and sexual development? What can you do now to adopt healthy attitudes, behaviors, emotions, and values?

When did you first hear about the female-male equity model? Who did you hear it from and what was your reaction? Most males do not take female-male sexual equity seriously nor do they feel it is relevant. Some give the "socially desirable" response, but the majority blow it off, especially in the context of male friends. This is her issue, not his issue.

Many men (especially college-educated) think of themselves as progressive, but don't discuss sexual equity as a personally relevant issue. In mixed-sex groups, it is women who advocate for change. It is hard to give up power and entitlement, especially when you don't believe that it is a personally relevant issue. You make fun of traditional double standard men and take pride in being a sexually liberated man who is sensitive to women's issues, especially female orgasm.

Talk about these learnings. Don't fall into simplistic and adversarial arguments with charges and countercharges. No one wins a power struggle.

As you wrap up this exercise, be honest with yourself and your partner about the effects of the double standard on your attitudes, behaviors, emotions, and values. Discuss the effects of the female-male sexual equity model on your attitudes, behaviors, emotions, and values. Most important, what do you need to do to confront the double standard and replace it with the female-male sexual equity model?

The Context for an Emotionally Meaningful Dialogue

A core strategy is a personal dialogue about the individual and cultural legacy of the double standard. Be honest and forthcoming, not blaming, adversarial, and certainly not shaming. Sharing personal learnings makes it easier for your partner to share. Focus on awareness, not blaming. A core understanding is that you can learn from the past, but cannot change the past. The power of change is in the present and future.

What does female-male sexual equity mean to each of you? It is easier to say what sexual equity isn't. It does not mean that you are clones of each other. It does not mean that every sexual experience must be mutual and synchronous. It does not mean that you have to compensate for past sexual inequality.

The essence of female-male sexual equity is recognition that both partners are first-class sexual people whose attitudes, behaviors, emotions, and values matter. Embrace sexual similarities and honor sexual differences. Value intimacy, pleasuring, and eroticism – there is not a split or competition. Celebrate mutual synchronous sexual encounters and enjoy asynchronous sexuality. Turn toward each other as an intimate sexual team whether the experience was wonderful, very good, okay, dissatisfying, or dysfunctional. Confront self-defeating gender and cultural stereotypes. Embrace your uniqueness as sexual individuals and a sexual couple.

Marcella and Jose

In many ways, Marcella, 38, and Jose, 39, were a typical American couple with typical sexual problems. In other ways, they are challenged by a growing awareness of female-male sexual similarities and gender equity. This was a second marriage for both. They have a five-person blended family, including a four-year-old son from this marriage. Marcella was a college graduate whose career as a human resource manager was thriving. Jose had an associate degree in law enforcement and was a police detective. He had a nine-year-old son from his first marriage whom he had custody of two weekends a month and six weeks during the summer. Marcella had a 19-year-old daughter from a non-marital relationship whom she raised as a single parent. The daughter was three years old at Marcella's first marriage and six when Marcella divorced.

When Marcella and Jose married, they were aware that the odds were against them, but were committed to creating a satisfying, secure, and sexual marriage. They wanted to be a cohesive, flexible family. Before marrying, they attended a skill-oriented 12-session blended family psychoeducational program. Jose had been anti-therapy due to his negative experience in couple therapy. He felt that the therapist sided with the ex-wife and unfairly characterized him as a blue-collar man who was an emotional neanderthal. Jose feared that therapy would be anti-male and blame him for marital and family problems. He was pleasantly surprised by the structure of the group and that the co-therapists were respectful and non-judgmental. Marcella had positive experiences with therapy, finding it challenging yet supportive. Her first experience was individual therapy dealing with the pressures of being a single mother balancing work, school, and parenting. Her second therapy experience was as a couple during her first marriage. Marcella had been hopeful about the marriage, but through couple therapy realized that it was a fatally flawed relationship. Her husband would show up for sessions, but he made promises he had no intention of keeping. His answer to Marcella's discovery that he was having an ongoing affair was to propose having a baby to shore up the marriage. She was disappointed in both her husband and herself, but realized that this was not a relationship worth saving.

When Jose came into her life, Marcella felt open to a relationship, but no longer believed that romantic love and sexual attraction were the core components of marriage. The blended family group program increased confidence and commitment to each other and their family.

Both Marcella and Jose grew up with the traditional double standard from their families and culture. Marcella's experiences as a single mother and in a college class challenged the double standard. Her first husband assumed the double standard, especially the right of men to have affairs and the "naturalness" of women having a child to validate the marriage. Marcella was proud she rejected those models. She wanted more for herself and her daughter than those repressive assumptions. She and Jose created female-male equity for themselves and their family. She felt like a first-class sexual woman in a first-class marriage. Marcella could not do this alone. She trusted that Jose would be her intimate ally and join in establishing an equitable bond, including sexually.

A key factor was accepting desire/pleasure/eroticism/satisfaction. Both valued intimacy and eroticism. They enjoyed sexual similarities while honoring sexual differences. An example of honoring differences is that Jose's sexual response was reliable and predictable, while Marcella's was variable and flexible. Jose was turned on by Marcella being turned on. Both enjoyed partner interaction arousal. Jose reliably had one orgasm during intercourse. Marcella was usually orgasmic before intercourse, although she could be orgasmic during intercourse. The keys for orgasm during intercourse were feeling erotic flow (subjective arousal of eight) before beginning intercourse, giving and receiving multiple stimulation during intercourse (especially giving testicle stimulation and receiving clitoral stimulation), utilizing private erotic fantasies, and using her orgasm triggers of verbalizing "I want to come" and Jose increasing speed of clitoral stimulation. Jose enjoyed her being orgasmic during intercourse (more than Marcella did). A crucial factor was turning toward each other whether the sex was wonderful or disappointing. Afterplay was an integral part of their lovemaking. Most of the time, afterplay was warm and caring; other times playful and creative. Afterplay enhanced feelings of satisfaction and secure attachment. Marcella was embarrassed to be more sexually responsive than Jose. Both the female-male sexual equity model and the Good Enough Sex (GES) model with emphasis on the multiple roles, meanings, and outcomes of couple sexuality were appealing to Marcella. Her enthusiasm won Jose over. Jose was a well-educated, third-generation Hispanic-American, but the cultural narrative of sexually dominant men and modest women still influenced him. Marcella was committed to rid herself and her family from those oppressive stereotypes.

One of their most difficult dialogues involved monogamy. Jose expected Marcella to be faithful, but as a Latin man, he wanted freedom to be sexual with other women as long as there was no emotional relationship – "just sex". Marcella was proud of being a "new woman", including feeling sexually free and expressive. The old myth that pro-sexual women would be vulnerable to affairs did not scare Marcella, although it did Jose. She assured him of her commitment to marital sexuality. She asserted her right to sexual daydreams, erotic fantasies, and "crushes". She did not fear that this would cross a line and result in an affair.

Marcella would not accept monogamy as a one-way agreement. Jose assured Marcella that he too was committed to a secure marriage. However, he would feel silly and less of a man if he committed to monogamy. For example, if he went on a weekend trip with male peers and there was an opportunity for sex, how could he say no? Part of Jose's learning was that "real men don't say no to sex". He did not want to embarrass himself, have Marcella feel hurt by his sexual "dalliances", or misunderstand his intentions. This is an example of how deep the double standard runs.

Rather than giving in or demonizing Jose, Marcella was clear that the double standard wasn't right for their marriage, especially not in regard to affairs. They needed an agreement that applied to both spouses, not one which meets his wants at her expense. If he had affairs, she had the right to have a sexual life apart from the marriage. A "sex only" affair would not fit her values. She did not want an affair, but if she had an affair, it would be a sexual friendship. This made Jose anxious. He didn't want Marcella to have an emotional or sexual involvement with another man. Marcella said, "Why should we have one set of rules for you but not for me. I thought we agreed on sexual equity?" She didn't need to beat Jose in an argument. She wanted an agreement both were committed to. She wouldn't accept him saying one thing but meaning something else. This was a very important dialogue, but not an easy one. Jose didn't want to give up the traditional masculine privilege of the right to an affair. He feared being the target of jokes by male peers. Who did he want acceptance from – Marcella or male friends? The traditional unspoken norm was that men were allowed "high opportunity/low involvement" affairs as long as it did not subvert the marriage or family. Jose's belief was that an affair was harmless male sexual fun, while her sexual friendship could subvert their marriage. She advocated for female-male equity. The traditional male approach to affairs treated her as a second-class citizen. In her experiences before marrying Jose, Marcella was aware that affairs could take on sexual and emotional meanings that were not intended. She did not want marital intimacy and family security disrupted. Jose agreed, but worried about pressure from friends.

Marcella and Jose had a dialogue about what to say to others. Jose was surprised to learn that on occasion Marcella felt pressured by female peers and by men coming on to her. Marcella told female friends that she was proud of her monogamy agreement. She enjoyed feeling attractive to men – this increased her sense of desirability and for her served as a bridge to sexual desire for Jose. If the man persisted or she felt pressured, Marcella was assertive in telling him he was being a bore and to stop. Jose admired her clarity and coping strategies. He affirmed monogamy, but this would require different coping strategies for him.

It was Jose who suggested that they establish a yearly ritual of going away as a couple for a long weekend. Marcella's daughter or a relative would watch the younger children. They set aside at least two hours to talk about their marital bond of respect, trust, and intimacy and their sexual bond of desire/pleasure/ eroticism/satisfaction. They discussed what went well in the last year, what had been problematic, and each spouse's goals for the next year.

These were not easy conversations, but were worthwhile. Marcella and Jose realize that they cannot treat their relationship with benign neglect. Marriage is a challenging process that they were committed to for themselves and their family. They wanted a better quality of life than their backgrounds and for their children to thrive in a loving, cohesive (although non-perfect) family.

The Challenges of Female-Male Equity

It is easier to confront the double standard than meet the challenges of the female-male sexual equity model. Each person is responsible for yourself. It is challenging to share your life emotionally, practically, and sexually.

In the double standard, the assumption was that the man's career came first — he made money; she was the homemaker and mother. If the economy changed or he got a better job offer, they moved. In equity relationships, both people work and sometimes the woman's career and income is greater than the man's. Is this acceptable? Negotiate agreements that work for you, your relationship, and your family. The rules of the double standard were clear. It did not promote psychological, relational, or sexual well-being, but received social and family support. The equity model requires more thought and dialogue as well as using all your resources so each person and your relationship thrive. Sexuality has a 15–20% role of energizing your bond and reinforcing feelings of desire and desirability. Sexuality provides energy to deal with life issues. An example is if both have work obligations and there is an ill child, who takes time off or works from home? You need flexibility and adaptability. If your wife makes more money, how do you integrate this into your self-esteem and relationship? If one of you is a caretaker for a family member, how does that impact your relationship?

The decision of whether to have children is the factor which most impacts your relationship. Can you be an emotionally and sexually equitable couple when going through the complex challenges of balancing parenting with autonomy, relationship, career, household, and sexuality? Equity does not mean splitting everything 50-50 nor should you expect perfection.

Traditional roles and functions continue while adding flexibility and adaptability. Within this complexity, sexual equity energizes your bond so that you are open to new roles and challenges.

The equity model involves respect, trust, and intimacy as you deal with the vicissitudes of life. This is considerably more of a challenge than assuming the traditional roles dictated by the double standard. It takes more thought, time, dialogue, and negotiation. However, the outcome will be more satisfying. Family relationships and children thrive with the female-male equity model.

Relational Equity and Sexual Equity

Although this book focuses primarily on sexual issues, the foundation of an equitable relationship is psychological and relational. Sexual equity cannot substitute for a relationship struggling with a power imbalance. There is a positive, reciprocal association between relational and sexual factors. The traditional belief about causality is that relational factors come first and sexuality naturally follows. The new understanding supports an interactive (both-and) process (Byers & McNeil, 2006). Desire/pleasure/eroticism/satisfaction as an equitable team promotes individual and couple growth. Relational and sexual equities reinforce each other in a reciprocal rather than hierarchical manner. In the traditional view, female sexuality was contingent on everything being in order. The new view of female sexuality allows her to express intimacy and eroticism to affirm her worth and energize your bond (McCarthy & McCarthy, 2019a). Sexuality is not contingent on everything being positive – she has a right to her sexual voice during stressful and difficult times. Sexuality energizes you in promoting psychological and relational equities. This helps navigate the complexities of a shared life.

Summary

Female-male sexual equity is a cornerstone of your understanding of male, female, and couple sexuality. It confronts and ends the traditional double standard which has oppressed couples over generations and across cultures. Equity redefines the core connection between the man, woman, and couple. This facilitates being intimate and erotic allies. Confront myths about male dominance and eroticism as your domain. The empowering guideline is sharing desire/ pleasure/eroticism/satisfaction.

A core message of the equity model is that female sexuality is first-class, not inferior and not contingent on everything being perfect. Each partner deserves to have a sexual voice and value pleasure. Relational and sexual equities are different dimensions, but reinforce each other. The double standard limits and oppresses you. The female-male sexual equity model affirms and energizes you, your relationship, and your sexuality.

5

THE SEXUAL DEVELOPMENT
OF BOYS AND ADOLESCENTS
Healthy and Unhealthy Learnings

In our culture, boys learn about sex in a very different way than girls. Some learnings are positive, but most are harmful. Understanding the complexity and confusing nature of childhood sexual socialization increases empathy as well as motivation to confront sexual issues as an adult.

An important learning is the prominence of the penis as opposed to the "hidden" nature of the clitoris. Insecurities about penis size are not discussed with anyone. Sexual jokes and name-calling are a negative legacy. A particular negative learning is that males do not admit weakness or ask sexual questions. This is driven by fear of being made fun of or belittled by peers.

The average male experiences first orgasm between ages 10 and 14. This is a result of masturbation or nocturnal emissions. First experiences with ejaculation/orgasm can be affirming, but often are confusing or even frightening. A powerful negative learning is that in our culture (and most cultures), males do not have the opportunity to process negative experiences or failures. Above all, boys are not supposed to have sexual questions or doubts.

For most males, childhood (up to age ten) is a happy time with few sexual stresses. Intellectual, athletic, and social growth are encouraged. Healthy development is supported by family, school, and community. The exception is sexual development. Health educators believe that sex education for children should be an integral component of human development. Unfortunately, this is not true in our culture.

There are two major problems with sexuality in childhood and adolescence. First, rather than a comprehensive sexuality education involving family, school, and religion, sex topics are ignored or treated with benign neglect. Second, male and female children are treated as if they were a different species. This increases with adolescence (ages 13–17). The notion that "boys will be boys" is the common approach. Sexual questions or concerns are avoided. Sex problems, especially in adolescence, are viewed as a female concern.

Sexual Identity for Boys

By age three, the great majority of children identify as either male or female. This means the boy accepts he has a penis which makes him different than girls. This gender acceptance is congruent with the biological reality of his body. Congruence and acceptance are crucial. There is a growing literature on gender dysphoria and gender fluidity which is an important topic (Chivers, 2017), but involves a small proportion of male and female children. For the great majority, gender acceptance sets a healthy foundation for sexual development.

What is unhealthy is the contentiousness and put-downs about the opposite gender. As is true in much of psychology and sexuality, healthy attitudes and development begin with acceptance. Conflict with girls, put-downs, or discrimination against sexual minorities interferes with healthy development. The cultural trap is to emphasize rigid differences between the genders, a trend which accelerates with adolescence. This mistaken belief is reinforced by family, adults, peers, and the culture.

There is a good deal of empirical and clinical evidence to support that among adults, especially in married and partnered relationships, there are many more similarities than differences between men and women (Hyde, 2005). A healthy developmental trajectory would create a foundation of similarities during childhood and adolescence. Unfortunately, traditional male socialization emphasizes a very different developmental trajectory. This is driven in large measure by fear. As boys enter adolescence, the emphasis on competition increases. An example is the "circle jerk" where the adolescent who ejaculates fastest and farthest is the most masculine. Fears about delayed physical development, not being athletically or socially skilled, and unsure of masculinity subverts male development.

Far and away, the chief fear involves penis size. Over 80% of males believe that their penis is smaller than average. In addition to the statistical unreality, this fear is illogical. There is no evidence that penis size has an impact on the man's, woman's, or couple's sexual function. Yet, this mistaken belief is a major theme for boys, adolescents, young adults, and adults. It reinforces feelings of not being "good enough" sexually. This is one of the most destructive learnings for adolescents.

Child Sexual Abuse

The paradox is that although sexual abuse in childhood and adolescence is less frequent for males (7% vs. 25% for females), male victims treat this as a shameful secret. This has a powerful impact on adult sexual relationships. There are four major factors in this paradox. First, female sexual abuse is a better-known problem, more written and talked about. Second, the myth is that abuse should not happen to males. If abused, this means there is something wrong with you – you are weak, vulnerable, or easily taken advantage of. Females who experience sexual abuse are also stigmatized, but stigma and secrecy are greater for males. Third, the great majority of perpetrators are adult males or male adolescents, so there is the guilt-inducing question of why it happened to you. Fourth, a common form of sexual abuse is being manually or orally stimulated to orgasm. How could it be abuse if you were aroused and orgasmic?

The best way to understand child sexual abuse is that the older man's sexual wants are met at the expense of the boy or adolescent's emotional needs. Abuse is the shameful secret that cannot be disclosed or processed. You disavow an important part of your sexual history. You have a "contingent sexual self-esteem" believing if your partner knew your sexual history, she would not love or respect you. The fear is she would be disgusted.

Two other factors have a major impact. First, the relationship with the perpetrator. Although it can be a stranger, most of the time it is someone the child knows, including a teacher, cousin, neighbor, uncle, mother's boyfriend, minister. Often, the perpetrator manipulates or threatens the boy. He says that no one would believe you and disclosure would cause great conflict and disruption. Second, the issue of physical force. Sex associated with force is psychologically destructive and a powerful negative learning. Secrecy and shame multiply the impact of child sexual abuse. The most painful issue is feeling you cannot share your abuse history. Rather than the woman being a "partner in healing", she feels left out and frustrated by your emotional distance. In the majority of cases, she is willing and eager to have a role in processing the abuse history and developing couple sexuality. When dealing with sexual trauma or negative sexual experiences, the theme is being a "proud survivor" not an anxious, angry, shameful, or depressed "victim" (Maltz, 2012).

In a healthy culture, sexual abuse would not occur – an example of primary prevention. If sexual abuse did occur – secondary prevention involves facing it at the time, processing it in an empathic, respectful manner (not engaging in victim blaming), emphasizing positive sexual information, and becoming a proud survivor. What usually happens is tertiary intervention. This involves dealing with trauma as an adult. The core strategy is processing abuse in a non-shaming manner and being a proud survivor who values consensual sexuality involving desire/pleasure/eroticism/satisfaction.

Healing occurs in the context of an intimate sexual relationship. Healing begins with the courage to share your psychological/relational/sexual history, including abuse and trauma. Can your partner be your emotional and sexual ally, responding in an empathic and respectful manner? You need her respect and empathy; you do not want sympathy or for her to "freak out". She cannot do it for you, but can be your partner in healing. The abuse was not your fault. You coped as well as you could with the resources you had at the time. As an adult in an intimate relationship, you have greater awareness, insights, and resources.

The most important awareness is that you deserve sexuality to have a positive role in your life. A specific strategy is the power to veto 1–3 sexual scenarios with confidence that she will honor your veto. This frees you to enjoy intimate, pleasure-oriented sexuality. That is the opposite of abusive experiences. You are a proud survivor who embraces desire/pleasure/eroticism/satisfaction. A favorite adage is "Living well is the best revenge".

When the Woman Has an Abuse/Trauma History

The same strategies and guidelines apply in the more common case where it is the woman with a history of child sexual abuse, rape, or incest. A major guideline is "Don't blame the victim". This is particularly important because in our culture, the norm is to blame women for acquaintance rape, sexual harassment, unplanned pregnancy, or incest. Blaming and shaming multiply the trauma. No one deserves to be raped or abused.

Be sure your partner is on your side and is trustworthy. Barry remembers a couple where the woman's abuse history involved an uncle rubbing his penis against her breast. Her veto involved any breast stimulation. Her partner described himself as a "breast man" but said, "Your emotional needs are more important than my sexual wants". They created and maintained an intimate sexual bond.

When you feel desire/pleasure/eroticism/satisfaction in the context of an intimate relationship, you have taken back your body and sexuality; it is no longer controlled by trauma.

Special Issues in Childhood Sexuality

You are a sexual person from the day you're born until the day you die. Male children have erections in utero. It is normal and healthy to enjoy touching and being touched, including children exploring and touching their genitals. Accept this rather than slap the child's hands. The child learns proper words for penis and vagina. Unfortunately, this is not the norm. Don't be harsh on your parents or culture. Developing sexual comfort is not easy for either adults or children.

Did you learn that genital touch in private (your bedroom or the bathtub) was acceptable, but not genital touch in public? Curiosity is normal and healthy. Hugs and affection are integral to healthy development. Did you learn the model of good touch/bad touch? What do you remember from elementary school? Were you encouraged to interact with both genders? Was touch and exploration accepted?

Acceptance of genital differences in childhood is an important learning. Did your family, school, and neighborhood promote healthy developmental learnings? Health educators advocate for educational programs beginning in first grade, including parental involvement (although in reality this is rare). The theme of health/sex educators is to begin with positive sexual learnings. Unfortunately, educational programs begin with topics like sexual abuse, fear of strangers, bad touch, and negative consequences of sex. Negative sexual messages target females, not males. Start with positive sexuality education for both males and females.

There are substantial age differences in physical development (height, genital hair). Male children fear being behind. A significant event is first orgasm whether with nocturnal emission or masturbation. Few children are educated about what to expect or what orgasm means. There are jokes and bragging, but no real discussion about orgasm/ejaculation. Feeling frightened or ashamed is unnecessary. Ideally, a father, father figure, or older sibling would reassure the child that orgasm/ejaculation is normal and healthy. First orgasm serves as a cue for sex education. Adolescents complain that school and family sex education was too little, too late. The "sex talk" is usually uncomfortable, uninformative, vague, and judgmental.

Ideally, both your father and mother were "askable parents"? A crucial guideline is "Never lie to your child". This is especially true for sex issues.

By the time the boy reaches adolescence (age 13), he has heard confusing and often contradictory information about sexuality from peers, family, religion, boy scouts, athletic teams, teachers, and the media. The number of 13-year-olds who are satisfied with their sex education is very small. Most of their education was informal – on the street or from the internet. A surprising number have been exposed to porn (without a context about the differences between the reality of sex and the erotic fantasy world of porn). Few had a serious discussion of sex issues with an adult. One of the most negative childhood legacies is that males are not supposed to ask questions or have sexual problems.

Sexual Issues for Male Adolescents

Scientists believe that ages 13–16 are the most confusing and disruptive in life. Much of this is attributed to sexual confusion and pressure. Adolescent males lie about their sexual experiences. No one admits that they are a virgin, although most are. They brag about what a wonderful sex partner they are, how strong their erections are, and their lasting power. In reality, most adolescents begin their sex lives as premature ejaculators with some experiencing orgasm before the penis enters the vagina. This is nothing to be ashamed of – sex like any other human skill requires practice and feedback. Ideally, your first relationship is a sexual friendship with an adolescent girl where you treat each other well and the relationship ends in a kind manner. A first relationship can involve a "hook-up" or a paid sex experience. On the other extreme, some men have a three-year relationship or marry their first partner. For the majority, the relationship lasts weeks or months. Most men remember their first intercourse positively, but not all. Be aware that first partner orgasm usually occurs with manual, oral, or rubbing stimulation rather than intercourse.

The question is whether sexual learnings were helpful or not. For most adolescents, there was a mixture of good, mediocre, and bad sexual experiences. This is the norm and is true with most learnings whether academic, athletic, or social. Two questions Barry asks when conducting a sex history, "What was your best psychological, relational, or sexual experience before you left home?" Then, "What was your most confusing, negative, guilt-inducing, or traumatic psychological, relational, or sexual experience before leaving home?" Most males (and females) had both positive and negative experiences. The most common positive experiences were feeling attractive and cared for, being in a healthy sexual relationship, confidence you can navigate life and relationships, enjoying personal freedom, feeling good about your body and sexuality, growing appreciation of women and sexuality. The most common negative experiences were feeling sexually rejected and put down, contracting an STI, causing an unwanted pregnancy, caught masturbating and made fun of, fearing that there is something sexually wrong with you, sexual abuse and feeling it had to be kept secret, feeling guilty for sexually harassing a woman. Remember the core adage, you can learn from the past, but cannot change the past. Your power for change is in the present and future.

Issues for Female Adolescents

The message for adolescent women is "don't". Don't get pregnant, don't contract an STI, don't be raped, don't be sexually harassed. Although not clearly stated, a common parental fear is don't become obsessed with the wrong man and let your life be sidetracked. There is little to no emphasis on growing as a female, valuing pleasure, enjoying arousal and orgasm, or assuming responsibility for yourself and your sexuality. The double standard is bad for females at any age, but especially during adolescence. It is hard to identify a healthy developmental trajectory psychologically, relationally, and sexually. Almost no one would choose to return to adolescence, even if they knew then what they know now.

Exercise – Healthy and Unhealthy Sexual Learnings

This is not an easy exercise, but is motivating and empowering.

List as many positive learnings as you can – be sure you have at least five. Then, list negative learnings. Most men find it easy to list many more than five negatives and some have to be reminded to stop at 20. Make the positive and negative learnings as specific and personal as possible; don't give vague or socially desirable responses.

Positive learnings include:

1 Pride in being a man, including your penis
2 Enjoying orgasm
3 Freedom to be sexual and enjoy intercourse
4 Feeling attractive to females
5 First partner orgasm
6 Learning to touch and kiss
7 Enjoy being orgasmic with manual or oral stimulation
8 Feeling good about being a sexual man
9 Joking with male friends about sex
10 A close relationship with an older sibling or cousin who provided sexual guidance.

Make your list personal and concrete, and acknowledge positive experiences and learnings.

Examples of negative learnings include:

1 Being made fun of by an ex-girlfriend and her friends
2 Caught masturbating and shamed for it
3 Fear your penis is small or oddly shaped
4 Being sexually abused by an uncle
5 Forced to be passive in anal intercourse
6 When 12-years-old having your pants pulled down by a group of males
7 Watching porn with fear you are addicted
8 Fear that you might be gay
9 Believing you must have a spontaneous erection to impress a woman
10 Fear that you can't live up to double standard demands.

Be honest. What adolescent learnings interfere with your adult sexuality?

We encourage the woman to do this exercise about her positive and negative adolescent learnings.

The real test is willingness to share your lists/learnings with your partner, especially the negative learnings. Doing so increases your vulnerability. More importantly, it builds a respectful, trusting, and intimate bond because it invites your partner to be your ally in confronting and changing destructive attitudes and values. The man who is vulnerable and open to his partner's positive influence is a better man, better sex partner, and better life partner.

Adolescence to Adulthood

Adolescence is a crucial developmental time in the lives of both males and females. The traditional approach to adolescence brings out the worst in people, especially sexually. The destructive learnings of the double standard are reinforced. Fears about negative sexual consequences are much higher for females. The learnings for males, especially fears of not being good enough and shameful secrets, subvert sexual self-esteem. The sad reality is that many men have a contingent sexual self-esteem and are in a contingent relationship. You fear if your partner or male peers knew about your sexual past they would not respect you. This is a very hard way to live. Self-acceptance involves acknowledging strengths and positive learnings as well as accepting and processing vulnerabilities and sensitive issues. Acceptance is the key to healthy sexuality. This gives you courage to confront toxic male sexuality and the oppressive double standard. Affirm a new model of male sexuality which allows your sexual relationship to thrive.

Daniel and Rachel

Rachel and Daniel met in their mid-twenties – they were an idealistic limerence couple. This was a wonderful way to begin, but not a healthy way to establish an intimate relationship. It was Rachel who pushed the importance of processing each person's psychological, relational, and sexual past. She could not commit to Daniel until she understood who he really was, including vulnerabilities from childhood and adolescence. Male friends warned him against self-disclosure. They said Rachel wanted to know this so she had leverage to force him to change.

Daniel prided himself on being a "regular guy" who valued a girlfriend and sexual relationship. Daniel knew that they were a special couple, and felt ready for a marital commitment. However, he was fearful of Rachel's motives – did she love him or was she searching for reasons to back away? Self-disclosure and vulnerability can strengthen the man and intimate relationship or it can be used in a destructive manner.

Rachel assured Daniel that she did not have a manipulative or hidden agenda. She disclosed two major vulnerabilities from her adolescence – an abortion when she was 17 and being sexually abused over a period of months by an older cousin when she was 13. Rachel regretted both experiences, but was not shameful nor did she allow these to subvert her sexual self-esteem. Daniel felt closer to Rachel after those disclosures and open to sharing his life with her. However, he felt that his "shameful secret" was much worse and feared that she would not accept him. Daniel wrote a four-page letter to Rachel describing his experiences of being fellated to orgasm two to three times a week at ages 14–16 by a married man who lived in the neighborhood. Daniel had never spoken about

44

this to anyone. The man told Daniel that this was just harmless fun which he enjoyed because he was so easily orgasmic. The neighbor said that if Daniel's parents found out, they would be ashamed of Daniel. The neighbor had young children and told Daniel that disclosure would destroy the neighbor's family.

As an adult, Daniel had no contact with this man who had moved to another state. Daniel still could not make sense of these experiences. At the time, Daniel feared that he was gay. His adolescent, college, and young adult sexual experiences were driven by the need to prove that he was straight. Although Rachel enjoyed giving and receiving oral sex, Daniel strongly preferred intercourse. He was much more comfortable giving oral sex than receiving.

After reading the letter, Rachel invited Daniel to dinner at her apartment. She was appreciative that he shared this traumatic experience. Daniel broke into tears – he had never labeled those experiences as traumatic, but she was right. He was the victim, not responsible for the abuse. The neighbor's sexual wants were met at the expense of Daniel's emotional needs. It was the burden of keeping these experiences secret that caused Daniel the most harm.

They discussed the difference between regret and shame. They did not want their adolescence defined by negative incidents. Rachel wanted Daniel to know that he could veto oral sex, but that for her giving oral sex was a loving, erotic experience. Again, Daniel cried. He associated fellatio with being sexually serviced, not loved. It reminded him of the way fellatio is shown in porn videos – oral sex had nothing to do with intimacy or pleasure.

As Daniel and Rachel processed healthy and unhealthy learnings, they didn't get stuck on the details but did process themes. Daniel felt pride in being a sexual man intermixed by a great deal of regret and guilt over abusive experiences. Rachel urged him to commit to intimate, pleasurable, and erotic sexuality. This was not a conversation that Daniel was used to, but was crucial. It was the opposite of fears and shameful secrets. Ultimately, Daniel became comfortable and turned on by receiving fellatio in the context of synchronous erotic scenarios. Daniel was not interested in asynchronous fellatio.

Just as important, Rachel and Daniel processed positive sexual learnings and experiences. Rather than making jokes or one-upping, they spoke as sexual allies highlighting what each needed if they were to maintain healthy couple sexuality. A prime task in the first two years of marriage is to transition from the limerence relationship phase to develop a couple sexual style with strong, resilient desire. Sexuality has a 15–20% role in their lives. Both Daniel and Rachel were committed to a satisfying, secure, and sexual marriage.

Summary

Childhood and adolescence are when males (and females) develop a foundation for adult sexuality. Few people have the benefit of comprehensive sex education involving the school, family, and religion. Sex education typically emphasized child sexual abuse, STIs, and unwanted pregnancy. The message to female children is don't be sexual and be afraid of negative sexual consequences. The message to male children is don't ask questions or appear uncertain. The message of gender sexual socialization is that boys and girls are very different. This reinforces the traditional double standard.

Males are encouraged to be sexual with masturbation and taking sexual risks with girls. Sex is the man's domain and sexual problems are the woman's issue. Females are taught sexual avoidance. Sexual abuse is a problem for girls, not boys. If boys are abused, it must stay a "shameful secret". The negative effects of splitting by gender are multiplied during adolescence.

The sexual socialization of males and females is very different. Sexual issues are a prime cause of the drama and struggles so many adolescents experience. Negative psychological, relational, and sexual learnings from adolescence interfere with adult sexuality. You need to confront these attitudes, behaviors, emotions, and values.

A crucial reality is that sexual differences are the greatest in adolescence and young adulthood. These negative learnings have to be challenged so that as adults, men and women are intimate and erotic allies.

6

YOUNG ADULT SEXUALITY
Time for Change

Major gender differences in sexual socialization and experience dominate young adulthood (ages 18–25). As adults, especially in marriage and partnered relationships, there are many more similarities than differences between men and women. This is true psychologically, relationally, and sexually. However, this is not true with young adult sexual experiences.

There are three major factors contributing to male-female sexual differences in young adulthood: (1) double standard learnings and expectations, (2) autonomous vs. intimate, interactive sexuality, and (3) negative sexual consequences (which have a greater impact on women). Be aware of psychological, bio-medical, and social/relational factors which subvert young adult sexuality.

Male-Female Double Standard

There is nothing natural or inherent in the male-female double standard. It is a socially learned set of rules passed down culturally as if the double standard was based on fact. The double standard subverts sexual desire and satisfaction for adults. It is unhealthy not just for the woman, but also for you. The double standard emphasizes that you are the "sex expert". Sexual initiation is your role, with intercourse frequency the prime focus. You are in charge of foreplay to get her ready for intercourse. Intercourse is "real sex". With the double standard, the woman's role is inhibited – she is passive and follows your lead. This is viewed as "normal" and even celebrated. In the double standard, negative sexual consequences are her fault and burden – whether pregnancy, contracting an STI, being sexually abused, raped, labeled a "slut", or being mistreated in a relationship.

The only advantage of the double standard is that the rules are clear, wrong but clear. In the double standard, sex is your domain with sexual problems her fault and burden. Your male pattern of sexual response is the norm – spontaneous desire and erections, highly predictable intercourse and orgasm, with freedom to be sexual in a guilt-free manner. Sex is a performance to prove yourself to the woman and to male peers.

The rules of the double standard mimic the concept that there is a totally different set of gender attitudes, behaviors, emotions, and values. The double standard makes it clear that males are the sexually dominant gender; females are submissive and second class. You are ready to "have sex with any woman, any time, any place". Foreplay is to get her ready for intercourse – she is in the one-down position, trying to catch up.

Autonomous Sex vs. Intimate, Interactive Sexuality

The second major negative learning from young adulthood is that male autonomous sex response is superior to female variable, flexible sexual response. You obtain an easy, spontaneous erection and proceed to intercourse and orgasm on your first erection. Sexual response is in your control and is highly reliable. The most important factor is that sexual response is autonomous. You experience desire, arousal, and orgasm, needing nothing from her.

The great majority of young adult women learn sexual response as interactive rather than autonomous, variable and flexible rather than totally reliable. The "common sense" notion is that the man's sexual response is the norm. The message is that male sex is totally predictable and superior. This is a prime cause for you to feel embarrassed and stop being sexual whether at 45, 65, or 75. The flexible, variable, pleasure-oriented Good Enough Sex (GES) approach (Metz & McCarthy, 2012) is compatible with female sexual socialization. The challenge for you is to adopt GES. GES promotes sexual desire and satisfaction, especially after age 50 in married and partnered relationships.

Negative Sexual Consequences

The third powerful, destructive learning from young adulthood is that the negative consequences of sexuality are the woman's burden. One reason that 35-year-old women are much healthier sexually than 15- or 25-year-old women is that they feel free to express themselves sexually with less fear of negative consequences or judgments. She feels increased sexual self-acceptance. She owns her sexual voice and values a satisfying, secure, and sexual relationship. Her partner is an intimate ally rather than someone she has to prove something to or meet your expectations.

Her body image is more accepting and positive than at 25, even though by media/social desirability standards she is no longer viewed as "hot". Ads, media depictions, and movies focus on beautiful, thin, erotic women between 18 and 25. These images are intimidating, not empowering. The message is she's not "good enough sexually". Anxieties about STI/HIV, unwanted pregnancy, and gossip dominate young adult female sexuality. A common way to deal with this stress is to use alcohol and/or drugs to reduce sexual self-consciousness.

This risks creating more emotional, behavioral, and sexual problems. Too many young adult men and women associate sex with being drunk or high. There is nothing wrong with one or two drinks to reduce self-consciousness, but associating sex with alcohol ultimately subverts sexual self-esteem and couple sexuality. From a biological perspective, alcohol is a central nervous system depressant so lessens sexual response. That is not the reality for young adult men and women. Alcohol "greases" the social and sexual milieu. Psychosocial factors override negative biological effects. However, this changes for middle years and older men (and women). Alcohol abuse is a major cause of sexual dysfunction.

Positive motivation promotes sexuality. Pressure to sexually prove yourself subverts sexuality. Few men want to return to their young adult years. This is even truer for women.

Sexual Development and Growth

Rather than demonizing young adult sexuality or feeling intimidated by it, a healthy approach is to accept this as a developmental phase which will require personal and sexual growth as he (and she) enter adulthood. Rather than envying or demonizing young adult sexuality, understand and process this in the context of development in the same way that you proceed through other developmental stages. For both men and women, psychological well-being improves after age 25. This is due, in part, to having a better sexual self-esteem. In adulthood, you have fewer social and sexual fears. You have a healthy sexual voice (autonomy) so you make better sexual decisions. Adults say that if they knew now what they should have known at 25, they would do things very differently. Almost no one would choose to return to adolescence and few would want to return to young adulthood. There is too much angst and drama, much of which is driven by relational and sexual issues.

The core concept is that healthy sexuality has a 15–20% role in a person's life and relationship. This is true whether you are male or female, 16, 26, 46, 66, or 86. The paradox is dysfunctional, conflictual, or avoidant sexuality has an inordinately powerful negative role, a 50–75% factor, subverting you and destabilizing your relationship. The most disruptive time is during adolescence and young adulthood. This includes issues such as STIs, HIV, and unwanted pregnancy. Psychological factors include low sexual self-esteem, sexual trauma, poor body image, and confusion about the roles and meanings of sexuality. Relationships are unstable during this period, including conflicts about intimacy and sexuality, feeling emotionally or sexually betrayed, dramatic break-ups, feeling unloved, fears of not being able to maintain a sexual relationship, and cynicism about sex and relationships.

Knowledge is a powerful resource. You learn to make wise psychological, relational, and sexual decisions. Young adulthood is a challenging time for sexual health and psychological well-being. Yet, it can be a time of psychological, relational, and sexual growth.

A motivating strategy is to view positive and negative sexual learnings during young adulthood as less important in themselves and more important from the perspective of what you learned about yourself, sexuality, and relationships (O'Sullivan, Cheng, Harris, & Brook-Gunn, 2007). A prime issue is setting the stage for adult sexuality. Does sexuality have a positive role in your life and relationship? The journey was a bumpy one, with positive and negative learnings and experiences. Are you a healthy adult in a healthy relationship?

Healthy Sexual Learnings from Young Adulthood

The core learning is that sexuality is a good thing in life, not bad or evil. Second, sexuality is a positive, integral component of your personal identity. Third, the experiences you had, especially dating and sexual, are lessons about becoming a healthy sexual adult. Positive learnings include owning your sexual story with its strengths and vulnerabilities, affirmative and difficult experiences. The majority of young adult men (and women) engage in masturbation. Accept your body, enjoy sexual touch, and through masturbation learn your unique desire/pleasure/eroticism/satisfaction pattern. The great majority of males learn to be orgasmic through masturbation. However, they negate the value of these learnings by associating masturbation with secrecy and shame. In contrast, emphasize an open approach to body exploration, sensual touch, playful touch, erotic touch, and orgasm as a whole-body experience. Learning sexual response and orgasm through masturbation makes it easier to enjoy partner sex.

A positive learning is to value yourself in the context of an intimate relationship. Even during the romantic love/passionate sex/idealization phase, do not lose your sense of self. Your sexual self-esteem is not governed by the partner and her judgment. A healthy relationship allows you to feel desire and desirable, contributing 15–20% to life satisfaction. Sex should not dominate your life. This is easier to accept and implement at 25 than 18. This involves psychological, relational, and sexual growth.

Another healthy learning is to value integrated sexuality – intimacy, pleasuring, and eroticism. Unfortunately, at this life phase, male sexual socialization focuses on sexual performance and eroticism to the exclusion of intimacy and pleasuring.

We urge you to value female sexuality. Female sexual response is more variable, flexible, complex, and individualistic than male response, especially during young adulthood. Complex and different does not mean worse. A theme is that female sexual socialization emphasizes intimate, interactive, variable, and flexible sexuality. This is compatible with the GES approach which is a better fit for couples than the autonomous male individual performance approach.

Debbie and Scott

Scott and Debbie became a couple their sophomore year in college. Six years later, they married. The marriage was supported by both family and friends. Debbie and Scott were committed to a satisfying, secure, and sexual marriage based on emotional and sexual equity.

Coming to this point required a great deal of psychological, relational, and sexual growth. Scott grew up in an intact family, but his parents were a poor marital and sexual model. There were chronic marital conflicts over a number of issues. As an adolescent, Scott realized that sex was an underlying problem in their marriage. His father drank with male friends, and the hidden agenda often involved paid sex or "hook-up" sex with women at bars. Mother attacked father as acting like an adolescent and he counter-attacked calling her "frigid". He blamed her for all marital and sexual problems. Scott and his younger brother attempted to shut out these conflicts. Scott tried to prove his manhood by "hooking up" starting at age 13. Scott and his friends joked that they would never need paid sex. Scott felt that he treated girlfriends well and believed that "hook-up" connections were consensual.

Scott's world view dramatically changed freshman year at college when he was forced to withdraw based on accusations of sexual harassment issued by two sophomore women. In Scott's view, these incidents were nothing more than sexual hook-ups. This was strongly confronted by the dean of students and the two women, with powerful negative consequences. Scott's mother encouraged him to learn from this experience and be resilient. She urged Scott to apply to a new college, and more importantly focus on life lessons, especially emotional and sexual boundaries. Scott needed to learn the red line between coercive sex and sexual consent. A problem with Scott's hooking up experiences was that those boundaries were blurred. Adding to this was that most of Scott's sexual experiences, including with the two sophomore women, occurred when he was drunk or high. This further confused boundaries, especially in light of sober reflection the next morning.

Scott was proud that he was resilient. He enrolled in a college which was a better fit for him and where he established a relationship with Debbie. This had been a painful learning, but a valuable outcome. A mature Scott valued intimacy, touching, and sexuality in the context of healthy boundaries.

Debbie had a very different life story and sexual socialization. She was 8 when her parents divorced and 13 when her mother remarried. Debbie was fortunate in that her parents were in the minority of couples – they had a "good divorce". The prime factor was her father accepting his sexual identity as a gay man. Instead of blame or shame, her parents sadly realized that the marriage was fatally flawed because of sexual orientation. The good divorce involved wishing each other well and not being involved in the ex-spouse's emotional, relational, or sexual decisions. Mother was the prime custodial parent, but father was an involved co-parent who maintained financial and emotional responsibilities. He reinforced a loving father-daughter relationship and encouraged Debbie to develop a positive relationship with her stepfather. Both parents supported Debbie's emotional and sexual development.

Debbie's first intercourse was as an 18-year-old high school senior. She introduced her boyfriend to her parents after they'd been dating for six months. Debbie obtained birth control pills and used condoms to guard against STIs. This relationship ended during her freshman year of college. The strain of a long-distance relationship and her desire to date at college motivated her to terminate the relationship. Debbie continued to utilize safe sex and birth control even when she was having sex on an irregular basis. She did not want to risk a pregnancy.

Debbie and Scott met sophomore year. They began as friends and two months later had their first official date. After three months, they became a sexual couple, but not before going to the student health center for an STI screen and HIV test. Debbie and Scott were free of STIs. They used birth control pills, but there was not a need for condoms. If either was sexual with another person, this was a cue to resume condom use. This occurred twice over the six years they dated. When they returned to being a monogamous couple, they were again jointly tested. Both felt good about following their agreement and being a safe sexual couple.

They married when Scott was 27 and Debbie 26. Like over 60% of American couples, they cohabitated before marriage. They didn't just slide into marriage, but made an affirmative decision to share their lives as a respectful, trusting couple. They were committed to a satisfying, secure, and sexual marriage. Less than one in four couples discloses and discusses sensitive psychological, relational, and sexual information before marrying (McCarthy & McCarthy, 2004). Debbie insisted that she and Scott have that conversation. She wasn't worried that Scott had a major secret, but wanted to be aware of personal and relational vulnerabilities. Although this was an emotionally difficult series of conversations, it was valuable. They were not burdened by negative sexual learnings from adolescence or young adulthood. The hardest issue for Debbie was Scott's belief that the man should be the initiator because sexual desire and function is easy for him. She enjoyed Scott's obvious attraction and sexual response, but insisted that he treat her as a first-class sexual person. Intimacy and pleasuring were not just to please her, but a valued part of their couple sexual style. Scott was not comfortable talking about sexual issues, but Debbie said she wanted to be sure they would be a healthy couple throughout their lives. Establishing this foundation was a wise emotional investment. When Debbie told him she'd read that it was men who stopped couple sex in their 50s or 60s because they'd lost sexual confidence, Scott didn't believe it or want to talk about it.

One day while watching football on TV, Debbie asked Scott how old he thought the couple in the Viagra commercial was. Scott guessed the man was

60, the woman 35. Debbie said they were in their 50s. Debbie didn't want to be like that couple – she wanted Scott to turn toward her, not to a pill. Scott was a certified physical therapist who advocated for primary prevention which made sense when thinking about sexual desire and function. Sexuality which integrates desire/pleasure/eroticism/satisfaction is the best primary prevention strategy. Scott had come a long way since adolescence and felt very lucky to have a pro-sexual wife to share his journey.

Eroticism: The Most Controversial Issue

In young adult male sexual socialization eroticism is the focus. This has always been true whether traditional Playboy centerfolds or the plethora of erotic pictures and videos on the internet. One of the core themes of porn is the crazier the woman, the more erotic she is. What is the best way to understand the erotic dimension of couple sexuality? Is it to be as sexually dramatic as possible? To reject eroticism as anti-feminist? To view porn and eroticism as unhealthy male sexuality? To hope you will outgrow this fixation on eroticism?

We suggest a very different strategy. Accept the mantra of desire/pleasure/eroticism/satisfaction as relevant for both men and women. Eroticism is an integral component of each partner's sexual voice. Eroticism is not the domain of male sexuality; eroticism is important for women. That does not mean that she adopts the male approach. Be sure eroticism is integrated into her sexual voice (McCarthy & McCarthy, 2019a). Integrated eroticism is much superior to the traditional porn version. Eroticism is a core component in the desire/pleasure/eroticism/satisfaction mantra for both women and men.

Let's be specific about what integrated eroticism means (whether at 20, 40, or 60). It is very different than a porn version. Eroticism is compatible with intimacy and pleasuring. Eroticism is not at the expense of the partner or relationship. Eroticism can include partner interaction arousal, self-entrancement arousal, and/or role enactment arousal. Eroticism involves creativity, mystery, unpredictability, lust, taking emotional and sexual risks, not being politically correct, and sharing vibrant, vital sexuality.

How is this different from porn eroticism? The porn message is that the best sex is dirty, kinky, out of control – totally divorced from intimacy and pleasuring. The crazier the scenario, the more erotic and the crazier the woman, the more erotic. Porn eroticism knows no boundaries; it's about sexual risks with no reality consequences. Porn eroticism lives in a world where the man is dominant, the woman submissive. Sex is about power and control, used to subjugate and humiliate women. There is no boundary between fantasy and reality – eroticism is controlling and has no conscience.

With integrated eroticism, there is a clear boundary between erotic fantasy and real-life sexual behavior. By its nature, erotic fantasies are about unacceptable sexual behaviors – violent sex, watching people having sex, sex with an inappropriate partner, orgies, double penetration sex, sex with two women, sexually humiliating the woman, being sexual in front of a group. Is this the behavior you want with a real-life partner? No, erotic fantasies (whether his or hers) are a totally different realm than real-life sexual behavior. Integrated eroticism recognizes that distinction.

Women want the freedom to enjoy erotic fantasies whether at 15, 25, 45, or 75. The best-selling book series "Shades of Gray" vividly illustrated that. The sales reflect the power of women's freedom to enjoy erotic sexuality, specifically socially unacceptable fantasy themes.

The split of eroticism by gender is an example of the importance of the need for you to confront the destructive learnings that occur in young adulthood. These destructive learnings have more negative impact on men than women. You mistakenly believe that "first class male sex" is controlled by autonomous sex response and porn eroticism. This limits and inhibits male sexuality. In contrast, the challenge for women is to incorporate eroticism into their sexual lives and couple sexuality.

Exercise – Assessing Healthy and Unhealthy Male Sexual Learnings in Young Adulthood

Do this exercise with a person you like and respect – a spouse, partner, sibling, minister, good friend, counselor – who is thoughtful and offers honest feedback about your sexual learnings (whether similar to or different than traditional learnings).

Start with positive learnings. Be as specific and concrete as possible. What were your psychological, relational, and sexual learnings as a young adult which promoted male and couple sexuality. Examples include valuing sexuality, seeing sex as a positive dimension in life, learning sexual response and orgasm through masturbation, enjoying a range of erotic fantasies, learning from sexual problems rather than feeling burdened or shameful, enjoying dating, seeing sexuality as an integral component of masculinity, admiring female beauty and sexuality, enjoying intercourse and orgasm, learning about women and relationships, using condoms and practicing safe sex. Don't talk just about socially desirable or politically correct learnings. What were your positive learnings?

The second part of this exercise is more challenging and difficult, but equally important.

What are the negative learnings from young adult sexual socialization which interfere with male and couple sexuality? Be specific and concrete – not the traditional war between men and women with attacks and counter-attacks.

Common negative male learnings include avoiding serious conversations about sexuality, feeling your penis is smaller than average, pressure to perform for the woman or to impress male peers, not be tested for an STI, avoid responsibility for an unplanned pregnancy, not use condoms in an effective manner, brag and lie about sexual experiences, label women as "sluts" or "whores", insist that you are the sex expert, put down the woman for not being as desirous or orgasmic as you, labeling other men as "wimps", engaging in coercive or forced sex, putting down gay men, stalking or harassing an ex-girlfriend, putting down women and telling sexist jokes, feeling that it is your job to be sure that she has an orgasm each time, insisting that a real woman must orgasm during intercourse, believing that men are better than women – especially sexually, believing intimacy and affection are for the woman, feeling that giving oral sex is a chore, insisting she swallow semen as a sign of submission, preferring porn to couple sex, pretending to enjoy a sexual scenario but in reality disliking it, having sex questions or doubts but not raising them, lying about whether you've had an STI, splitting intimacy and eroticism, treating "relationship women" different than "erotic women".

Once these lists have been created, focus on what it means to be a sexual man. What are the problematic legacies from young adult socialization? How can you deal with these negative learnings? Even more challenging is dealing with your partner regarding disparate sexual and relational learnings. A crucial guideline is to avoid "right-wrong" power struggles. Each partner is responsible for your sexuality, but ultimately sexuality is a team sport. As adult partners, process healthy and unhealthy, common and different, sexual learnings. The challenge is integrating these learnings in your intimate sexual relationship.

Looking Back Fondly, Resentfully, or in an Empowering Manner

You can learn from the past, but can't change the past. Take responsibility and enjoy sexuality in the present and future.

Many men (and some women) look back fondly at sexual experiences in young adulthood. That is fine as long as you acknowledge negative learnings and be open to sexual change. The trap of fond memories is that it makes it too easy to deny or minimize problematic experiences. Carefully process positive and negative learnings from young adulthood.

The problem with resentful processing is that you stay stuck in the "victim role". You are caught in the angry, anxious, or shameful victim cycle which subverts your sexuality. It is crucial to process hurt, angry, and abusive feelings about past sexual experiences. Recognize and grieve psychological, relational, and sexual losses. You cannot allow these experiences to control your sexuality. It is women who commonly fall into depressive, angry, or resentment traps. It is men who fall into the shameful secret trap (especially in regard to sexual trauma).

Process young adult sexual experiences and learnings in an empowering manner. Be open. Recognize both healthy and unhealthy learnings. Processing all your experiences allows you to increase understanding. Address male and couple sexuality to promote desire/pleasure/eroticism/satisfaction.

Summary

Major differences in sexual socialization occur in young adulthood. The challenge is to confront and learn from the disparities in psychological, relational, and sexual socialization. A key to healthy couple sexuality is an equitable female-male model which emphasizes respect, trust, and emotional and sexual intimacy. You are intimate and erotic allies who value desire/pleasure/eroticism/satisfaction. When you engage in the traditional war between the sexes – for example, intimacy is the woman's domain, eroticism the man's domain – couple sexuality is the loser. The male-female double standard is strong in young adulthood. A challenge of adult sexuality is to confront these self-defeating learnings. Adopt female-male sexual equity which promotes a satisfying, secure, and sexual relationship.

7

THE NEW SEXUAL MANTRA

Desire/Pleasure/Eroticism/Satisfaction

In the traditional approach to sexuality, the mistaken assumption was that eroticism, intercourse, and orgasm were the man's domain; intimacy, pleasuring, and stability were the woman's domain. "Foreplay" involved the man stimulating the woman so that she would be ready for the "real thing" – intercourse. The traditional view was "sex = intercourse".

There is a new mantra in the sexuality field – desire/pleasure/eroticism/satisfaction (Foley, Kope, & Sugrue, 2012). This empowering mantra is applicable to both men and women. The great majority of young adult men learn that sex is easy, highly predictable, and in their control. Male sexual response is autonomous – he experiences desire, erection, intercourse, and orgasm needing nothing from his partner. This learning backfires with aging. When couples stop being sexual – whether at 50, 60, 70, or 80 – it is almost always the man's choice – made unilaterally and conveyed non-verbally (McKinlay & Feldman, 1994). He has lost confidence with erections and intercourse. Sex is filled with anticipatory anxiety, intercourse as a pass-fail performance test, leading to frustration, embarrassment, and eventually avoidance.

Typically, the woman feels confused, abandoned, and unsure whether to blame herself, you, or the relationship. Approximately one in three couples stops being sexual between 60 and 65 and two in three between 70 and 75. This is preventable if you adopt the mantra of desire/pleasure/eroticism/satisfaction in your 50s (ideally in your 30s).

Male sexual socialization emphasized that a "real man is able to have sex with any woman, any time, in any situation". What made a man a man was spontaneous erections and perfect intercourse performance. This mistaken notion has oppressed men across generations and cultures. Those who challenge this demand are belittled as "wimps", "inadequate", "not man enough". Few men have the awareness and courage to challenge the perfect individual sex performance model, especially not with male peers. The psychologically healthy man accepts broad-based couple sexuality. This is especially true if you are committed to a satisfying, secure, and sexual relationship.

Sex as a Team Sport

A core concept is that the essence of couple sexuality is giving and receiving pleasure-oriented touching. Sexuality is a team sport, not an individual performance. Sexual desire involves intimacy, pleasuring, and eroticism. Sex is best when you approach it as intimate and erotic allies. Why is sexuality as a team sport so hard to accept? In part, it's because as adolescents and young adults, sexual socialization is so different for males and females. A major reason is the oppressive and destructive male-female double standard. As people age, especially after 40, and in a married or partnered relationship, there are more psychological, relational, and sexual similarities than differences. The over-learned double standard damages the sexuality of women, men, and couples. Yet, it is difficult to confront and change. The adolescent/young adult learning must be challenged as you grow as intimate and erotic friends.

Desire

Desire is the core dimension of healthy sexuality. The key to desire is positive anticipation and that you deserve for sexuality to energize your relationship. Desire is facilitated by freedom, choice, pleasure, and unpredictable scenarios and techniques.

Males learn about sexual desire in a very different way than females. Sexuality is an integral component of being a man. Sex is associated with spontaneous erections, intercourse, and orgasm. Most males begin masturbating between 10 and 14 and are orgasmic daily or every other day. The typical male will experience orgasm during couple sex between 15 and 21 whether through manual stimulation, intercourse, or oral stimulation. Men have less fear of pregnancy, contracting an STI, and don't worry about their reputation – it is women who are labeled "sluts". A sexually active man is a "stud".

This works for adolescent and young adult males, although we do not believe that it is a healthy developmental learning. It does not serve the adult man, especially after age 40 and in a relationship.

Rather than pretending that gender stereotypes are true of all males, let us examine common positive and negative learnings about desire/pleasure/eroticism/satisfaction. Remember the crucial gender guideline – there are more psychological, relational, and sexual similarities than differences. It is not true that men and women are a different species.

Desire is the core factor in healthy sexuality. Women experience more desire problems than men. Sexual dysfunction, especially erectile dysfunction and ejaculatory inhibition, causes secondary low desire. This results in avoidance of partner sex. When couples stop being sexual whether at 55 or 75, it is almost always your choice, made unilaterally and conveyed non-verbally. You have lost confidence in erections, intercourse, and orgasm. Sex is frustrating and embarrassing. You are stuck in anticipatory anxiety, performance anxiety focused on intercourse as a pass-fail test, and frustration and shame eventually leading to sexual avoidance. You say to yourself, "I don't want to start something I can't finish".

Desire is the focus of the new mantra, specifically desire for pleasure-oriented touch. For both men and women, touch and emotional awareness lead to sexual desire. Rather than male spontaneous arousal (erection) driven by fantasy and visual stimuli, the new understanding is "responsive male sexual desire". Unlike the focus on spontaneous erection as the "right' or "natural" way to experience desire, this sophisticated, nuanced approach to desire reflects similarities between men and women and recognizes the multiple roles and meanings of sexuality. With aging, "responsive male sexual desire" is an empowering strategy.

Desire includes psychological, bio-medical, and social/relational factors. You can promote or subvert desire. Desire is an active, complex process which waxes and wanes, but is resilient.

Desire is facilitated by positive anticipation, intimacy, and touching.

A core psychological factor that promotes desire is feeling that you deserve sex to be positive in your relationship. Desire is facilitated by choice, freedom, and unpredictable scenarios and techniques. Unfortunately, desire is easy to kill. Psychological factors that negate desire include performance pressure, coercion, fear of negative consequences, anger, guilt, anxiety, routine, and the demand that all touching result in intercourse. It is a challenge to keep desire vital and resilient as well as being sure sexual poisons stay out of the system.

Bio-medically, this includes that anything which is good for your physical body is good for your sexual body. In addition to good health, this includes behavioral habits of sleep, exercise, eating, no smoking, and moderate or no drinking. It is not aging which subverts desire, but the side-effects of medications (especially hypertensive and anti-depressant medications). Poor behavioral health habits – loss of sleep, lack of exercise, unhealthy eating, obesity, smoking, alcohol or drug abuse – interfere with sexual desire and function (this is true for both men and women). Illness and disability do not stop desire, but do alter sexual function.

Socially and relationally, attitudes, values, and expectations have a major impact on sexual desire. A core factor is whether you value a satisfying, secure, and sexual relationship. For example, movies seldom feature marital sexuality; "hot sex" involves pre-marital or extra-marital couples. Hot sex is new, dramatic, illicit, and idealized. Marital sexuality where intimacy and eroticism are integrated in a secure bond is ignored. It is crucial for maintaining desire to turn toward each other as intimate and erotic allies. Sexual desire cannot be taken for granted nor treated with benign neglect. Maintaining strong, resilient desire is an individual responsibility and a couple challenge.

Communication, loving feelings, and intimacy are emphasized with the false assumption that these automatically generate sexual desire. In relationships, whether married or partnered, straight or gay, the challenge is integrating intimacy and eroticism. Traditionally, there has been a gender split where men valued eroticism and women valued intimacy. This split subverts sexual desire. Strong, resilient desire is facilitated when both partners value intimacy and eroticism.

Pleasure

The second component of the new mantra is nondemand pleasuring. This involves sensual and playful touch both inside and outside the bedroom. Pleasuring is a crucial dimension of sexuality whether it proceeds to intercourse or not. This is a core concept in the broad, flexible approach to couple sexuality. Of course, pleasuring can be a path to arousal, intercourse, and orgasm. However, intercourse is not the sole or even chief function of pleasuring.

Sensuality is the foundation for sexual response and a facilitator of sexual desire. Sensual touch involves non-genital massage, cuddling on the couch while watching a DVD, touching when going to sleep or on awakening, giving and receiving back or foot rubs. On a 10-point scale of sexual pleasure where 0 is neutral and 10 is orgasm, sensual touch involves 1–3 levels of sensations and feelings.

Playful touch involves both genital and non-genital pleasuring, 4–5 on the subjective pleasure scale. Examples of playful touch include whole-body massage, touching while bathing or showering, romantic or erotic dancing, and games like strip poker or Twister. Playful touch is seductive and energizing. It has value in itself as well as a bridge to arousal and intercourse.

Nondemand pleasuring validates the role of touch for both attachment and sexuality. Pleasuring reinforces touch as a core component of desire as well as promoting unpredictable sexual scenarios. Touch can have a number of roles, meanings, and outcomes.

Pleasure (as opposed to performance) validates touch. Sex is not a pass-fail test of erection or orgasm; sexuality is sharing pleasure-oriented experiences with a range of outcomes. Foreplay is a one-way experience of preparing the woman for intercourse. Performance-oriented foreplay subverts desire. A pleasure-orientation involving giving and receiving touch is a bridge for desire.

Eroticism

Erotic scenarios and techniques can be a confusing and controversial aspect of couple sexuality. On the pleasure/arousal scale, erotic touch involves feelings and sensations in the 6–10 range. A crucial strategy is to transition to intercourse at 7 or 8 rather than rushing to intercourse as soon as you are erect or she begins lubrication. You can enjoy the erotic flow of manual, oral, or rubbing stimulation, allowing it to culminate in orgasm.

Eroticism is different than pleasuring, complementary, not oppositional. Eroticism involves taking personal and sexual risks, creativity, intense emotions and sensations, mystery, unpredictability, and vitality. Nondemand pleasuring is sensual and playful, warm and sharing. Eroticism is explicitly sexual-intense and lustful, embracing erotic flow, intercourse, and orgasm.

Eroticism involves three arousal styles:

1   partner interaction arousal
2   self-entrancement arousal
3   role enactment arousal.

These are three very different ways of experiencing eroticism (Mosher, 1980).

Partner interaction arousal is the most common. This involves giving and receiving erotic stimulation. It is the arousal pattern shown in R-rated movies. It is an erotic extension of the "give to get" pleasuring guideline. One partner's arousal plays off the other's erotic responsivity. Partner interaction arousal is illustrated by the adage "an aroused partner is the major aphrodisiac". Some couples only use partner interaction arousal; others also use self-entrancement and/or role enactment arousal.

The second most frequent pattern, especially as people age, is self-entrancement arousal. The key to self-entrancement arousal is taking turns – one is the giver, the other the receiver. Self-entrancement arousal is very different than you doing foreplay (where she is passive and dependent). In self-entrancement arousal, you are mindful and focused on feelings and sensations. Couples, especially with aging, utilize self-entrancement arousal on a regular basis.

Self-entrancement arousal emphasizes the receiver (whether the woman or man) being relaxed, taking in pleasure, being open to and mindful of erotic feelings, allowing you to enjoy erotic sensations with the freedom to let go and orgasm. Some couples switch roles during an erotic encounter, others transition to intercourse at high levels of erotic flow, and still others enjoy an erotic, asynchronous orgasmic experience. Self-entrancement arousal is positive for the giving partner even though less erotically intense. Self-entrancement arousal confronts the "tyranny of mutuality" – not all sex has to be serious, intimate, and mutual. Self-entrancement arousal is an integral component of your sexual relationship.

Role enactment arousal receives by far the most attention in sexuality books and internet sites. The essence of role enactment arousal is bringing something external to your sexual repertoire. This can involve sex toys (blindfold, vibrator, paddle, dildo, handcuffs), x-rated videos, playing out an erotic fantasy, being sexual in front of a mirror, taping a sexual scenario, using fetish material, or sex while cross-dressed. The Emotionally Expressive couple sexual style is most amenable to role enactment arousal. The couple sexual styles where it is not a good fit are Traditional and Best Friend (couple sexual styles are described in Chapter 11).

Some couples find that role enactment arousal enhances their sexual repertoire. It spices up your relationship and adds an unpredictable, vital dimension. However, we are concerned that the way role enactment arousal is promoted intimidates rather than empowers couples. For example, porn videos can serve as a bridge to sexual desire or an erotic charge to orgasm. Porn works best when both partners recognize that erotic fantasy is very different than real-life couple sexuality. Erotic fantasies and scenarios are charged because they are different from real-life couple sexuality. In the great majority of cases, what charges an erotic fantasy is totally different than your actual sexual experience. In many cases, playing out an erotic fantasy results in a sexual "dud" rather than an erotic high.

The message of porn is the crazier the scenario, the more erotic it is and the crazier the woman, the more erotic she is. This causes women to fear eroticism whether from a video or on the internet. She worries that this is what her partner wants and she cannot measure up to this crazy, erotic woman. What is the reality? Erotic fantasies, images, videos, and scenarios are all about fantasy and not about what the man wants from a real-life woman with whom he has an intimate relationship. It is worth repeating – erotic fantasies/videos are a totally different dimension than real-life couple sexuality. This is true for men and couples. It is an "apples-oranges" comparison which has no real meaning or importance.

What is the essence of eroticism and what is its importance? Eroticism is an integral dimension of couple sexuality. Eroticism allows you to experience arousal, erotic flow, intercourse, and orgasm. Sexual pleasure naturally flows to eroticism and orgasm whether with partner interaction, self-entrancement, or role enactment arousal. Eroticism enhances sexual vitality and energizes your bond.

Satisfaction

Does orgasm $=$ satisfaction? No, satisfaction is much more than orgasm. You can have a satisfying sexual experience even when you and your partner are not orgasmic.

The essence of satisfaction is reinforcing feelings about you as a sexual person and feeling bonded and energized as a sexual couple. Orgasm is an integral component of healthy male, female, and couple sexuality. However, when orgasm is a pass-fail individual performance test, this subverts satisfaction.

The essence of satisfaction is feeling good about yourself personally and as a couple. Pleasure, eroticism, and orgasm are positive, integral components which enhance satisfaction.

Satisfaction is a complex phenomenon involving cognitive, behavioral, physical, emotional, and value components. Satisfaction involves different dimensions – from highly satisfying and meaningful to good to okay. It is possible to be orgasmic yet feel alienated. More commonly, you do not have an orgasm yet feel emotionally bonded. In fact, sometimes the sexual experience is more satisfying for the non-orgasmic partner than the orgasmic partner.

One of the most neglected components of sexuality is afterplay. Afterplay is an integral component of couple sexuality. Afterplay facilitates satisfaction. You have just shared an intense physical experience; satisfaction is enhanced when you share an involved afterplay experience.

The most common afterplay scenario is warm and cuddly. There are a range of possible emotions and scenarios. Afterplay can be playful or intimate, serious or light-hearted, verbal or non-verbal, involve a glass of wine or a snack, lying together, sitting and reminiscing, or your unique way of sharing.

Can or should afterplay be a prelude to a second sexual encounter? Yes, but only if both partners are open to an erotic or intercourse scenario. One reason people avoid afterplay is the fear that it will be misinterpreted as a sexual initiation. The majority of afterplay experiences are to share, bond, and enhance satisfaction, not a second sexual encounter.

Is sex sometimes better for one partner than the other? Not only is that normal, but it is true for the majority of sexual encounters. Almost all couples prefer mutual, synchronous sexual experiences where both enjoy desire/pleasure/ orgasm/satisfaction. However, among happily married, sexually functional couples, this ideal scenario occurs less than half the time (Frank, Anderson, & Rubinstein, 1978). This does not mean that the sex wasn't satisfying (more than 85% of sexual experiences are positive). Asynchronous sex means that it wasn't equally positive. A key to sexual satisfaction is awareness that it is normal for sex to have different roles and meanings (including in the same encounter) for each partner. The foundation for sexual satisfaction is positive, realistic expectations. Often, there are differences in psychological, physical, and relational satisfaction – that too is normal and healthy.

Exercise – Implementing the New Mantra

This exercise asks you to make personal and concrete the mantra of desire/ pleasure/eroticism/satisfaction. This is both an individual and couple exercise. Whether your relationship has existed for 1 or 40 years, each person describes when each dimension was most positive. Usually, it is different for each dimension. Often, the partner has a different remembrance. For example, people remember desire being highest in the first few months, pleasuring best in the present, eroticism best when on vacation, and satisfaction best when you feel emotionally understood and accepted.

Be specific and concrete; share attitudes and feelings. Some find it easier to write about sexual dimensions and others to speak about sexuality. The important thing is to own your experience and share it with your partner so she "gets it". What do you value sexually and what makes a sexual experience satisfying for you? This exercise requires courage to be transparent and vulnerable. Don't be vague, politically correct, shy, or inhibited. Allow yourself to be sexually known by your partner. This enhances trust in yourself, your partner, and your relationship. It is especially important if your sexual feelings and experiences are atypical or "socially undesirable".

One of the most interesting and challenging aspects of being a sex therapist is listening to the range of people's feelings and experiences about what makes a sexual experience special. Let us explore examples from the pleasuring dimension. There are common scenarios such as being in a bath with a glass of wine, receiving a whole-body massage with a sensual lotion, mutual stroking while dressed in a sexy outfit, a 20-minute back massage while listening to your favorite jazz tape. Examples of atypical erotic experiences include being on a nude beach with people admiring your bodies as you seductively play with each other; going to a sex-themed motel where there are mirrors and scented candles; being sexual at 2 am under the Christmas tree; "making out" for an hour in a car parked by the lake as the sun goes down.

Identify special experiences for each dimension. This is not a matter of "right-wrong" or proving something to yourself or your partner. Be open in sharing sexual feelings and experiences. Perhaps the most valuable learning is that the desire/pleasure/eroticism/satisfaction dimensions were experienced at different times and in different ways. Another critical learning is that your partner's experiences and what she prefers are different than yours. Sexuality is complex and individualistic. You are not clones of each other, a motivating and empowering concept.

The second part of this exercise is even more important. What are positive, realistic goals to enhance desire/pleasure/eroticism/satisfaction? Do not set romantic, Hollywood goals or crazy, porn goals. What goals are you committed to personally and as a couple? Desire is the core dimension. A common desire goal is to increase the frequency of sensual and playful touching with the hope that these become a bridge to sexual desire. This makes personal and concrete the concept that touch (nondemand pleasuring) is the key for responsive sexual desire. Does this work in your relationship? Do you enjoy nondemand pleasuring for itself as well as a bridge to intercourse?

Do these strategies and techniques facilitate your desire? If not, find sources for desire which are a good fit for you.

Let's explore atypical sources for sexual desire. An example is planning a special erotic date. It can involve you watching the children in the afternoon so she can get a pedicure or a massage. Instead of going home, she does something she enjoys whether a swim, kayaking, shoe shopping, meeting a girlfriend for a drink, reading a romance or erotic novel. If it's she who usually arranges for a babysitter, you contact the sitter and take care of logistics. Instead of the usual dinner, movie, and home for sex, do something different. Rent a hotel room from 7 to 10 with sex before and/or after dinner. Go dancing and later be sexual in the car in a safe, secluded place. Go to a sex store and purchase a sex toy to use after taking the babysitter home. Some couples find these scenarios elicit desire, others find only one does (the others are turn-offs), while other couples design their unique scenario.

Whether focusing on desire/pleasure/eroticism/satisfaction, this exercise encourages you to implement scenarios and techniques to promote vibrant, satisfying sexuality that has a 15–20% role in your life and relationship.

Arousal, Intercourse, and Orgasm

People read this chapter and find it interesting, but come back to a basic question – What about arousal, intercourse, and orgasm? Isn't that the essence of sexuality (especially for you)? Are desire/pleasure/eroticism/satisfaction just the politically correct words? Doesn't it all come down to whether sex works or not? Meaning old-fashioned arousal, intercourse, and orgasm.

Let us be clear – we are in favor of arousal, intercourse, and orgasm. And, yes, most sexual experiences involve those components. But, no, this is not the essence of couple sexuality. Couples have functional sex which neither energizes your bond nor promotes desire. The new mantra, with its emphasis on desire and satisfaction, is motivating and reinforcing. Pleasuring often transitions to arousal, intercourse, and orgasm. Yet, nondemand pleasuring has value in itself. Erotic sexuality is vital and energizing whether it leads to intercourse or not. Asynchronous (including one-way) eroticism can enhance desire and satisfaction.

Let us explore this from a different perspective. Mutual, synchronous sexuality involving arousal, intercourse, and orgasm is the most highly valued. However, if that is the only acceptable sex, it will subvert desire. By its nature, couple sexuality is variable and flexible, with a number of roles, meanings, and outcomes. Couple sexuality is much more than arousal, intercourse, and orgasm.

Rebecca and James

James and Rebecca were a religious, socially conservative couple in a 32-year marriage. For the first time in 26 years, they were a "couple again" after they launched their last child into college. The "empty nest" phase is a myth for most couples. The majority find the "couple again" phase an impetus for personal, relational, and sexual satisfaction. For 70% of couples, sexual satisfaction goes down at the birth of a first child and does not go up again until the last child leaves home. This does not mean that Rebecca and James regretted having three children. Although stressful at times and reducing opportunities for couple and sexual time, they enjoyed parenting and were proud of their five-person family.

In the couple again phase, James and Rebecca had an opportunity to embrace desire/pleasure/eroticism/satisfaction after 32 years of marriage. Like many couples in their 50s, they had fallen into the pattern of sex once a week, usually late on a Saturday night. Sex was functional but not special. The sexual encounter was a routine of five minutes of foreplay, five to seven minutes of intercourse, and two to three minutes of afterplay. Good, but not vital.

Rebecca lobbied James to come to a session with her individual therapist (she hoped that this would lead to couple therapy). James agreed to meet Rebecca's therapist (he wanted to see who she was as well as give the therapist a better idea of who he was as a person and spouse). During a subsequent session, the therapist told Rebecca that meeting James was valuable. He was much different than the image the therapist had of a "closed down" man. James suggested that he and Rebecca commit to a six-month effort to enhance their emotional and sexual relationship. If that was not helpful, he was open to couple therapy. One effect of that consultation was Rebecca's therapy refocused on her individual issues. The therapist encouraged Rebecca to value James, their marriage, and couple sexuality. The trap for a woman in individual therapy is to blame the husband and marriage for most, if not all, problems.

James and Rebecca were committed to improving their relational and sexual lives. She missed feelings of attachment and sexual desire. James had largely ignored these issues because of worry about not having spontaneous erections and concern about maintaining his erection. He feared a humiliating intercourse failure. Rather than enjoying the pleasuring/eroticism process, James rushed intercourse because he worried that he would lose his erection and let Rebecca down.

James and Rebecca had a predictable sexual pattern. She had been orgasmic during intercourse, especially when they used manual clitoral stimulation with his or her fingers. With decreased foreplay, rush to intercourse, and worry about erection, sex was less fun. Rebecca was orgasmic less than a third of the time. James saying "what's wrong" made the situation more tense and performance-oriented. Although erectile failures were infrequent, fear hung over their sexual relationship. Neither was having fun sexually.

Unknown to Rebecca, James had consulted their internist to obtain a Viagra prescription with the hope that this would restore reliable erections. When

James was subjectively aroused and in an erotic flow, Viagra did ensure maintaining his erection. However, he subverted the positive Viagra vascular effect by rushing intercourse. Negative motivation (fear of erectile dysfunctional or female genital pain) subverts couple desire and pleasure.

Rebecca wanted to focus on intimacy and nondemand pleasuring. James worried that this would decrease sexual frequency and increase erectile anxiety – a fear that was not verbalized and Rebecca was unaware of. This is a common dilemma for couples regardless of age.

Rather than falling into the traditional intercourse power struggle, Rebecca made an insightful suggestion. Each read the same material (a short article) about desire/pleasure/eroticism/satisfaction. They shared feelings and ideas about how to enhance their sexual relationship. This reading and discussion helped James and Rebecca speak the same language about intimacy, touching, and sexuality.

A crucial factor was their commitment to rekindle sexual desire. They built anticipation, felt they deserved to enjoy sexuality at this time in their lives, took advantage of the freedom of when and how to be sexual, and moved away from the performance pressures of erection and intercourse. They put fun, pleasure, and unpredictability into their sexual relationship. Rebecca wanted James to turn toward her as his intimate sexual ally rather than feel that he had to perform for her and fear disappointing her.

The nondemand pleasuring encounters included a commitment to not rush intercourse. Rebecca would initiate the transition to intercourse when she felt subjectively aroused and into an erotic flow. James was open to multiple stimulation during intercourse. Rebecca liked giving and receiving stimulation, especially clitoral stimulation. He valued kissing and testicle stimulation. The entire sexual encounter, including intercourse, was engaging and vital. Pleasuring and erotic flow enhanced orgasmic response.

Afterplay had been routine. Now afterplay was involving, meaningful, and less predictable. Sometimes, it was warm and cuddly, other times fun and silly, and occasionally intimate and bonding. Not all sexual encounters had to be mutual. The vibrancy of desire/pleasure/eroticism/satisfaction was markedly improved. Rebecca and James were committed to couple sexuality in their 60s, 70s, and 80s.

Summary

The new mantra of desire/pleasure/eroticism/satisfaction is valuable to men, women, and couples. You speak a common language about sexual feelings and scenarios as well as the roles and meanings of sexuality. Especially important is the recognition of female-male sexual similarities. Although not clones of each other, both value desire/pleasure/eroticism/satisfaction. Desire is the core dimension and is best approached as a couple issue.

8

ADULT SEXUALITY

A New Model of Masculinity

This is one of the most important and challenging chapters. What does it mean to be a healthy sexual man in 2021?

The dual challenges are to build your sexual self-esteem and develop a couple sexual style which integrates intimacy and eroticism. Maintain sexual autonomy while being an intimate sexual team.

It is crucial that you confront the traditional model of masculinity which emphasized perfect sex performance, total control, and sex as a pass-fail test. The challenge of the new male sexuality model is to embrace a positive, realistic approach which affirms the value of pleasure, consent, and sharing as intimate and erotic allies. Sexuality is a couple process of sharing pleasure. Value erections, intercourse, and orgasm, but you do not need to prove that you are a man. A core concept is being a "wise man" who makes psychological, relational, and sexual decisions which promote pleasure and satisfaction. Your partner is your intimate and erotic friend whether sex was wonderful, good, mediocre, or dysfunctional. The wise man adopts the Good Enough Sex (GES) model and rejects the individual perfect performance approach.

In adopting the new model of male sexuality, it is necessary, but not sufficient, to confront the traditional double standard. It is a one-two combination of confronting the old model based on control and performance and creating a new model of masculinity based on acceptance and pleasure. This is healthy for men, women, couples, and the culture.

Confronting and Changing the Traditional Model of Male Sexuality

Why is it so hard to change the traditional male model? Traditional roles are easy to understand and there is tremendous pressure from male peers and the culture to prove that you're a "real man". This is particularly true sexually. Male sexual socialization reinforces the message that male sex is natural and superior. Masculinity and sexuality are closely associated. The emphasis on testosterone, spontaneous erection, easy intercourse, reliable orgasm, and meeting performance demands is a given. The most important factor is "autonomous" sexual response. You need nothing from your partner in order to function sexually. The message is that sex is simple and totally predictable. Women are complex, but not men. This simplistic belief is scientifically wrong and harmful to men, relationships, and the culture (Zilbergeld, 1999). Yet, it is widely accepted. Men are afraid to challenge the traditional view because they will be labeled weak, wimps, not man enough, or "feminized". The truth is just the opposite. It takes courage to say to peers that the traditional approach to masculinity is oppressive and unhealthy. It requires self-acceptance to advocate for a new model of masculinity based on the diversity of men rather than a rigid performance approach. Feel genuine pride in being a self-accepting man rather than maintain a contingent sexual self-esteem based on a false sense of power and control.

Genuine sexual self-esteem is based on the belief that sex is a good thing in life, that sexuality is an integral dimension of being a man, and you accept yourself with your sexual strengths and vulnerabilities rather than denying vulnerabilities and not questioning sexual demands. It is very important to not allow shameful sexual secrets.

We advocate core guidelines for being a proud, self-accepting sexual man. Accepting yourself as a first-class man allows you to accept your partner as a first-class woman. You are intimate and erotic allies rather than adhering to the traditional split between intimacy and eroticism. You honor intimacy and pleasuring in addition to eroticism and intercourse. Intimacy and pleasuring are valued, not seen as "feminine". This model of male sexuality is humanistic and comprehensive, not subverted by a narrow definition of masculinity. This approach motivates and empowers you to be an accepting, healthy human being.

Challenges to Implementing the New Model of Male Sexuality

The biggest challenge to implementation is overcoming fears of change. The traditional model was clear and simplistic. The new model is complex, individualistic, and requires awareness and acceptance. The new model is healthy for men, women, couples, and the culture. It promotes psychological, relational, and sexual well-being. It recognizes gender similarities, affirms pleasure, integrates intimacy and eroticism, and accepts the multiple roles, meanings, and outcomes of couple sexuality. You are proud to be a sexual man. Rather than male sexuality as superior, accept the female-male sexual equity model. This requires dropping the double standard. The biggest challenge is giving up the need for autonomous sexual performance and replacing it with awareness of variable, flexible couple sexuality with a focus on pleasure. Totally predictable erection, intercourse, and orgasm were the basis of the myth of male superiority. Men fear giving up control and superiority.

The fact that GES ensures being sexual with aging has little appeal for a 30-year-old man who enjoys sex without self-consciousness. The majority of men will not transition to GES until they have a "sensitizing" sexual experience. This means that he does not get or maintain an erection sufficient for intercourse. Typically, this occurs in his 30s or 40s, but can occur in adolescence or not until his 60s. This does not mean that he has erectile dysfunction (ED). After a sensitizing experience, you become more aware and a better lover. You enjoy couple sexuality more. Most men do not return to autonomous sex performance. You learn to value variable, flexible couple sexuality. The joke is that if sex was only about arousal and orgasm, men (and women) would masturbate and avoid couple sex. Sexuality becomes intimate, interactive, pleasure-oriented, and couple-oriented with aging. Your partner's stimulation and arousal is arousing for you. She is your intimate and erotic friend. The essence of the new male and couple sexuality is sharing pleasure, not individual performance.

This sounds inviting and liberating, so why is it so fearful? It is different than the way you learned to be sexual in adolescence and young adulthood. You give up control and total predictability for a more human and satisfying couple sexuality.

A good example is dealing with erectile anxiety. The bio-medical approach is in keeping with traditional male sexuality. You turn to a stand-alone medical intervention whether Viagra, penile injections, or testosterone. You are searching for a miracle cure which returns you to autonomous sex performance. This is self-defeating. In the new model of male sexuality, you are open to using all your resources to build erectile comfort and confidence. Your major resource is your partner who is your intimate and erotic friend. If you use medical interventions, these are integrated into your couple sexual style. You adopt GES expectations rather than sex as an individual pass-fail performance. GES attitudes, behavior, and emotions confirm the new male sexuality.

These challenges are also true in the psychological and relational realms. Your self-esteem is not based on being superior to the woman. Self-esteem is based on owning your authentic sexual self with vulnerabilities as well as strengths. Roles are not split by traditional gender rules, but are determined by your interests and skills. It is not a hierarchy where men are in control – the new model advocates equitable sharing. It is okay if she is more mechanical than you. It is okay if she is a better financial manager. It is okay for you to get on your hands and knees to play with your child. It is masculine to change diapers. Implementing these changes requires awareness and dialogue.

A particularly sensitive issue is money and decision-making. In the traditional double standard, the man made more money and had the power to make major decisions. A core guideline in the new model is that power, money, and decision-making are shared based on interests, skills, preferences, and reality factors. Themes include complexity vs. simplicity and dialogue vs. assumptions. The fear is that men (and women) will feel confused and overwhelmed, resulting in poor decisions, poor relationships, and chaos.

The new model of masculinity emphasizes finding the "right fit". We suggest personally relevant "guidelines" not simplistic "rules".

These concepts are particularly challenging in regard to sexuality. Most men under 40 choose to stick with the male performance model, although we strongly believe that the new model is superior whether at 25, 35, or 55. Accepting yourself as a man who values your partner is important even when your sex function is autonomous. Accept the complexity of GES, including meanings and outcomes of couple sexuality, even when your sexual response is highly predictable. The new model of masculinity and sexuality is healthier and more human. Ideally, it is adopted as a young adult rather than waiting for a problem to occur. Primary prevention is always preferable. This is in your best interest psychologically, relationally, and sexually. Adopt a self-acceptance model of male sexuality.

Ian and Alexa

Ian was the first member of his family to earn a graduate degree. He grew up in a working-class family in a small city. He was proud of his family and community roots. His father was a factory worker who, like his peers, experienced a great deal of economic turmoil. Father told Ian and his siblings that to maintain a good standard of living would require advanced education and skills. Ian's older brother was trained as an electrician and older sister was a college-educated nurse.

Ian was nine years old when his mother was killed in an accident caused by a drunk driver. Memories of his parent's marriage were positive, but their marital and parental roles were governed by a strict double standard. Father was not prepared to be a single parent or manage the household, especially cooking for the family. Unfortunately, he quickly remarried a woman who had her agenda which did not include being a nurturing parent for Ian. Ian planned to be a fully functioning adult, not trapped in the rigid male role. This included learning to cook and manage a home.

Sexually, Ian was eager to date and be involved with girls. His older brother married at 21 because of a pregnancy. They worked hard to establish a secure marital bond and family. His sister took advantage of her nursing training to be a successful IUD user and had a four-year relationship before marrying. Ian appreciated the guidance and advice of both siblings, but had to be his own person. As a college junior, Ian enrolled in a human sexuality class. There were 35 females and 5 males in the class. Male friends teased him about why he needed to take the class. Ian was the only cisgender heterosexual male with mainstream values in the class.

Ian felt supported by the academic material and by female peers. He wanted to do more than question the traditional male role; he wanted to carefully and comprehensively explore what it meant to be a "new man". He affirmed the female-male sexual equity model. Ian appreciated the emphasis on female empowerment, but did not like that class members of both genders engaged in "male bashing". Relationships are not a "zero-sum" game. Men do not have to lose for women to win. Both genders benefit from the female-male equity model. You join forces in confronting unwanted pregnancy, STIs, sexual abuse, rape, and sexual harassment. There is nothing inherent in the male role which is destructive for women or relationships. This generated dialogue and conflict which challenged Ian to be a strong spokesman against toxic male sexuality. More important was to be a spokesman for healthy male and couple sexuality. The foundation for healthy sexuality is consent and pleasure, a value shared by both genders.

A measure of psychological well-being is integrating healthy attitudes, behaviors, and emotions. Academic learnings made it easier to implement this in his life. This class was a turning point in Ian's young adult development.

Ian had a double major in economics and computer technology. He wanted to be successful professionally and economically. Being successful psychologically, relationally, and sexually was also a high value. Ian was a diligent student who was involved in internships and special projects. During college, he avoided the "hook-up" culture, preferring sexual friendships which lasted one or two semesters. He took his sister's advice about establishing his life before considering marriage.

Ian was 26 when he began dating Alexa who was 27. They met during a volleyball tournament. Alexa came from a college-educated upper-middle-class family. She was ambivalent about her life organization. She wanted a work-life balance and worried that being a litigation associate in a large law firm was not the right fit for her. She eventually wanted marriage and children, but first needed to decide on a career path.

The group went on a weekend hike followed by a beer and pizza party (Ian and Alexa chose to skip the party). Instead, they went with two friends to a small bistro. As they talked about careers, they realized that although in different fields, they had a lot in common. Feeling proud and successful was important for both as was defining self-esteem as more than job and money. Ian enjoyed the field of economic analysis and wanted a career where he was in control of the type and quantity of work. He knew people who had 80-hour work weeks – Ian wanted a career with a 50-hour work week. At this point, Alexa worked 80 hours. Although intellectually stimulating, she did not feel passionate about the litigation field.

There was a clear attraction. They didn't want to immediately have sex, deciding to proceed in a conscious manner. During the next three weeks, they communicated by phone and text. They scheduled a hike close to Ian's favorite small town and made reservations at a B&B. This was a romantic, sexual weekend. Both Ian and Alexa had experienced the limerence phase in earlier relationships. From the beginning, Ian knew that this relationship was special. Sex is not the most important dimension in their relationship, but sexuality was vital and energizing. Alexa owned her sexual voice and was enthusiastic about sharing intimacy and eroticism. She didn't expect Ian to make her orgasmic. She joyfully shared eroticism and orgasm with him. If she didn't like something in a sexual scenario (for example, Ian had always enjoyed playing with a woman's hair), she let him know and shared what she did find pleasurable.

After the limerence phase, it takes most people three to six months to develop a couple sexual style of desire/pleasure/eroticism/satisfaction. Ian knew that this was a healthy relationship – it was easy to talk sexuality while hiking and to play out sexual scenarios whether in the bedroom or camping under the stars. This integration of intimacy, pleasuring, and eroticism was the goal he established in his college class.

A healthy relationship brings out healthy parts of each person. It gave Alexa the courage to leave her law firm and join a quality boutique firm focused on business succession planning. This was an appealing area of law and a good way to help clients avoid litigation. Ian was pleased that they would be a two-career couple. The marriage limited his ability to transfer cities, but allowed him to be a successful economic consultant.

Their hardest decision involved children. In marriage, there are many issues couples need to negotiate. The three core issues are children, money, and where to live. Of all the decisions, the child decision is the hardest to change. It is easier to switch jobs, houses, even marital partners. When the child is five, you can't decide not to parent. Children are a couple's decision. In the double standard, it was the woman's decision because child-rearing was her domain. In the new model of masculinity, contraception, pregnancy, and raising children (including sex education) are a shared domain.

Both Alexa and Ian wanted children. Sex with the goal of pregnancy is an aphrodisiac. She was glad to be free of the IUD. They were fortunate to become pregnant after only three months. They enrolled in prepared childbirth classes. Ian was present at the birth of their daughter (and four years later the birth of their son).

For the majority of couples, sexual frequency and satisfaction goes down at the birth of the first child and doesn't rebound until the last child leaves home. The "empty nest" syndrome is a misnomer. The "couple again" phase heralds an increase in sexual satisfaction. Ian and Alexa committed to "beating the odds" – balancing parenting, careers, marriage, and sexuality. This is an example of the anti-perfectionism, GES approach which requires dialogue, flexibility, and emotional problem-solving. It is a complex, challenging life organization compared to his father, brother, and peers, but Ian was committed. He was a "wise" man willing to adopt flexible roles which worked short and long terms, emotionally and practically. Life is less predictable than in the traditional male role, but facilitates personal, parental, relational, and sexual satisfaction. He valued his career, but unlike many of his colleagues, life was not defined by his career. Ian was glad that they had two careers rather than being the primary income earner. Alexa was in charge of investments, Ian in charge of household expenses and bills.

Ian and Alexa created a very important couple tradition. They vacationed with friends and extended family, but the most valued time was a four-day-three-night yearly couple hiking trip. This was Ian's time to check in with Alexa about personal, career, family, marital, and sexual issues. Was he maintaining a balanced, quality life? Was he living out his values as a new man? Ian relied on Alexa to be honest and confront him if he was falling into psychological, relational, or sexual traps. There were two hard issues for Ian. First, accepting himself and GES. Ian was seduced by movies and tv shows which featured dramatic sex. Alexa affirmed the value of intense sex, especially on their couple weekend, but felt that sexuality was more genuine and satisfying at home. They felt good about the range of roles, meanings, and outcomes of marital sexuality. Ian knew that Alexa masturbated one to two times a month; she treated this as her special sexual time. In contrast, Ian's masturbation was for tension reduction.

The second challenging issue involved career and money. Ian's income was somewhat less than Alexa's. He felt ambivalent about this role reversal. He knew that he could earn considerably more if he committed to a 60-hour work week, but this would unbalance his life and parenting. He liked the luxury of two successful careers but was uneasy about passing up prestige and money. Ian realized that he couldn't have a "perfect life" and celebrated his balanced life. He was committed to the female-male equity model. Alexa accepted and valued Ian and their marriage which made these challenges easier for him to accept.

Vulnerabilities and the New Man

All people have strengths and vulnerabilities. This is a core issue in the new model of masculinity. Can you be both strong and vulnerable? The message of the traditional male model was clear – be strong, admit no vulnerabilities. The message of the new model is emphasize your strengths and accept your vulnerabilities. Some vulnerabilities can be resolved and turned into strengths. Most vulnerabilities can be modified. Other vulnerabilities are neither changeable nor modifiable, accept these and work around them. The wise man implements the acceptance model and is healthier for it. Barry cites his personal example. A vulnerability I resolved was fear of public speaking. Now a favorite professional activity is presenting all day workshops. A modifiable vulnerability was inability to cook. When Emily is away, I have two to three dishes I prepare, enjoy going to ethnic restaurants, and make salads, scrambled eggs, and English muffins at home. Not great, but functional. An example of a vulnerability I have to accept and work around is my perceptual-motor learning disability. Although I love to write, I cannot type nor use computers. This is a major problem and makes me very inefficient. I regret this vulnerability/disability, but am not ashamed of it. This vulnerability does not make me less of a man.

The issue of strengths and vulnerabilities is especially important sexually. In the double standard, the man was not allowed to have a vulnerability (or at least admit to one). In reality, every man has sexual vulnerabilities. It could be sexual shyness, premature ejaculation, an idiosyncratic masturbation pattern, a misshapen testicle, uncomfortable talking about sex, feeling unsure of self sexually, poor at using condoms, embarrassment about genital hair, sexual anxiety, taking a medication which interferes with sexual response, guilt over erotic fantasies, overweight, history of sexual trauma, fears about penis size, a body scar, discomfort looking at partner's vulva. Should these vulnerabilities be a shameful secret causing you to have a contingent sexual self-esteem? Absolutely not. Process your vulnerability whether with your partner, best friend, counselor, physician, or minister. Is it resolvable, modifiable, or do you need to accept and work around it? Don't allow your sexual self-esteem to be controlled by a vulnerability. Play to your relational and sexual strengths, but be aware of your vulnerabilities. Be sexually self-accepting. Do not be controlled by performance-oriented myths about male sexuality.

Exercise – Establishing a New Male Sexual Model

Psychosexual skill exercises are meant to make concepts real and concrete. Exercises challenge you to create new attitudes, behaviors, emotions, and values. This exercise focuses on developing a positive, realistic, sexual self-esteem.

Do you have a role model for what it means to be a healthy sexual man? Most of us don't, but if you do, that's a great resource. Whether or not you have a model, your challenge is to clearly and specifically list what being a new man involves psychologically, relationally, and sexually. This is not a socially desirable/politically correct exercise, but what it means to be a proud man with a positive, balanced view of yourself. Focus on self-awareness and self-acceptance. Psychologically, what is it about you, your job, home, and values which promote being a proud man? Relationally, what is it about your relationship with your spouse (life partner), friends, children, community which enhance your life? Sexually, are you pro-sexual and proud of being a sexual man? Do you value the female-male equity model? Do you value intimacy, pleasuring, and eroticism? Do you accept GES? Do you turn toward your partner as your intimate and erotic friend whether the sex was great, good, mediocre, or dysfunctional? Do you accept the mantra of desire/pleasure/eroticism/satisfaction?

Be sure your answers are truthful and comprehensive, including problematic and vulnerable components. Choose at least one issue (three at the most) to change which would enhance your sexual self-esteem? Set a positive, realistic goal.

Ask your partner to review your answers. Don't be surprised if your perspectives are new to her. This is an opportunity to dialogue about masculinity, sexuality, and your relationship. It is particularly important to get her input on change plans and how she can support you in reaching those goals.

She has the opportunity to suggest at least one and up to three changes that would be healthy for you and your relationship. She is your respectful, trusting, and intimate friend who wants to help. Listen respectfully to her observations and suggestions. You have the option of agreeing, modifying, or saying no and developing a different strategy or goal. Remember, a key to masculinity is valuing your partner and being open to her positive influence.

The Poison of Male-Female Power Struggles

This chapter, and the entire book, emphasizes a positive approach to men, couples, and sexuality. A healthy relationship and healthy sexuality enhance your well-being. Conversely, people caught in power struggles – whether relational or sexual – find this demoralizing and emotionally painful. Negative emotions – hurt, anger, anxiety, depression, alienation – subvert you. If your relationship is controlled by power struggles, our recommendation is sex, couple, or individual therapy (suggestions for finding a therapist are in Appendix A). Power struggles undermine the strategies and techniques we advocate. Seeking therapy is a sign of strength.

Summary

A new view of men and male sexuality is growing in the United States and throughout the world. You have opportunities for psychological, relational, sexual, and physical health that your grandfather and father did not. Yet, with opportunities come challenges. It is necessary, but not sufficient, to confront and rid yourself of the individual male performance model and the double standard. The challenge is to adopt a model based on genuine pride in being a man, self-acceptance with awareness of strengths and vulnerabilities. Many men have a contingent self-esteem and a contingent relationship based on a false sense of control centered on perfect sex performance. The wise man embraces the female-male sexual equity model and turns toward your partner as your intimate and erotic ally. The essence of sexuality is sharing pleasure rather than individual sex performance. The new male sexuality embraces variable, flexible GES. Create positive, realistic expectations rather than demand perfect performance. A wise man realizes the range of roles, meanings, and outcomes of male and couple sexuality. If there is a sexual problem, rather than hoping for a stand-alone medical intervention (Viagra, penile injections, testosterone) to return you to perfect performance, your partner is your primary emotional and sexual resource. Celebrate erection, intercourse, and orgasm while realizing that couple sexuality is inherently variable and flexible. With the new male sexuality, you need not panic or apologize. The essence of being a healthy man is acceptance and pleasure.

9

DESIRE

The Core of Sexuality

The traditional understanding of what makes you a sexual man is erection, intercourse, and orgasm. The new sexual mantra is desire/pleasure/eroticism/satisfaction (Foley, Kope, & Sugrue, 2012). Desire is the core dimension for male and couple sexuality. This is very different than the traditional approach. Men learn desire as autonomous, manifested by a spontaneous erection. Desire is easy, predictable, in your control, and most important – autonomous (needing nothing from the woman). Traditionally, desire was driven by erotic fantasy, visual stimuli, testosterone, and the promise of totally predictable sex.

The Masters and Johnson sex therapy model (Master & Johnson, 1970) took male sexual desire for granted. Therapy focused on premature ejaculation and erectile dysfunction (ED). Male desire was assumed to be simple and robust, totally different than female desire.

Low sexual desire and desire discrepancies are the most common sexual problem couples bring to therapy (McCarthy & McCarthy, 2020). One in three adult women complains of secondary low desire, i.e. she once felt desire, but has lost her "sexual voice". What few health professionals or the public realize is that when couples stop being sexual, it is the man who causes the relationship to become non-sexual. The most common cause is loss of confidence in erections and intercourse. You feel frustrated and embarrassed and say to yourself, "I don't want to start something I can't finish". Stopping sex is a unilateral choice, conveyed non-verbally. You unfairly blame the partner which compounds the relational damage.

Secondary low sexual desire is a common problem for both men and women, shrouded in secrecy and shame. Its impact is worse for males because men are not supposed to experience desire problems. The great majority of male desire problems are secondary. You don't admit desire problems to friends, physicians, a minister, and certainly not your partner. It is easier to admit to premature ejaculation, ED, or ejaculatory inhibition than low desire.

Primary Male Desire Problems

Primary sexual dysfunction means that the man has a life-long history of the problem. Total lack of sexual desire for anyone or any sexual scenario is very rare. Asexuality is a sexual orientation which impacts less than 1% of males. The man might want to marry and/or be a parent, but does not value sexuality. Sadly, he does not tell his partner about his sexual orientation. The woman deserves to know that asexuality is the core problem. When she learns this, she usually feels relieved.

Most cases of primary low desire involve a sexual secret. The most common secret is a variant (atypical) arousal pattern. This includes approximately 4% of men. The most common secret is a fetish arousal. Sex desire is very high with fetish materials and fantasies, but low or non-existent for intimate, interactive couple sexuality. The novelty of a new relationship provides a temporary sexual impetus, but it disappears after weeks or months. This dramatic change in desire is very confusing for the partner. The great majority of men do not disclose anything to their partner. The combination of high secrecy, high eroticism, and high shame controls the man's sexuality. Other variant arousal patterns involve cross-dressing and BDSM (bondage and discipline/sadomasochism). You have a secret sexual world. Chapter 15 describes the phenomenon of variant arousal more completely. Unlike asexuality, there is strong desire, but not for couple sex. The three strategies for dealing with variant arousal are acceptance, compartmentalization, and necessary loss. We encourage you to share the sexual secret so that you can dialogue about how to deal with this problem. The partner feels relieved to know that she is not the cause of low desire and has a voice in deciding how to approach the issue.

A second pattern is that you have a high rate of masturbation (20–40 times a month). You feel sexually confident with masturbation (you are a "A" masturbator), but anxious and uncomfortable with couple sex (you are a "D"). This is misunderstood as a "porn addiction" because you masturbate using porn. The core issue is low desire for couple sex and high desire and confidence with masturbation.

A third pattern is that you have a "shameful secret" involving abuse and trauma. Few men share this with the partner because you fear her judgment. Like other sexual secrets, this needs to be disclosed and processed. Most women are accepting and supportive, willing and able to be your "partner in healing" (Maltz, 2012).

Sexual orientation issues are another cause of low desire. This is discussed in detail in Chapter 16.

Primary low desire is usually tied to a sexual secret. Disclosing and processing with your partner and/or in therapy is crucial to address these sexual desire issues.

Secondary Male Low Sexual Desire

The great majority of adolescent and young adult men find sexual desire easy and robust. You experience first orgasm through masturbation or nocturnal emissions. This builds desire and anticipation for partner sex. The symbol of desire is a spontaneous erection. Although a source of jokes and embarrassment, it reinforces masculinity. First partner orgasm whether occurring with manual, oral, rubbing stimulation, or intercourse reinforces desire. Masculinity is tied to easy and predictable desire. A crucial understanding is that for the great majority of young men, desire, erection, intercourse, and orgasm are autonomous. You need nothing from the woman.

Unfortunately, expectations of totally predictable sexual response set you up to develop secondary low desire, especially after age 40. Spontaneous erections, visual stimuli, eroticism, and predictable sexual response are not a solid foundation for male sexual desire. Friends, male physicians, and drug company reps mislead men into believing that a medical intervention will magically return you to an intense desire you experienced in adolescence. It can't.

The new model of male sexuality is motivating and empowering, but challenging. The core concepts are valuing your partner as your intimate and erotic friend; being open to touch to elicit desire rather than depending on visual stimuli; accepting variable, flexible Good Enough Sex (GES) not sex as a pass-fail individual performance; expanding your definition of sexuality to include sensual, playful, and erotic scenarios in addition to intercourse; openness to his, her, and our bridges to sexual desire; and valuing both synchronous and asynchronous sexuality. The essence of desire is positive anticipation, feeling deserving of sexual pleasure, freedom to embrace pleasure-oriented touching, and unpredictable sexual scenarios and techniques.

Desire is both an individual and couple concept. Rather than returning to autonomous desire, desire is a couple process focused on touch and pleasure. The breakthrough concept for women was "responsive sexual desire". Rather than expecting desire to be spontaneous and autonomous, when the woman is receptive and responsive to sensual and playful touch and aware of her (and your) feelings, she experiences subjective arousal of two, three, or four. That is when she feels desire. Desire flows from touch and receptivity rather than desire being the initial cue. Responsive sexual desire is a motivating and empowering concept.

"Responsive male sexual desire" is a new and empowering concept, especially for men over age 50. Responsive desire is not inferior to spontaneous desire. It reinforces couple sexuality as intimate and interactive. GES and responsive desire is the foundation for sexuality in your 60s, 70s, and 80s. Embracing responsive desire is a core strategy for changing male (and female) low desire.

Causes of Secondary Low Sexual Desire

The major cause of male secondary low desire is sexual dysfunction, especially ED. The cycle of positive anticipation, easy and totally predictable erection, and transitioning to intercourse and orgasm on the first erection, is replaced by the cycle of anticipatory anxiety, performance anxiety, rush to intercourse caused by fear of losing the erection, frustration, embarrassment, and eventually sexual avoidance. ED can be caused by psychological, bio-medical, or relational factors. Commonly, a combination of factors are in play. Your low desire is controlled by the cognition "I don't want to start something I can't finish". Over time, ED becomes chronic and severe. Desire is no longer associated with pleasure; it is controlled by frustration and failure. Sexual self-consciousness dominates and destroys desire.

A second cause is intermittent ejaculatory inhibition (delayed ejaculation). This increases with aging, up to 15% of men over 50. You maintain an erection but are unable to establish erotic flow and reach orgasm. This is misdiagnosed as ED because eventually you lose your erection. When intercourse lasts more than two minutes before your erection dissipates, the problem is ejaculatory inhibition, not ED. You have intercourse the way you did as a young adult focused on thrusting. If you want sex to be satisfying, you need to increase involvement and stimulation, specifically multiple stimulation before and during intercourse. Intercourse thrusting is important but is not enough. Multiple stimulation involves receiving (testicle stimulation, buttock stimulation, and kissing) and giving (clitoral stimulation, anal or buttock stimulation, and breast stimulation). The most common form of multiple stimulation for both men and women is private erotic fantasies. Fantasies serve as a bridge to arousal and orgasm. The majority of men utilize erotic fantasy during couple sex to enhance erotic flow.

Other causes for secondary low desire include alcohol abuse, side-effects of medications, fatigue, conflict regarding parenting, routine and mechanical sex, poor eating and sleep habits, job and financial distress, depression and boredom, and not valuing marital sexuality. Desire is easy to kill. The good news is that desire can be revitalized, especially if you adopt GES and a broad-based approach to intimacy, pleasuring, and eroticism. Identify psychological, bio-medical, and relational factors which inhibit desire. Schedule a consultation (ideally as a couple) with your internist or specialist. Use medications which have fewer sexual side-effects. Improve sleep patterns so you have more energy to be sexual. Have sex in the afternoon or early evening rather than late at night.

Exercise – Rekindling Sexual Desire

Rekindling sexual desire is one of your best investments to improve psychological and physical well-being. Sexuality energizes your bond and reinforces feelings of desire and desirability.

Rather than hoping that your partner will give you desire, a testosterone patch will restore desire, or something magical will happen – take an emotional problem-solving approach. You are responsible for your desire. This requires a one-two approach. First, confront and change the factors that "poison" desire. Second, build bridges to desire and use all your psychological, bio-medical, and social/relational resources to promote desire and pleasure.

Identifying and changing poisons is the easier task. An example of confronting a psychological poison is to masturbate only when your partner is not receptive rather than masturbating in a secret, compulsive manner. Another example is identifying thoughts, fantasies, or erotic material which serve as sexual cues; drop narrow, compulsive, and shameful fantasies. Erotic fantasies are normal and healthy. By their nature, erotic fantasies represent non-socially desirable sexual behavior such as being sexual with a forbidden partner or engaging in triadic sex. Illicitness provides an erotic charge. Fantasies which are narrow, compulsive, and shameful poison desire for couple sex.

An example of a bio-medical poison is needing to be drunk or high in order to feel sexual. Another example is depending on a pill or injection for desire. Confront bio-medical poisons and break the self-defeating cycle.

Relationally, what subverts sexual desire? One poison is a secret arousal pattern such as a fetish involving long fingernails. This results in walling off your partner. You are not sexually present. You need the fingernails rather than her. A common relational poison is de-erotizing your partner. She is not your intimate and erotic friend, but a woman robbed of her sexuality.

Discuss poisons with your partner. What is your partner's perspective? Does she have concerns about psychological, physical, or relational poisons? Be clear and specific about what poisons desire. What can she do to help you in the change process?

The second phase of this exercise is more challenging. What psychological, bio-medical, and relational factors can help build desire?

Psychological examples include developing a new initiation scenario such as joining your partner for a shower or bath or mixing non-genital touch with a request to "get together". Another example is buying a pillow saying "tonight" on the one side and "rain check" on the other. You can create a new bridge to sexual desire involving a self-entrancement arousal scenario where she receives first.

An example of a bio-medical intervention to facilitate desire is you taking Cialis and she using a Vylessi injection an hour before being sexual. Use that hour to talk and share nondemand pleasuring. Another example is being sexual after a nap where you wake to genital stimulation.

Examples of relational interventions to facilitate desire include taking a two-mile walk as a couple followed by a shower so you are fresh for oral sex. Another scenario is coming home to a beer and as you sit watching the sunset, she stimulates you to orgasm. Meet at a funky hotel and pay the day rate so you can have an "afternoon delight". Sit and talk for 30 minutes about your intimate relationship. Make couple sexuality inviting so desire has the space to thrive.

As you review this list with your partner, are the strategies and techniques clear and can you implement them? Do they allow you to feel desire? Your partner has her perspective and suggestions. Do you approach desire as a couple issue? Can you work together to rekindle and strengthen desire?

Is Sexual Desire Really a Couple Issue?

Each person has a right to sexual desire. You partner is not responsible for your desire. Desire involves a combination of personal responsibility and being an intimate sexual team. Remember, sex is a team sport.

The traditional male model of spontaneous erection and autonomous desire confuses the issue and creates the intercourse or nothing power struggle. This eventually leads to low desire. Desire as a couple issue is empowering for the man, woman, couple, and culture. You are an intimate and erotic team. Sexually, you win or lose as a team. You cannot make your partner desirous, but you can facilitate your desire and your partner's desire by touching, sexual openness, and responsivity (Nobre, Carvalho, & Mark, 2020).

Be intimate and erotic allies in keeping poisons out of the system and building bridges to desire. This is even more important when the man is the low desire partner. She cannot force or cajole you to be sexual. She can help you confront the poisons which subvert desire and be your sexual friend in rekindling desire. Do not expect to return to autonomous sex or spontaneous erections. Develop a new approach to male and couple sexuality. Focus on pleasure and turn toward your partner rather than hoping a stand-alone medication or a porn video will restore desire. Be sexually aware, emotionally and physically open, and focus on giving and receiving touch. Be open to broad-based sexuality which includes sensual, playful, and erotic scenarios in addition to intercourse. From this foundation, it is easier to be an intimate team who revitalize desire. Men who cling to the old model stay stuck in a low sex or no sex relationship. The wise man accepts desire as a couple issue and is ready and able to create vital, resilient desire.

Henry and Brianna

Forty-seven-year-old Henry had a very common name, but a unique life story. He came from a working-class double standard family. He was the first to graduate college, earn an MBA, and be an amazingly successful entrepreneur. Three years ago, he sold his company and is now a semi-retired multi-millionaire.

Henry had been married to 43-year-old Brianna for three years. This was Henry's second marriage and Brianna's third.

Although financially and professionally successful, Henry thought of himself as a failure. He was the youngest and shortest of three brothers. His brothers were a "man's man" – strong and athletic who bragged about sexual prowess. The oldest brother experienced a pregnancy, marriage, and divorce before age 20. He joined the military and was disabled in a training accident. He has been divorced twice more and lives on disability payments and part-time work. He still thinks of Henry as the weak little brother. Sex is his favorite topic for jokes, often at Henry's expense. Henry's middle brother is a heavy-duty driver of construction equipment. He is in a first marriage with three children, but brags that he's a "sexual player". He belittles Henry, saying even though Henry has more money, he has more sex. Henry's ex-wife left after nine years and blamed Henry for the divorce. Brianna feels that Henry was taken advantage of. He still pays alimony to the ex-wife (even though they had no children). In many areas of life, Henry was a successful man, but not relationally or sexually.

The problem which brought Henry and Brianna to therapy was his fear that she would divorce him because of his sexual failings. They had a very different way of handling conflict. Brianna was vocal with her complaints. When she felt that Henry was avoiding issues, she would accelerate her emotional demands. The cycle was clear – Henry ignored conflict which served to increase Brianna's emotional intensity. After arguments, Henry would give her a gift as a peace offering. This further agitated Brianna. She felt that he was trying to placate her rather than deal with problems.

When they began as a couple, sex was a strength. Brianna fell in love and was impressed with Henry's success and financial generosity. She had been very disappointed with both of her husbands, especially ignoring their daughters (one from each marriage). In contrast, Henry was a solid stepfather, especially to the 19-year-old. He was generous with tuition and college costs, and encouraged her to be a successful young adult.

Henry viewed Brianna as smart, attractive, and pro-sexual. This was his healthiest and most satisfying relationship. When she initiated sex, Henry was receptive and responsive. Brianna was puzzled why 90% of the sexual initiations were hers. In one way, she found that refreshing but made her wonder what was wrong. Her history was very different than Henry's – the only thing the ex-husbands would show up for was sex. Brianna's experiences were the opposite of the stereotype – good sex, bad relationships. She felt that Henry and she had a good marriage and good sex.

Brianna was pleased that Henry was open to therapy and glad that he valued her and their marriage. However, Henry's approach to relational and sexual problems made no sense to her. How could such a nice, generous man be such an emotional and sexual avoider? When they started talking about desire issues two years ago, Brianna had been patient and empathic, but at this point she was blunt and confrontative.

At the first session, the therapist asked Henry what he wanted relationally and sexually. He tried, but what came out were not his desires, but his fears. He was overwhelmed by fear that she would leave him because of sexual failures. Brianna fought her impulse to attack. She followed the therapist's guidance in trying to understand why he was so negative about masculinity and sexuality. A core issue is that he didn't feel he deserved sexual pleasure. Henry enjoyed arousal and orgasm – his problem was desire and pleasure. He felt that she deserved pleasure, but not he. Henry was controlled by the fear that sexually he was not a real man. Brianna could not convince him that he deserved to feel good about himself sexually.

What Brianna could do was understand Henry's vulnerabilities and help him challenge and change these. His view of masculinity was defined by his brothers' view of him rather than Henry's view of himself. He gave others, including the ex-wife and Brianna, power over sexuality. Henry had a contingent sexual self-esteem. He was afraid of other's judgment. Henry was hyper-vigilant about any negative feedback. This is what drove sexual avoidance and his inability to initiate or take sexual risks.

As this pattern became clear, Henry realized that he would never allow this in his professional or financial life. Masculinity and sexuality brought out the worst in Henry.

The therapist suggested five individual therapy sessions and then couple sex therapy. Henry needed to develop a positive sexual self-esteem, including finding his "sexual voice". This would affirm him as a sexual man and create a positive rather than fearful view of couple sex.

Henry found individual therapy (including readings about male sexuality, psychosexual skill exercises, and erotic fantasy exercises) of great value. His view of masculinity and sexual desire was controlled by performance myths, intimidating expectations, and fear of harsh judgment. Henry had the right to own his body, sexual experiences, and pleasure. For the first time in his life, Henry accepted himself as a first-class sexual man.

Henry could turn toward Brianna rather than see her as someone he needed to prove something to. He need not fear her judgment and rejection.

Henry's newfound sexual autonomy was appealing. Brianna was open to his sexual voice, especially sexual initiations. She had the freedom to say no without worrying about intimidating him. She initiated sexual scenarios with confidence that he would tell her if it wasn't right for him. The power to say no to sex is crucial in creating desire. Henry's ability to initiate, play, experiment, and say no made him an attractive sexual partner. Their sexual experiences were genuine, with each present and involved. They had vital, energizing sex. Just as important, when the sexual experience was a "dud", Henry did not apologize. Brianna no longer felt that she had to tiptoe around Henry. She could say "that was a bummer" and laugh without fear that he would be devastated.

Henry had a good life and a good marriage. Now he had a good sexual life, feeling open to a range of feelings and experiences. For the first time in his life, masculinity and sexual desire had a 15–20% positive role.

The Reality of Adult Sexual Desire

Male sexual desire is complex, not simple. Don't be intimidated by the myth of sex with any woman, any time, any situation. You are a proud man who values your sexuality, not controlled by oppressive performance myths and demands.

A crucial understanding is that male sexual desire is resilient. You don't need desire 24 hours a day, 7 days a week. When you feel anxious or sad, fatigued or experience medication side-effects, have a conflict with your partner or exhausted from attending children's events, low desire is normal. The key to desire resiliency is receptivity and responsivity to pleasure-oriented touch. Another key is awareness of sexual stimuli such as a sexy outfit, an erotic fantasy, an attractive person you see on the street, an R-rated movie, dancing, taking a shower together. Other keys for desire are being on vacation, the children out of the house, camping under the stars, taking your partner on a business trip and enjoying an upscale hotel room. Rather than depending on spontaneous desire, create bridges to desire. Sexuality is an integral part of your life. Be open to a range of roles, meanings, and outcomes of couple sexuality.

Summary

Men are prone to take sexual desire for granted. This is both a strength and a vulnerability. Sex is not just for young men, but for middle-years and older men. Welcoming your partner as your intimate and erotic friend, being open to her touch, and accepting responsive sexual desire facilitate strong, resilient desire. The traditional double standard demands male desire; in the long run, this subverts desire. The new model of masculinity reinforces desire/pleasure/eroticism/satisfaction. By its nature, couple sexuality is variable and flexible with a range of roles, meanings, and outcomes.

A key for genuine male desire is to approach sex as a team sport and turn toward your partner in giving and receiving sensual, playful, and erotic touch in addition to intercourse. Don't fall into the trap of demanding spontaneous erection with totally predictable intercourse. That ultimately leads to low desire and giving up sex. Embrace GES and turn toward your partner whether the sex was wonderful or disappointing. Don't apologize for sex. Resilient desire is based on openness to touch, creating bridges to desire, and accepting a range of sexual experiences.

10

INTEGRATING INTIMACY, PLEASURING, AND EROTICISM

Broad-Based Sexuality

Traditionally, intimacy and pleasuring were the woman's domain, with eroticism and intercourse being the man's domain. An easy to understand split, but destructive for the man, woman, couple, and culture. An important sexual decision is to adopt an integrated intimacy, pleasuring, and eroticism approach to male and couple sexuality. Being an intimate sexual team promotes desire and satisfaction. Rather than splitting by gender, value intimacy and pleasuring as well as eroticism and intercourse. This is crucial for the growth of male sexuality. You are a fully functioning man psychologically, relationally, and sexually. Broad-based sexuality is healthy for you and your relationship.

Intimacy, pleasuring, and eroticism promote the desire/pleasure/eroticism/ satisfaction mantra. The myth that men don't need or value intimacy is one of the most destructive learnings from the double standard. The fear that intimacy will "feminize" you is an example of the destructive role of rigid gender stereotypes. Intimacy is integral to being a sexual man. Needs for intimacy are core to your sexuality. In a cross-cultural study of couples from six countries who had been together for more than 20 years, what men most valued was confidence that the partner "has your back" and feeling secure with your intimate bond (Heiman et al., 2011). What women valued most was a vital sexual relationship. This is the opposite of traditional gender stereotypes. Intimacy, pleasuring, and eroticism are not split by gender, but are integrated and shared. Intimacy is about feeling close and secure. You feel accepted for who you are with psychological, relational, and sexual strengths and vulnerabilities. Intimacy is a foundation for your relationship and promotes desire, but is not enough. The old view was the more intimacy, the better the sex. The trap is that too much intimacy and closeness cause you to "de-eroticize" your partner and relationship. The challenge for couples, married or partnered, is to integrate intimacy and eroticism. Find a comfortable level of intimacy which facilitates rather than smothers sexual desire. How to balance intimacy and eroticism is a challenging issue for both couples and mental health professionals. Couple therapists advocate intimacy, while sex therapists advocate eroticism. Women advocate intimacy; men advocate eroticism. This splitting is bad for couple sexuality. The issue is finding the right balance and integration. Find the level of intimacy which allows you to feel open and receptive as well as affirm being a sexual team.

The second dimension is nondemand pleasuring. In addition to affectionate touch, pleasuring involves sensual and playful touching. Traditionally, this was the woman's domain, not the man's. Nondemand pleasuring involves subjective arousal in the 1–5 range. This is valuable for itself. You don't need erotic stimulation or intercourse to enjoy being a sexual man. Sensual massage and genital play are affirming. The woman can enjoy pleasure without having an orgasm. This is a crucial learning for you – value pleasure for itself. Erection is a sign of pleasure, not a demand for intercourse or an orgasm. Women avoid sexual play because of the pressure felt when you have an erection. The answer to this paradox is simple, enjoy your erection for what it is – a sign of pleasure. Your erection and her vaginal lubrication is a natural response to pleasure. The core of nondemand pleasuring is accepting pleasure. This reinforces a major concept – the essence of couple sexuality is giving and receiving pleasure-oriented touching. Of course, pleasure can lead to arousal, intercourse, and orgasm. However, this is not the chief function of pleasure.

The third dimension, eroticism, is the most contentious and can cause confusion and alienation. Eroticism involves intense sensations and feelings in the 6–10 range. Traditionally, eroticism is the man's domain; the woman's role is to promote male eroticism. What nonsense. Like intimacy and pleasure, eroticism is a shared domain. The issue is how to integrate eroticism into couple sexuality (McCarthy & McCarthy, 2020). The woman's role is not to sexually perform for you, but to find her "erotic voice" and integrate it into couple sexuality. Integrated eroticism is very different than the porn depiction or the focus on illicitness and drama. Eroticism is integral to the desire/pleasure/eroticism/satisfaction mantra. Erotic scenarios are often asynchronous, better for one partner than the other. As long as the erotic scenario is not at the expense of the partner or relationship, enjoy it. If it's a 10 for you and a 3 for her, this is fine. What is not healthy is if it's a −3 for the partner.

As with other dimensions of sexuality, mutual, synchronous eroticism is the ideal. An aroused, orgasmic partner is a powerful aphrodisiac. Eroticism is a natural extension of the "give to get" pleasuring guideline. Eroticism belongs as much to the woman as the man.

The Whole Is More than the Parts

Intimacy, pleasuring, and eroticism are three different dimensions. When integrated and implemented, the whole is more than the parts. It is not a hierarchy; all three dimensions enhance your sexuality. Not all dimensions need to be present at each encounter. For example, you experience a high level of eroticism, so there is no time for pleasuring. More common is an intimate encounter focused on pleasure where eroticism follows. The most satisfying sex integrates intimacy, pleasuring, and eroticism, but if that were necessary for each encounter you would have much less sex. This is a complex message, but a very important one. When all three dimensions are valued, it is easier to accept a sexual experience where one or two dimensions are missing. A healthy couple embraces the variability and flexibility of sexuality. Couples with the traditional intimacy/eroticism split are vulnerable to sexual conflicts and low desire. Each partner valuing all three dimensions provides a solid sexual foundation. You have confidence in yourself and your partner. If a dimension is missing from an encounter, you accept this rather than overreact. An example is the woman who has two drinks and has a strong reaction to pleasuring which leads to a powerful erotic response. He enjoys this, but feels strange. He thinks, "Does she respond more to alcohol than me"? She is confused by your reaction because she assumes that all men are turned on by female erotic response. Gender assumptions and misunderstandings subvert the best-intentioned couple. It is normal to have sexual encounters which are more or less intimate, more or less pleasurable, more or less erotic. You are not a perfectly functioning sexual machine nor are you clones of each other. Be aware that intimacy, pleasuring, and eroticism is not a recipe you need to follow each time nor does it need to be the same for each partner. Asynchronous sexual encounters (positive but better for one partner than the other) are the norm, not the exception. There are times the man craves more intimacy and there are times the woman craves more eroticism. This is normal and healthy. Both partners valuing intimacy, pleasuring, and eroticism is the basis for variable, flexible couple sexuality.

Jeremy and Emma

Jeremy met Emma when he was 32. They have been a couple for more than five years. He identifies as a non-traditional man both in his job and approach to women and relationships. He works four to six months at a job site, returning to his one-bedroom apartment in their small city on occasion. He likes this lifestyle and saves a significant part of his salary (including travel bonuses). He does not plan to marry nor have children. When he was 27, Jeremy had a vasectomy so did not have to worry about an unwanted pregnancy. Jeremy had sexual friendships but was not interested in a serious relationship. Sometimes, the sexual friendship lasted the whole time he was at the job site, but more often there were a series of short-term relationships – from one night to two months.

Emma was a dental hygienist in a thriving dental practice. She enjoyed her two-bedroom condo where she had solid friendships and community ties. Emma valued economic stability and like Jeremy was a saver. She came from a chaotic family where her parents, two siblings, and four half-siblings had multiple divorces. Emma had an eight-year-old niece she was close to, but kept distance from other relatives. Like Jeremy, Emma had no interest in marriage and children. Unlike Jeremy, Emma valued a serious intimate relationship. She had no interest in multiple relationships. She had friends, both married and partnered, who engaged in consensual non-monogamy, but that was not for Emma. She viewed Jeremy as a sexual friend, not as a life partner. Emma was pleased that Jeremy had a vasectomy.

Relationships change over time. For most dating couples, satisfaction is lowered eventually leading to ending the sexual friendship. A sign of a healthy relationship (whether a marriage or life partnership) is that it becomes better over time, including sexually. Jeremy and Emma felt that their relationship, especially their sexual friendship, was healthier after five years. Integrating intimacy, pleasuring, and eroticism made their relationship more satisfying than in the limerence phase. Jeremy enjoyed the limerence phase with a new woman, but over time felt that he was letting her down because their relationship wasn't moving in the direction she wanted. With Emma, he found a partner who shared his values of a sexual friendship, engagement when he was in the city, and willing to travel to his work site. Emma shared his life organization and not having children.

Jeremy thought of sexuality as a strength. He had good ejaculatory control which he believed was the key for female sexuality. Jeremy used the woman's orgasm as his measure of being a good lover. Emma valued orgasm, but for her the issue was not length of intercourse. Like many women, Emma could be orgasmic during the pleasuring phase, during intercourse, or during afterplay. Like the majority of women, her orgasmic response was variable. She was orgasmic in 70–80% of partner experiences.

The intimacy, pleasuring, eroticism model was more easily accepted by Emma. They were more in synch on eroticism than the other dimensions. Both enjoyed giving and receiving erotic stimulation. Emma enjoyed mutual oral sex, while Jeremy preferred taking turns. Emma went with his preference. When receiving oral stimulation, she wanted two things. First, begin with manual stimulation and intermix oral stimulation when subjective arousal is a 7. Second, his openness to her touching and moving rather than being passive. When she is the giving partner in oral sex, she prefers the position where she is kneeling, him standing, with her setting the rhythm of oral pleasuring. She enjoys Jeremy verbalizing sexual feelings and saying when he is about to "come". She finds ejaculation in her mouth a turn-off, so switches to manual stimulation before orgasm. This is not a rigid set of rules, but variable guidelines.

The issue of intimacy was challenging. Jeremy's sexual experiences followed the traditional role of the woman emphasizing intimacy. Jeremy did not want to be sexually selfish, but felt no need for intimacy – intimacy was to placate the woman. Emma disliked feeling that she was being placated; she does not want to be viewed as "emotionally needy". She wants a genuine emotional connection. This meant being a sexual team with intimacy as a shared dimension. Finding the "right fit" for emotional and sexual intimacy is a couple challenge. This is not about marriage; it's about feeling emotionally attached and sexually valued. When they are sexual, whether at her condo, his apartment, or on a trip, Emma wants to feel that they are genuinely sharing themselves. Jeremy saying, "What can I do so you don't complain", was the opposite of emotional intimacy. She wanted a genuine emotional dialogue. For Emma, genuine is the operative concept. Jeremy had viewed intimacy as a foreign idea; it was a reason the woman felt hurt and demanding. Ideally, emotional intimacy bonds the couple; sexual intimacy energizes the couple.

When Jeremy is on a job site, they speak by phone two to three times a week. They meet for a long weekend once a month. She wanted to know whether that level of intimacy fit for Jeremy. This was a question he had never asked himself. What was the right balance of autonomy and intimacy for him? He was so used to feeling controlled by the woman's intimacy needs that he ignored his own intimacy preferences. He did not want a marital commitment, but now felt open to a genuine intimate relationship. He particularly valued that "Emma has my back".

Jeremy was proud to balance autonomy and their relationship. He respects that Emma has a life of her own – career, friends, condo, financial independence. The incident that strengthened their relationship was her support when he injured his back in a work accident. Emma urged him to return home and consult a rehabilitation medicine specialist rather than the general practitioner the company wanted him to see. Emma accompanied him to the appointment and picked him up after physical therapy. She urged him to use all his resources to ensure a full recovery. Jeremy trusted Emma to listen and give feedback on the rehab program. Jeremy feels he is a better, healthier person with Emma in his life. In addition, they developed a new sexual scenario so that he could enjoy sex without back stress.

The hardest dimension for Jeremy was nondemand pleasuring. This was not part of his sexual socialization. Women focused on pleasure, not men. Jeremy viewed foreplay as strictly for the woman. Pleasuring made no sense to him and had no role in his approach to sex.

Learning to value pleasuring for himself as well as a couple was a major breakthrough. Emma had a central role in advocating for nondemand pleasuring. Emma disliked "foreplay" where she was passive. A key to Emma's receptivity and responsivity is giving and receiving touch. She wants Jeremy to be actively involved in the pleasuring process rather than the controlling partner.

A benefit of nondemand pleasuring was that it confronted routine, predictable sex. Emma enjoyed playful scenarios without the demand that it end in intercourse. She enjoys his erection rather than feel pressured by it. Emma suggested that at least once a month, they have a playful date with a prohibition on intercourse and orgasm. At first, Jeremy felt that was silly and unnecessary, but found this a special experience. Nondemand pleasuring is something Jeremy has learned to value.

Jeremy and Emma committed to a life partnership. They emphasize a satisfying and sexual relationship as more important than relational security. Jeremy knows too many married men who complain about the spouse and marriage. Emma has too many friends with "stable" relationships, but did not feel "secure". Secure means you value your partner and the intimacy of your relationship. Stable means you stay together for convenience, continuity, children, finances, social norms, but do not feel valued relationally or sexually.

Jeremy was proud that he and Emma had grown as a couple. They value intimacy, pleasuring, and eroticism. Sex has a 15–20% role of energizing their bond and reinforcing feelings of desire and desirability.

Integrating Intimacy, Pleasuring, and Eroticism into Your Couple Sexual Style

We emphasize guidelines rather than sexual rules. This is particularly true for the integration of intimacy, pleasuring, and eroticism. Each couple develops their unique way to integrate these dimensions, often changing over time. Intimacy and pleasuring take a more important role as the couple mature. You want eroticism to be vital whether you've been a couple for 1 or 50 years. Some couples emphasize intimacy, others emphasize eroticism; some emphasize pleasuring. Be sure all three dimensions remain present. The traditional male trap is downplaying pleasuring. The traditional female trap is downplaying eroticism. The most common trap is the gender split between intimacy and eroticism. This split is overlearned in adolescence and young adulthood. It does damage to men, women, couples, and the culture. An advantage of integrating intimacy, pleasuring, and eroticism is having a shared language and a shared value. It allows you to confront the "intercourse or nothing" myth. It provides three distinct ways to feel connected and be present. Men and women are not clones of each other, but are allies who embrace intimacy, pleasuring, and eroticism. The challenges are different by gender. The goal is finding common ground so you experience enhanced humanity and sexuality. Intimacy, pleasuring, and eroticism are particularly challenging for men, but also particularly rewarding. They facilitate male sexuality which is more human and genuine. In addition, they promote a broad-based approach to desire and satisfaction, especially with aging.

Exercise – Implementing Intimacy, Pleasuring, and Eroticism

This exercise asks you to take responsibility for your sexuality and clearly define what you value about intimacy, pleasuring, and eroticism. This is a challenge because intimacy and pleasuring have traditionally been the woman's domain, not yours. Let's begin with intimacy. What type and degree of intimacy fit your needs (rather than your partner's)? For you, is emotional and sexual intimacy different? Does sexual intimacy enhance emotional intimacy? Does emotional intimacy enhance or inhibit sexual desire? Be clear, specific, and genuine; do not give socially desirable answers. Does it matter if you are the one initiating an intimate encounter?

Next, focus on your preferences for nondemand pleasuring. This includes affection, sensual, and playful touch. Is your preference mutual touching or taking turns as giver and receiver? How often do you want pleasuring to be a bridge to arousal and intercourse – 20%, 40%, 60%, 80%, or 95%? If you have an erection during pleasuring, do you rush to intercourse or can you accept the erection for itself? Do you enjoy pleasuring clothed, semi-clothed, or nude? What is the meaning of pleasure for you? What are your partner's preferences for pleasure?

What does eroticism mean for you? Is eroticism valuable for itself or as a bridge to intercourse? Do you prefer partner interaction arousal/eroticism, self-entrancement arousal/eroticism, or role enactment arousal/eroticism? What is your favorite synchronous erotic scenario? What is your favorite asynchronous erotic scenario? Does your partner know what you value about integrated eroticism?

Share learnings with your partner. What is her feedback about your approach to intimacy, pleasuring, and eroticism? What are her perceptions and suggestions to enhance intimate, pleasurable, and erotic sexuality?

This exercise illustrates that what initially sounds like an easy concept is in fact multi-dimensional and challenging. It is such a different approach to being a sexual man than the traditional double standard. Be sure that intimacy, pleasuring, and eroticism fit personally and relationally.

Broad-Based Masculinity vs. a Narrow Approach to Masculinity

This new model of being a sexual man and broad-based masculinity opens you to a human, genuine understanding. It promotes acceptance and valuing male and couple sexuality. The disadvantage is that it's more complex and challenging than the old model and is not supported by male peers. The old model was simple and required little thought or dialogue. In truth, it was narrow, unrealistic, and oppressive. You kept doubts, questions, and fears to yourself. Barry remembers a client saying, "What matters in life is making as much money as you can, having as much sex as you can, and being strong and independent-I know who I am". This narrow view of masculinity negates your humanity and choice in expressing who you really are. The traditional approach leaves no space for doubt, vulnerabilities, doing something non-traditional, or the courage to say no. It gave fears and stereotypes inordinate power, especially in regard to sexuality. Sex was a simple pass-fail performance that left no room for intimacy and pleasuring.

The new model of masculinity is based on acceptance of the reality and complexity of being a man. An example is receiving fellatio. The myth is that all men love being fellated to orgasm, want to ejaculate in the woman's mouth, and want her to swallow your semen as a sign of submission. Fellatio is viewed as erotic sexuality with the man dominant and the woman subservient. Is that a turn-on for all men? Absolutely not. We estimate that one in five men does not enjoy fellatio to orgasm, but would never say that to the woman and certainly not to male friends because you fear being judged. The traditional view of masculinity does not give you the right to your sexual feelings and preferences. You are trapped in an intimidating, rigid role.

The challenge of the new masculinity is to be your authentic sexual self. This includes your approach to intimacy, what you value about nondemand pleasuring, and preferred erotic techniques and scenarios. When you are open about who you are, your partner is likely to be open about who she is. Women feel pressured by traditional masculinity which treats her as a second-class citizen. She is blamed for any and all sexual problems. The new masculinity frees men, women, couples, and the culture. This is especially true of integrated eroticism. Both value the integration of intimacy, pleasuring, and eroticism.

Summary

Intimacy, pleasuring, and eroticism are separate dimensions, but are best when integrated and valued by both partners. The whole is more than the parts. The challenge is to identify for yourself what degree of intimacy promotes sexual anticipation and desire. Contrary to cultural myths, more intimacy is not better. A key is to balance intimacy and eroticism. Another key is to confront the traditional male (eroticism)-female (intimacy) split. Men have a need for an intimate, secure relationship. Women have a right to enjoy integrated eroticism and her "erotic voice". Nondemand pleasuring is a core factor in a healthy relationship. You and your partner decide what type of pleasuring and what type of eroticism are the right fit.

Both partners valuing intimacy, pleasuring, and eroticism promote strong, resilient sexual desire and couple satisfaction.

11

DEVELOPING YOUR COUPLE
SEXUAL STYLE

The Autonomy/Couple Balance

Sex therapy brings two major contributions to the relationship field. First, psychosexual skill exercises to enhance sexual comfort and confidence. Second, the importance of creating a couple sexual style (which is often different than your relational style). This chapter focuses on your couple sexual style.

There are two components of your couple sexual style. First, maintain your sexual autonomy ("sexual voice") while being an intimate sexual team. Second, how you integrate intimacy and eroticism into your relationship. This is different than your relational style which focuses on dealing with differences and conflicts. Your relational style involves how you organize your life as a couple, while your sexual style focuses on the 15–20% role of healthy sexuality.

The primary couple sexual styles (by frequency) are:

1   Complementary (mine and ours)
2   Traditional (conflict minimizing)
3   Best Friend (soul mate)
4   Emotionally Expressive (fun and erotic).

Each sexual style has strengths and each has vulnerabilities (traps). We urge you to adopt a sexual style that meets his, her, and our needs and preferences. Reach a mutual agreement on which couple sexual style is the best fit and then modify the style so that it meets your needs and preferences (McCarthy & McCarthy, 2009).

A common power struggle is that the man wants the Traditional sexual style and the woman wants the Best Friend style. The Complementary sexual style is the choice for the majority, but not all, couples. Sexually, one size never fits all.

We describe each couple sexual style focusing first on strengths and then vulnerabilities. Choose the sexual style which is the best fit for your feelings, preferences, and values. Enjoy the strengths of your chosen style while monitoring traps so they don't subvert couple sexuality.

Complementary Couple Sexual Style

The reason this is the most common sexual style is that it fits the therapeutic model of each person taking responsibility for your sexuality while being an intimate sexual team. Both the man and woman value intimacy and eroticism. In addition, you have "his", "hers", and "our" bridges to sexual desire. Complementary couples are not clones of each other. Both value pleasuring, eroticism, intercourse, and afterplay. You affirm the value of both synchronous and asynchronous sexual scenarios. Acknowledge the multiple roles and meanings of sex, including a shared pleasure, a means to reinforce attachment, a tension reducer, and to conceive a planned, wanted child. In addition, sex affirms attraction, a "port in the storm" when dealing with difficult parenting or financial issues, energizes your bond so you can deal with emotional conflicts, or provides comfort after the death of a sibling. Your sexual style acknowledges the inherent variability and flexibility of couple sexuality. The Good Enough Sex (GES) approach is easily compatible with the Complementary couple sexual style.

There are several potential vulnerabilities (traps) of the Complementary sexual style. The major one is treating your sexual relationship with benign neglect. This results in lowered desire and satisfaction even if sex remains functional. Another vulnerability is too much routine and predictability. The Complementary sexual style welcomes partner interaction and self-entrancement arousal scenarios. Role enactment arousal is more challenging to incorporate. A vulnerability is feeling resentful that the promise of an equitable sexual relationship was not met.

A satisfying sexual relationship requires continual awareness and energy. Don't treat your Complementary sexual style with benign neglect – sexuality cannot rest on its laurels.

Traditional Couple Sexual Style

This is the most stable sexual style. You adopt traditional roles. Initiation is the man's domain with an emphasis on intercourse frequency. Intimacy and affection is the woman's domain. There is little sexual fighting and no need for sexual dialogue – each partner is clear about your very different roles. Traditional sexual couples tend to be religious, family-oriented, and benefit from community support. Same-gender friends make jokes about the foibles of the opposite sex but are supportive of marital security. Paradoxically, this is the couple sexual style which most easily accepts a non-sexual relationship with aging, especially if you maintain an affectionate attachment.

There are several vulnerabilities with the Traditional couple sexual style. The most common is that sex roles become rigid, causing isolation and alienation. You believe that she does not value sexuality, especially intercourse. As you age and deal with illness, including side-effects of medications, you are not able to be sexually functional without her stimulation. Sadly, you turn away rather than toward her. The trap for the woman is resentment because your need for intercourse overrides her need for intimacy and affectionate, sensual, and playful touch. She loves you and feels loyal to the marriage, but does not feel that you're an intimate spouse nor does she value couple sex.

Another trap is dealing with infertility. Rather than seeing infertility as a medical issue where you support each other, infertility is viewed as god's punishment for past sexual transgressions. Even though religious Catholics, Jews, Protestants, and Mormons are not supposed to have extra-marital affairs, this occurs, including to happily married couples. Traditional couples find it hard to recover from an affair (especially the woman's affair).

In dealing with difficult issues such as infertility or affairs, you are urged to seek professional help and stay away from the traps of shame or feeling that this is god's punishment.

Best Friend Couple Sexual Style

When we wrote about couple sexuality years ago, we said that the Best Friend sexual style was superior. This is what mental health professionals believed at the time. We thought the Best Friend style would be the best fit for most couples. How wrong we were. The Best Friend (also called soul mate) sexual style has great strengths, but even greater vulnerabilities. The Best Friend relational style is usually the best fit, but not the Best Friend sexual style.

The biggest strength of the Best Friend sexual style is that you share intimacy and eroticism. Your partner knows your strengths and vulnerabilities and loves and accepts you. This is affirming. If something goes wrong sexually, you trust your partner "has your back". You enjoy mutuality and support. You reinforce the value of intimacy and touching.

The Best Friend sexual style has major vulnerabilities. There is so much intimacy that you de-eroticize each other. Mutuality is so crucial that you don't take personal or sexual risks. Thus, there is less sexual initiation and frequency. It is easier to be warm and cuddly than erotic and sexual. Best Friend couples experience the most difficulty recovering from an extra-marital affair. They stay stuck in feelings betrayal. Couples fall into the Best Friend sexual style because they mistakenly believe that if this style fits relationally, it should fit sexually. The Complementary couple sexual style is a better fit for most couples.

Emotionally Expressive Couple Sexual Style

This is the fun and erotic sexual style. People envy Emotionally Expressive sexual couples because they make their own rules, are filled with sexual energy, and have the most resilient sexual relationship. For example, they bounce back from an affair – they cry, yell, and have sex. They are the couple most likely to have a non-traditional life organization, enjoy role enactment arousal, and have a consensual non-monogamy agreement.

The Emotionally Expressive sexual style has the largest number of potential vulnerabilities, especially being less secure. Even though they are resilient, after recovering from the fourth affair, you feel emotionally worn out. The biggest vulnerability is breaking emotional and sexual boundaries. People are vulnerable, especially when fighting about sex, nude, in bed, lying down, after a negative sexual experience. When hurt, angry, or drunk, people say harmful things that are long remembered. An example is the man saying, "You pulled a sexual bait and switch-if I knew who you really were, I never would have married you". Or the woman saying, "If you can't keep it up why do you bother to stay alive"? The partner apologizes the next day, but this does major harm to self-esteem and your relationship. The best time to talk about sex is dressed, sitting, the day before being sexual, and a clear request of what you want to sexually try the next time.

The guideline is to play to the strengths of your chosen sexual style and be sure to not fall into traps. Your chosen couple sexual style allows sexuality to have a 15–20% role in your relationship – energizing your bond and reinforcing feelings of desire and desirability.

Mitch and Sarah

When they married four years ago, Sarah and Mitch were a loving, enthusiastic couple. After four years and one child, it was unclear whether they would be able to stay married. Rather than sexuality having a positive role, it was a major problem, a 50–75% draining role which threatened the marriage.

Mitch and Sarah had a wonderful beginning as a romantic love/passionate sex/ idealized (limerence) couple. Sex was special and energizing. Both sexual quality and frequency were excellent. This began to change after six months of living together, occurring five months before the wedding. As they shared their lives and negotiated emotional and practical details, including wedding planning, "magical" sex disappeared. The biggest issue was a common struggle – initiation patterns and intercourse frequency. Rather than a fun coming together, Mitch pushed sex almost every day. Sarah felt pressured and did not like being in the role of saying no. She did not want to be the sexual gatekeeper. She hoped that this pattern would change after the wedding, but instead the cycle intensified. Was it Mitch's fault, Sarah's fault, or was there something wrong with them as a couple?

Sarah looked forward to the honeymoon in Hawaii, hoping that it would break the problematic sexual cycle. Sadly, the honeymoon made the intercourse frequency problem worse. They argued every day. The two times they had intercourse, it was fine for Mitch, but not for Sarah, and both felt disappointed.

Sex with the goal of becoming pregnant was fun, but the conflict over intercourse frequency continued during the pregnancy and became worse after the baby was born. Mitch and Sarah were excellent parents and valued many aspects of their lives, but were not an intimate sexual team.

Over the past eight months, Sarah was thinking more about divorce. Mitch did not want a divorce, but tired of daily masturbation being his sexual outlet (in the past year, they'd had intercourse three times and no other sexual touch). Sarah did not feel sexual desire with Mitch, but was increasingly attracted to other men.

Sarah's sister did an extensive internet search and found a well-respected, pro-marriage sex therapist. They e-mailed the therapist who responded that she was willing to meet with Mitch and Sarah.

At the initial session, it was clear that Sarah and Mitch were a demoralized couple who turned away from each other. This is typical for couples in a non-sexual marriage. The clinician was not discouraged. She empathized with them about how demoralizing it was to go from being a loving, sexually vibrant couple to a non-sexual, alienated couple. She recommended that they commit to a six-month therapy contract with the goal of creating a marital bond of respect, trust, and emotional commitment. A crucial issue was developing a new couple sexual style. Sarah was motivated by the therapist's willingness to see them and especially her optimism that like three of four couples they could rebuild couple sexuality. Mitch was hopeful because the clinician was experienced and suggested realistic goals rather than promising a return to the magical sex of the first year.

Sex therapy requires focus and energy by both the couple and the clinician. There are five clients (dimensions) for the therapist to attend to: (1) Sarah, (2) Mitch, (3) their relationship, (4) their sexual relationship, and (5) the most difficult client – their emotional and sexual history.

A major challenge in working with Mitch was his anger at Sarah for blaming him for the sexual problem. The clinician noted that Mitch couldn't change the past, although he could learn from the past. Mitch needed to focus on the present and future and realize that low desire was the joint enemy. In her individual session, Sarah committed to focus on the marriage rather than allow herself to be diverted by an affair – including an emotional, unconsummated affair.

The challenge for Sarah was to find her sexual voice and rebuild positive anticipation – the core of sexual desire. A particularly empowering psychosexual skill exercise was Sarah having the power to veto a sexual scenario. Mitch honored her veto. Rather than go away and sulk, Mitch and Sarah developed a trust position where she put her head on his heart, he stroked her hair, and they were mindful of feelings of safety and attachment. This was a powerful healing experience, especially for Sarah.

An important understanding is that you do not have the freedom to say yes to sex unless you have the power to say no. You trust your partner will respect your veto. Her emotional needs are more important than your sexual wants. Rather than turning away, Mitch and Sarah would turn toward each other in an affectionate, sensual, or erotic manner.

The majority of couples in therapy choose the Complementary couple sexual style. Sarah and Mitch read about sexual styles, took a self-administered questionnaire, and discussed their sexual attitudes, experiences, feelings, and values. In retrospect, they understood the conflict – Mitch assumed that they would have a Traditional sexual style, while Sarah assumed that they would have a Best Friend sexual style. This misunderstanding and difference in assumptions almost guaranteed a power struggle. The "good-bad" struggle about sexual desire and frequency was unintended. The desire problem had not been caused by negative motivations or hidden agendas.

Sarah and Mitch (with the therapist's guidance) approached the issue of their couple sexual style from a positive knowledge base. Both were committed to finding a sexual style that fit them.

Sarah made it clear that she valued both intimacy and eroticism and realized how important it is to have her sexual voice. Mitch committed to intimacy and nondemand pleasuring. Each partner had preferences for sensual, playful, erotic, and intercourse scenarios. They developed afterplay scenarios which increased emotional and sexual satisfaction, even when the sexual encounter was mediocre.

Mitch and Sarah embraced the Complementary couple sexual style and integrated that with the Best Friend relational style. This provided a solid foundation for a respectful, trusting, intimate marriage from which to welcome a planned, wanted second child. Sex with the goal of pregnancy is an aphrodisiac.

Rather than taking their marital bond and sexual relationship for granted, Mitch and Sarah committed to a relapse prevention program. They agreed to attend six-month follow-up sessions for two years to be sure that changes were maintained and generalized. In addition, they set a new couple sexual growth goal for the next six months. If the relationship ran into a problem or they were concerned about a relapse, they would call for a "booster session". They had come too far psychologically, relationally, and sexually to allow a relapse.

Couple Discrepancies in Sexual Desire

You are not clones of each other, especially not sexually. There will be differences in what you value about intimacy, pleasure, and eroticism. Contrary to popular belief, these are not governed by traditional gender stereotypes. There are many men who value intimate sexuality. There are many women who value sexuality generally and erotic sexuality specifically.

Focus on yourself and your partner – your attitudes, behaviors, emotions, and values are more important than gender stereotypes. Be clear and specific about sexual feelings, especially what promotes desire.

An important guideline is don't fall into the pursuer-distancer trap. A sexual power struggle over intercourse or nothing is in no one's best interest. One of the reasons American couples have intercourse only a bit more than once a week is that they only have two dimensions (gears) – affection and intercourse. They ignore sensual, playful, and erotic touch.

In dealing with differences, focus on sexuality as an intimate team experience of sharing pleasure. Discussing the value of touch and attachment opens partners to affectionate, sensual, playful, and erotic touch in addition to intercourse. Touch is an invitation to connection rather than a demand for intercourse. An empowering guideline is to enjoy touch both inside and outside the bedroom without the expectation that touching must lead to intercourse. Many women dread the man's erection because the erect penis is viewed as a demand for intercourse or at least an orgasm. Welcome your erection as a sign of pleasure rather than a sexual demand.

Sexual desire is enhanced by freedom, choice, and unpredictability. Implement this into your couple sexual style. It is easiest for the Complementary style. For the Traditional and Best Friend styles, this needs to be explicitly stated and behaviorally implemented. This results in more sexual experiences because it allows her freedom to enjoy intimacy and touching rather than being afraid of turning you on unless she wants intercourse. The key to implementing this guideline with the Emotionally Expressive couple is to celebrate playfulness and unpredictability.

Exercise – Discovering Your Couple Sexual Style

Choosing the right sexual style is a very important decision. It will affect your relationship and couple sexuality for years. Be honest with yourself and your partner. Discuss the following questions:

1 How important is sex in your life? How important is having a satisfying, secure, and sexual relationship?
2 What is your preferred way to express affection – hand holding, kissing, or hugging?
3 What is the difference between affectionate touch and sexual touch?
4 Do you value sensual, non-genital touch? Do you prefer taking turns or mutual touching?
5 What is the meaning and value of genital pleasuring? Do you experience this as playful or is it always oriented toward arousal and intercourse? Do you have a favorite playful scenario? Do you enjoy mixing sensual and genital touch?
6 Do you value erotic scenarios and techniques that do not lead to intercourse? Do you prefer manual, oral, or rubbing stimulation? Do you enjoy multiple stimulation or one focused stimulation? Taking turns

or mutual stimulation? Using external stimuli (sex toys, erotic videos, playing out a fantasy)? Do you enjoy erotic sex to orgasm or is eroticism a prelude to intercourse?

7 Do you view intercourse as a natural extension of the pleasuring/eroticism process or a pass-fail performance test? Do you transition to intercourse as soon as possible or wait until you experience erotic flow? What is your preferred intercourse position? What types of thrusting do you enjoy? Do you value multiple stimulation during intercourse?

8 How much do you value afterplay? What afterplay scenarios and techniques enhance sexual satisfaction?

9 What is the preferred balance of your sexual voice (autonomy) with being an intimate sexual team?

10 How do you integrate intimacy (closeness, loving feelings, warmth, security, predictability) with eroticism (creativity, mystery, intense sensations, taking emotional and sexual risks, unpredictability)?

Share your feelings and preferences. Discuss areas of agreement and disagreement. In developing a comfortable, pleasurable, erotic, and satisfying couple sexual style, you need to take personal responsibility and share sexuality.

In choosing among the four couple sexual styles – Complementary, Traditional, Best Friend, and Emotionally Expressive – which affirms your sexual voice and allows you to be intimate and erotic friends?

Each partner states the one or two couple sexual styles which would be a good fit as well as one or two which are not right for you. This is not an analytic problem-solving process, but an attitudinal/behavioral/emotional commitment of who you are as a sexual person and a sexual team.

Ideally, both partners choose the same couple sexual style. When there is no agreement, engage in an exploration of why the couple sexual style you prefer would be a good fit. Do not fall into the demand/attack mode. Share the key dimensions of your sexual voice, what you value about being a sexual team, and your preferred way to integrate intimacy and eroticism. Listen empathically and respectfully to your partner's emotional and sexual preferences. This process increases understanding and empathy. Your intimate relationship is based on a positive influence process, with a commitment to not engage in power struggles. Find a genuine common ground, so sexuality has a 15–20% role in energizing your bond. Individualize components of your chosen couple sexual style so that sexuality uniquely fits your relationship.

Monitoring the Vulnerabilities of Your Chosen Couple Sexual Style

Each couple sexual style has vulnerabilities (traps). Individually and as a couple, commit to not failing into traps. An advantage of having chosen a sexual style is that you don't have to monitor all the traps, only the ones relevant for your sexual style.

The Complementary couple sexual style has many strengths which is why it's the most chosen. The biggest vulnerability (trap) is complacency – you take sexuality for granted and "rest on your laurels". Rather than devoting thought, energy, and communication so that your sexual style remains vital, sex becomes routine and stale. To address this vulnerability, each partner commits to introducing one new scenario each year. It could be a new pleasuring lotion or sequence, a new erotic scenario or technique, a new pattern of multiple stimulation during intercourse, a new intercourse position or thrusting rhythm, or a new afterplay scenario. Each partner initiates something new (at least two new sexual scenarios a year). This ensures that couple sexuality remains vital and satisfying.

The prime vulnerability for the Traditional couple sexual style is that the roles become rigid. Specifically, as the man ages and your ability to function autonomously is lessened, you become self-conscious and anxious. The trap for the woman is she resents that her needs for intimacy and touch are overridden by your need for intercourse. The suggested intervention is that once every six months, you initiate an intimacy date with a prohibition on intercourse. Every six months, she initiates a playful or erotic scenario and it's her choice whether to transition to orgasm or intercourse. Honor traditional roles while "spicing up" your relationship.

The Best Friend couple sexual style's major vulnerability is that with so much emphasis on intimacy, you "de-eroticize" your partner. A second vulnerability is that with so much emphasis on mutuality, you take few personal or sexual initiations, which results in low sexual frequency. The suggested intervention is that every six months, each partner initiates a "selfish" asynchronous erotic scenario. Own your sexual feelings – it is normal and healthy to have different sexual preferences. This confronts the "tyranny of mutuality" allowing you sexual freedom (as long as it's not at the expense of the partner or relationship). Another intervention is to initiate a playful sexual scenario – not all sex needs to be intimate and serious. Playfulness is a sign of healthy couple sexuality.

The vulnerability of the Emotionally Expressive couple sexual style is that you wear each other out with emotional and sexual drama. When hurt or angry, the partner drops a "sexual atomic bomb". The suggested intervention is to set boundaries. Each partner shares one to three "sexual atomic bomb" issues. You make an emotional commitment that no matter how hurt, angry, or drunk, you will not launch a sexual attack. A specific suggestion is to not talk sex when lying in bed, nude, after a negative sexual experience. In that situation, people say and do things which cause great damage.

The core guideline is to enjoy the strengths of your couple sexual style and monitor the traps so they do not subvert your sexuality.

Gender Issues with Couple Sexual Styles

The simplistic belief that women value intimacy and men value intercourse has done great damage to men, women, and couples. A core concept in choosing a couple sexual style is to speak the same intimacy and sexuality language. Each partner has their sexual voice and values being a sexual team. Each couple decides what is the right integration of intimacy and eroticism for you. The Complementary couple sexual style affirms female-male sexual equity. Each partner has the right to initiate, say no, and value both intimacy and eroticism. A key element of the Complementary sexual style is to disarm the male-female power struggle over intercourse frequency. The Traditional sexual style is organized along gender roles but affirms the importance of sexuality. The Best Friend sexual style emphasizes female-male equity, mutuality, and centers on intimacy. The Emotionally Expressive sexual style emphasizes both partners enjoying eroticism and taking sexual risks.

The issue is which couple sexual style fits your approach to sexual roles and expectations.

Summary

A major contribution the sexuality field brings to the relationship field is the importance of developing a couple sexual style which promotes and maintains sexual desire. There is not "one right" way to be a sexual couple. Choose the sexual style which is the right fit for you. Your couple sexual style breaks the power struggle over intercourse as the measure of sex, instead promoting desire/pleasure/eroticism/satisfaction.

Play to the strengths of your chosen couple sexual style as well as be aware of the vulnerabilities so you don't fall into those traps. Individualize your sexual style so it uniquely fits your feelings and preferences. Be sure your sexual style facilitates the 15–20% role of sexuality in your life and relationship.

12

GOOD ENOUGH SEX (GES)

Positive, Realistic Expectations

Traditional men stop being sexual in their 50s or 60s. "Wise" men can be sexual in their 60s, 70s, and 80s. A key strategy is to embrace the Good Enough Sex (GES) model. This empowers male sexuality, especially with aging.

Women find GES inviting and easy to accept because it is congruent with female sexual socialization and lived experiences. The great majority of women learn sexuality as an interactive, variable, flexible experience. In contrast, the great majority of men learn sexuality as easy, highly predictable, and in your control. You learn that sexual response is autonomous, i.e. you get a spontaneous erection and go to intercourse and orgasm on your first erection. You experience desire, arousal, and orgasm without needing anything from your partner. The traditional belief is that male sexuality involves the ability to have sex with any woman, any time, and in any situation with the expectation of perfect sex performance.

Male sex focuses on individual performance with total control and predictability. This might work for men in their teens, twenties, and thirties, but not for men in their forties and older, especially not in married or partnered relationships. The female model of intimate, interactive, variable, and flexible sexuality is superior to the male autonomous sex performance model (McCarthy & McCarthy, 2019b). Sadly, when men talk sex with peers, they brag, lie, and one-up each other. Male peers do not affirm GES.

Acceptance of GES in the Context of an intimate Relationship

What does GES mean? GES affirms that couple sexuality is inherently variable and flexible. The core of sexuality is giving and receiving pleasure-oriented touching. Couple sexuality is a team sport not an individual performance. The traditional sex performance approach demands predictable erection from you and predictable orgasm (during intercourse) from the woman.

The best sex is mutual and synchronous where both partners feel desire/pleasure/eroticism/satisfaction. We advocate for arousal, intercourse, and orgasm as well as mutual, synchronous encounters. Research indicates that although the great majority of sexual experiences are positive, even among happily married, sexually functional couples less than 50% are synchronous (Frank, Anderson, & Rubinstein, 1978). Couple sexuality is inherently variable, involving a range of motivations, roles, and outcomes. This is true for both men and women. For example, you view the sexual encounter as a means to reconnect and feel attachment, while for her, sex is driven by the desire for orgasm as a tension reducer. A sexual encounter later that week is better for you than her – sex is a celebration of your job promotion while she "goes along for the ride". The next week, a sexual encounter results in your orgasm, but is not particularly satisfying, while she feels warm and attached even though she is not orgasmic. These examples illustrate that GES is much more than sex function. GES involves roles, feelings, and meanings. Desire and satisfaction are more important than arousal and orgasm.

GES is a couple process focused on sharing pleasure, not an individual performance. GES becomes more important with the aging of the individuals and relationship. GES is particularly important for sexuality in your 60s, 70s, and 80s. The challenge is to embrace GES as first-class sexuality.

A key concept is that not all touching can or should proceed to intercourse. Perhaps 85% of sexual encounters will flow from pleasure to arousal to erotic flow to intercourse and orgasm. When sex does not flow, do not panic or apologize. There is nothing more anti-erotic than sexual self-consciousness and apologizing. Be open to a seamless transition to an erotic scenario or a sensual scenario. It is normal for 5–15% of sexual encounters to be mediocre, dissatisfying, or dysfunctional. GES is based on positive, realistic expectations. Romantic love and perfect sex demands ultimately subvert desire. GES allows you to thrive with positive, realistic sexual expectations.

GES Experiences and Expectations for Women

Most, although certainly not all, women find GES inviting. Perhaps the easiest concept to adopt is valuing sensual, playful, and erotic scenarios rather than all touching leading to intercourse. Most women, including those who are not orgasmic during intercourse, enjoy intercourse. However, the belief that all touching must end in intercourse promotes sex as a mechanical routine rather than as an anticipated pleasure. Alternative scenarios and erotic unpredictability put spice into your sexual life. Sensual scenarios are different than playful scenarios which, in turn, are different than erotic scenarios. Reinforce sensuality, playfulness, eroticism, and unpredictability in couple sexuality. In addition, freedom to enjoy both synchronous and asynchronous scenarios is empowering.

An example is pleasuring your partner to orgasm rather than having intercourse when you are not interested. Freedom to broaden your sexual repertoire builds comfort and reinforces pleasure. A particularly powerful scenario is requesting him to orally stimulate you to orgasm (or multiple orgasms) without the expectation that it must be reciprocated at that time. GES recognizes that not all sexual experiences need to be serious, mutual, or have the same meaning for both partners.

Positive, realistic expectations are particularly important in regard to intercourse. Sex involving desire/pleasure/eroticism/satisfaction is most valued. In addition, you can say, "This won't be an intercourse night-can we cuddle, play erotically, or take a rain check?" Celebrate sexual variability and flexibility. Even the 15% of women who are only orgasmic during intercourse welcome sensual and playful scenarios. Manual, oral, or rubbing stimulation can facilitate her (or his) orgasmic response. Variable, flexible scenarios are an important addition to couple sexuality.

GES Experiences and Expectations for Men

Men find adopting GES is a major challenge and welcome the woman's support and enthusiasm. Reading and talking about variable, flexible GES is necessary, but not sufficient. You need to experience the transition to a sensual, playful, or erotic scenario and the pleasure that comes from non-intercourse sexuality. Her sexual involvement and enthusiasm is good for your couple bond and helps you embrace GES. Be open to GES not to please her, but because it facilitates male and couple sexuality.

Carolyn and Ian

Ian and Carolyn had been a couple for 16 years. This was 44-year-old Ian's first marriage and 45-year-old Carolyn's second. Ian being a confident, involved lover was attractive for Carolyn. He was sensitive to Carolyn's emotional, touch, and sexual needs unlike her ex-husband who was a "meat and potatoes" sex man.

The first husband's sexual scenario involved breast and vaginal foreplay to get Carolyn ready for intercourse (as soon as possible). Sex was a source of contention. He would push intercourse four to five times a week, and she would reluctantly go along once or twice a week. At first, sex was functional, but after the second year, Carolyn's desire was low. Intercourse was a way to placate him with little pleasure for her. The marriage ended eight months after their daughter was born because Carolyn found him a disappointment as a person, spouse, and father. He further disappointed her by having marginal contact with the daughter and making irregular child support payments.

In the three years before meeting Ian, Carolyn found a renewed sexual interest with dating. She had two romantic love/passionate sex/idealized relationships, each lasting less than a year. The relationship with Ian started in that manner, but with time intimacy grew rather than burning out. Carolyn and Ian were open to a committed relationship.

At 38, Ian wanted more from life than a six-month to two-year relationship. He wanted a life partner. He had grown fond of Carolyn's daughter. Ian told Carolyn that the daughter deserved love and stability. Carolyn found this touching. It increased her attraction and desire for an intimate, secure relationship with Ian.

Almost all sexual touching led to intercourse, but it was a very different experience for Carolyn than with the ex-husband. Ian enjoyed touching both outside and inside the bedroom and sensed her feelings and needs rather than constantly pushing intercourse. Intimacy, touching, and sexuality had a 15–20% role in their relationship and continued to do so for 13 years, including Ian adopting the daughter and their having a son.

Ian had his first experience with erectile difficulty when he was 61. Carolyn realized that the cause was fatigue and alcohol. He tried twice more that night, but Carolyn lacked desire and Ian was sexually frustrated. The next night, intercourse went fine and Carolyn thought nothing about it. She had experienced low desire and low arousal many times. Like most women, Carolyn was orgasmic in many, but not all, sexual encounters. She was not aware of the negative impact of the erectile failure on Ian. He no longer felt sexually confident and unselfconscious. Although he continued to enjoy pleasuring and eroticism, Ian rushed intercourse because he feared losing his erection. Over time, erectile anxiety increased and the number of unsuccessful intercourse experiences also increased.

Carolyn and Ian did not speak directly about sexuality. Carolyn developed a pattern of manually stimulating Ian to orgasm if he wasn't aroused enough for intercourse. For a number of months, this worked fine, but Carolyn began resenting Ian's "sexual selfishness" and noticed a decline in her desire. She loved Ian, but sex was no longer fun. Ian's making sure Carolyn was orgasmic before intercourse had the paradoxical effect of increasing her orgasmic response but decreasing her sexual desire.

With the internet flooded with Viagra ads, Carolyn encouraged Ian to ask the internist for a prescription. The doctor was glad to do so, although he gave Ian no guidance about how to use it other than not to drink alcohol before taking Viagra. Pro-erection medications have two major effects. First, increase efficacy of the vascular system so that once aroused the erection is firm and lasting. Second, a psychological effect – Viagra reduces anticipatory anxiety. In the next four months, fun was back in their sexual relationship. Ian's sexual enthusiasm increased Carolyn's sexual desire. However, this came to a crashing halt when

Viagra failed to produce an erection sufficient for intercourse. Ian lost all sexual confidence and returned to avoidance. Carolyn begged him to try again and offered to stimulate him to orgasm, but to no avail.

After four months of a total sexual shutdown, Carolyn insisted that they make an appointment with a couple sex therapist. Ian literally had to be dragged to the session. Couple sex therapy is more effective than a stand-alone erection medication (Althof & Rosen, 2007). Ian was relieved that the therapist was empathic and respectful rather than berate or shame him. The therapist was clear that regaining erectile comfort and confidence was a couple challenge. Carolyn had an important role in the change process. The most important thing the clinician said was that Viagra would not return Ian to the autonomous, totally predictable erections of the past. The therapist introduced the GES approach, giving them materials to read and discuss. This offered guidance and positive expectations, rather than hoping for a "magic pill" which guaranteed perfect erections.

The next step in the therapeutic process was to schedule individual sessions for a psychological/relational/sexual history. Carolyn had a chance to voice her confusion, anxiety, and anger about what had happened relationally and sexually. The clinician was supportive and empathic, normalizing Carolyn's feelings as well as making clear her role in the change process. Carolyn valuing desire/pleasure/eroticism/satisfaction was a crucial factor in the success of sex therapy. She had an opportunity to ask questions and clarify feelings about sensual, playful, and erotic scenarios. The guideline that 85% of encounters would flow to intercourse was realistic. When sex did not flow, Ian and Carolyn could transition to an erotic or sensual scenario so that the experience ended in a positive manner. The therapist encouraged Carolyn to value mutual erotic scenarios in addition to pleasuring Ian to orgasm. Carolyn was hopeful that this would be a satisfying chapter in their sexual life.

Ian's individual session allowed him to develop a narrative about psychological and sexual strengths and vulnerabilities. The challenge was to give up the traditional male model of perfect erection and intercourse and embrace the "wise man" role which facilitates sexuality and erections. Ian liked the concept of "beating the odds" and valuing variable, flexible, pleasure-oriented GES. The therapist advised Ian to ask his internist for a prescription for Cialis rather than Viagra. Cialis was easier to integrate into their couple style of intimacy, pleasure, and eroticism, especially the daily low dose regimen. Cialis allows freedom of when to initiate sex (30 hours rather than 4). Ian was warned against expecting 100% predictable erections and strongly encouraged to accept GES as first-class male sexuality. Turning toward Carolyn as his intimate ally was integral to successful therapy. A major new learning was for Ian to "piggy-back" his arousal on hers.

In subsequent therapy sessions, these themes were discussed, modified, and implemented. Change is seldom easy or problem-free; it's a matter of "2 steps forward, 1 step back". GES was easier for Carolyn to accept. Ian wanted a return to predictable erections and intercourse. Carolyn's desire was enhanced by the variety and unpredictability of sexual scenarios. Choice, freedom, and unpredictability enhance sexual desire.

Ian made it clear to Carolyn that he preferred to transition to intercourse and orgasm on his first erection. The therapist affirmed this and added two suggestions. First, do not transition to intercourse until you are into an erotic flow and utilize multiple stimulation during intercourse. Second, practice transitioning to erotic and sensual scenarios so that you don't panic if sex did not flow to intercourse. Ian was positive about the first suggestion, but ambivalent about the second. Carolyn's enthusiasm about sensual and erotic scenarios won Ian over. Reading and talking about alternative scenarios are important, but the real learning occurs with practicing these scenarios. Ian enjoyed their new sexual style. Variable, flexible GES was good for Ian, Carolyn, and their bond.

Woman's Sexual Self-Acceptance

Traditionally, the woman felt that she had to catch up with your spontaneous erection and readiness for intercourse. New scientific findings and clinical insights establish that female sexual desire and orgasm are first-class (McCarthy & McCarthy, 2019a). Female sexual response is more complex, variable, flexible, and individualistic than male sexual response – different, not better or worse. Embracing desire/pleasure/eroticism/satisfaction is empowering. A prime guideline is to own your unique sexual voice.

GES recognizes that female desire and orgasm is healthy. Female sexual socialization and lived experiences reinforce the value of variable, flexible, pleasure-oriented GES. The male individual perfect performance model is in contrast to GES. Accept the core concept – couple sexuality is a variable, flexible, pleasure-oriented experience of sharing intimacy and eroticism. Orgasm is not a pass-fail test for her (and erection is not a pass-fail test for you). Intercourse is valued as the natural continuation of the pleasuring/eroticism process, not a pass-fail test. Desire and satisfaction are more important than arousal and orgasm. Self-acceptance of your body and touching is more important than performance. GES empowers you to embrace healthy sexuality rather than feel intimidated by performance demands.

The psychological challenge is to accept variable, flexible sexuality as healthy. Biologically, accept your body and adopt healthy behavioral habits of sleep, exercise, eating, moderate or no drinking, and no smoking. Relationally, turn toward your partner as your intimate sexual friend. You don't need to prove anything to him or yourself. Accept GES as first-class.

Male Sexual Self-Acceptance

Traditionally, your sexual self-acceptance was contingent on perfect performance. You were afraid of failing your partner and even more afraid of male peers knowing about your sexual anxieties and vulnerabilities. That's a hard way to live. If your penis could speak, it would say, "Treat me better, I am always one failure from feeling humiliated".

GES builds a new foundation for sexual awareness and self-acceptance. You and your penis are human, not a performance machine. GES emphasizes your right to sexual pleasure and approaching your partner as your intimate and erotic friend rather than someone to perform for. GES allows you to be self-accepting rather than afraid or shameful. You will not receive support for GES from male friends; you need it from your intimate partner. Her acceptance reinforces your acceptance.

Why is GES so hard for men to accept? The male performance model is powerful and oppressive. Adolescents, young adults, and adult men over learn the message that a "real man is willing and able to have sex anytime and anywhere". Is this really human? You are afraid to challenge this model because you fear being labeled a "loser", "wimp", or "not man enough". GES is viewed as "settling" because you can't "perform like a real man".

This irrational thinking and peer pressure subverts sexual self-esteem. She can't do it for you, but can urge you to embrace GES and increase self-acceptance. Be a healthy man in a healthy relationship. The challenge is to take the risk – show her you value variable, flexibility couple sexuality. Don't be a traditional man who falls into the trap of anticipatory anxiety, rushes to intercourse, experiences frustration, embarrassment, and sexual avoidance. A wise man anticipates intimacy, pleasure, and eroticism; enjoys giving and receiving sensual and playful touch; is open to erotic scenarios and techniques; transitions to intercourse at high levels of erotic flow; enjoys giving and receiving multiple stimulation before and during intercourse; lets erotic sensations naturally culminate in orgasm; and enjoys the afterplay experience. It is an involving, multi-dimensional sexual scenario, different than sex in your 20s. This is all to the good. When there is not an erotic flow rather than trying to force intercourse, seamlessly transition to a mutual erotic scenario, pleasure her to orgasm with your mouth or hand, or ask her to pleasure you to orgasm. Another option is saying that this won't be a sexual night – you can enjoy a sensual, cuddly scenario. Be sexual in the next few days when you feel comfortable and receptive. Women welcome and enjoy erotic and sensual scenarios as long as you are involved. GES is empowering for the man, woman, and couple.

Use of Pro-Erection Medications, Penile Injections, and Testosterone

Wise men are open to psychological, bio-medical, and relational resources to promote sexuality. Pro-erection medications, penile injections, and testosterone are compatible with GES. The reason medical interventions are not as successful as advertised is that no one (doctor or counselor) sits with the couple (or you alone) and discusses how to integrate the medical intervention into your couple sexual style. A major flaw in the medication/marketing approach overpromises easy, predictable erections. The GES 85% guideline for intercourse is applicable to men using Viagra or Cialis. Few men return to totally predictable erections and intercourse.

What are guidelines for using medical resources to improve sexual confidence and function? The ideal guideline is you meet as a couple with the internist, urologist, nurse practitioner, endocrinologist, psychiatrist, or sexual medicine specialist. The first doctor to consult is your primary care physician who will assess factors such as high blood pressure, cardiac problems, diabetes, depression, a pituitary tumor, alcohol or drug abuse among other bio-medical problems to consider.

In exploring pro-erection medications, many couples prefer Cialis to Viagra because it provides greater freedom of when to initiate sex. The crucial factor is feeling desire and subjective arousal before the vascular effects of the medication kick in.

A crucial psychosexual skill is not to rush to intercourse, driven by fears of losing your erection. Intercourse driven by fear increases the likelihood of ED. A positive strategy is to begin intercourse when you (as well as she) are into an erotic flow. Another technique is for the woman to guide intromission. Rather than being distracted by performance concerns, enjoy giving and receiving erotic stimulation. Multiple stimulation during intercourse facilitates the erotic experience for both partners.

The more intrusive the medical intervention, the more likely it will produce an erection. An example is penile injections. The reason injections have been disappointing, with a high dropout rate, is that the sex feels mechanical. You have difficulty ejaculating because you are not subjectively aroused. Your partner does not enjoy intercourse because she does not feel aroused. The sexual experience is not satisfying for either partner. If you use penile injections, do so in a manner which enhances involvement and subjective arousal. Schedule a couple consultation with the urologist or internist. Both partners learn to do injections in a safe and comfortable manner. Many couples prefer the woman administer the injection. The medical intervention can't be expected to provide everything sexually. A crucial psychosexual skill is to engage in pleasuring/eroticism to enhance your (and her) subjective arousal rather than assume that you are subjectively aroused because you have an erection. Remember the guideline – integrate the medical intervention into your couple sexual style. This is a couple challenge – the injection can't do it all.

Hormone enhancement is popular for both men and women. Although testosterone is sold at drug stores and on the internet, we recommend seeing a physician and obtaining a prescription. Consult a competent endocrinologist with a sub-specialty in hormonal and sexual function. The trend to overuse testosterone is one of the worst in our culture. Testosterone is usually pre-scribed in the gel form, but can be administered through patch or injection. Seldom is oral testosterone advised. From the psychobiosocial perspective, tes-tosterone is a resource to enhance desire for those with severe testosterone deficit. In those cases, testosterone is a necessary, but not sufficient, resource. Psychological and relational factors are addressed to promote sexual receptivity and responsivity. With the impetus of testosterone, you find it easier to reestab-lish anticipation and feel receptive to sexual pleasure.

Exercise – Accepting and Implementing the GES Approach

This couple exercise asks you to read, discuss, and, most importantly, implement the GES approach. Very few couples begin their sexual rela-tionship with GES. Commonly, you begin as a romantic love/passionate sex/idealized (limerence) couple. This provides special memories. How-ever, by its nature, limerence fades after 6–24 months. Replace it with a couple sexual style which promotes strong, resilient sexual desire. Ide-ally, you adopt the GES approach in your 30s. However, most couples do not until there are sexual problems, especially ED. Prevention is always superior, but the majority of men do not adopt GES until they experience a problem. The good news is it's never too late. Adopting GES is a wise choice for the man, woman, and couple.

Knowledge is power. Read about GES. Even more important is a couple dialogue about the role and meaning of GES. The best time to talk about sexual issues generally, and GES specifically, is the day before being sexual. Talk over a glass of wine or cup of tea, at the kitchen table or on the porch (clothed and sitting up). The worst time to talk sex is in bed, nude, lying down, after a negative experience. Agitation or anger causes people to say and do things which are hurtful and destructive. Sexual communication involves sharing information/attitudes, requesting sexual scenarios, and, most importantly, disclosing sexual feelings and values. Don't be politi-cally correct or give the socially desirable response. Share psychological, relational, and sexual desires as well as vulnerabilities. What is inviting about GES? What are your fears and concerns about GES? The suggested format to implement GES involves practicing three sexual scenarios:

1   Transition to a mutual or asynchronous erotic scenario
2   Transition to a sensual, cuddly scenario
3   Practice an intimate, interactive sexual scenario which promotes inter-course as a natural continuation of the pleasuring/eroticism process.

Transition to intercourse at high levels of erotic flow and enjoy multiple stimulation during intercourse.

Most couples (especially men) prefer the third scenario. This is fine as long as it is not a performance mandate.

Practice each scenario at least twice, and preferably three or more times. Ideally, develop comfort and confidence with all three scenarios. Having a variable, flexible sexual repertoire is a great relational resource, especially with aging.

It is common for one or both partners to reject a scenario or part of a scenario. An example is choosing to "take a rain check" rather than engage in a sensual scenario. Another example is a woman who prefers pleasuring her partner to orgasm than a mutual erotic scenario. Be honest with yourself and your partner about preferences and feelings as well as what does not fit. You can repeat this exercise in the future – reading, talking, and implementing.

Guidelines for Asynchronous Sexual Scenarios

Couples have a strong preference for mutual, synchronous sex involving intercourse and orgasm. In addition, be open to asynchronous scenarios (both intercourse and erotic experiences). Accepting asynchronous sexuality is crucial for GES.

A core guideline is that the asynchronous scenario cannot be at the expense of the partner or relationship. Said positively, the partner finds the scenario a 2, 5, or 8 on the pleasure scale. At a minimum, the asynchronous scenario is neutral. If it's negative, resentment will grow, and desire will be inhibited.

A common example is that you value intercourse, while she finds it pleasant – whether a 4 or 7. For couples over 60, female arousal and orgasm is often easier than for you. She enjoys being pleasured to orgasm – the experience is a 7 or 3 for you. A different example is that you find rear entry intercourse highly erotic, where she finds it a 1 or 3.

If you experience conflict regarding asynchronous sexuality, we suggest seeking couple sex therapy (Appendix A has guidelines for choosing a competent therapist). Sexual power struggles are destructive. Rather than share pleasure, the issue is not feeling like the loser. Asynchronous scenarios enhance your couple repertoire and are compatible with GES. However, some couples decide not to engage in asynchronous sex.

Summary

GES validates the reality of your relationship. Flexible couple sexuality recognizes that the essence of a sexual encounter is giving and receiving pleasure-oriented touching. GES acknowledges the multiple roles, meanings, and outcomes of sexuality for the man, woman, and couple. Intercourse and orgasm is highly valued, but not as an individual performance demand. Sexuality is much more than intercourse. Satisfaction is more than orgasm. Touching (affection, sensual, playful) is valued both inside and outside the bedroom. Not all touch leads to intercourse.

Her acceptance and enthusiasm for GES is affirming for you. Acceptance of GES promotes sexuality in your 60s, 70s, and 80s. GES helps rid you of the oppressive pass-fail performance demands of erection, intercourse, and orgasm. GES is valuable for both partners, and thrives as an intimate team experience.

13

MALE SEXUALITY IN THE 60s, 70s, AND 80s

Being a Wise Man

The good news is that there is solid scientific evidence that men (and women) can enjoy sexuality in their 60s, 70s, and 80s (Lindau et al., 2007). The bad news is that one in three couples stop being sexual by age 65 and two in three by age 75. In the great majority of cases, the choice is the man's, made unilaterally and conveyed non-verbally. It isn't that he wants to stop sex, but he has lost confidence with erections and intercourse. He feels frustrated and embarrassed, saying to himself "I don't want to start something I can't finish". This is a destructive choice for the man, woman, and couple.

One of your best emotional investments is reinforcing a broad-based, pleasure-oriented sexual relationship. With aging, you need each other in a manner you hadn't when younger. Sexuality is more human, genuine, and satisfying.

Rather than the "show-up" erections of youth, you need her touch and stimulation to develop "grown-up" erections. The essence of couple sexuality is giving and receiving pleasure-oriented touch. Sexuality is a couple process of sharing pleasure rather than an individual pass-fail performance test of erection and intercourse.

It surprises most people, including physicians, to learn that it is men who choose to stop sex. It is the opposite of the traditional gender belief about men having a stronger sex drive. It is another example how the double standard misleads men, women, couples, and the culture. Two mistaken beliefs lead to ceasing sex. First, the emphasis on erection as a measure of desire. Second, that intercourse is the only real sex. Adolescent and young adult sexual socialization "poisons" sexuality with aging. Sexuality in your 60s, 70s, and 80s is promoted by a focus on pleasure and being intimate and erotic friends. The Good Enough Sex (GES) model emphasizes sexuality as a couple issue with a variety of roles, meanings, and outcomes. GES facilitates acceptance of the variability and flexibility of sexuality after 60.

Confronting Myths about Sex and Aging

In dealing with sex and aging, you are confronting two stigmatized topics – aging and sexuality. Some cultures honor aging – sadly, the United States is not one of those. Traditionally, people over 60 were viewed as "over the hill". Their emotional and sexual needs were treated with benign neglect. They were thought to be living in the past rather than having a vibrant life. The belief was that sex belongs to the young and beautiful with a focus on exploration, breaking boundaries, illicitness, and drama. The fear is that sex disrupts people's lives and relationships rather than be a source of bonding and security. When Barry asks college students "How many of you believe people of your grandparents age are sexual", it is 1 in 13. That is a terrible cultural message.

A prominent myth is that the key to sexual desire is visual stimuli. This negates aging bodies. In truth, the key to sexual desire is touch, not visual cues. Enjoy giving and receiving pleasure-oriented touch throughout your aging.

Another prominent myth is that illness and disability, which becomes more common with aging, destroys desire and the ability to be sexual. Sexual function does change, but sexual desire continues no matter what the illness or disability. The challenge is to accept the "new normal", valuing sexual pleasure rather than sex performance.

Another myth involves menopause – that after menopause women lose their ability to enjoy sex. In reality, a fascinating role reversal with aging is that female arousal and orgasm is easier than for the male. An important learning is to "piggy-back" your arousal on hers. Another gender challenge is accepting GES – variable and flexible sexual response is easier for women to accept. Women can and do enjoy sexuality after menopause.

Anther myth is that "natural" male sexual response of predictable erection and intercourse without needing anything from the partner is superior. We are proponents of erection and intercourse, but not as an individual pass-fail performance. With aging, you need partner genital stimulation and to accept that erections are not totally reliable. This is normal male sexuality with aging, not a sign of ED. The experience of variable, flexible response is healthy for the man, woman, and couple.

A core myth is that "spontaneous sexual desire" is better than "responsive sexual desire". You can begin a sexual encounter at 0 (neutral). As you give and receive affectionate, sensual, and playful touch, your responsivity increases (2–4) which results in sexual desire. An involved, receptive partner is your major source of desire. You need each other to enjoy sexuality with aging.

There are many more myths regarding sexuality and aging. The good news is that there are clinically relevant, scientific guidelines about the value of broad-based male and couple sexuality with aging.

The Good Things about Sexuality Come to Fruition with Aging

Healthy sexuality comes into focus in your 60s, 70s, and 80s. Sexuality is more human and genuine. Sexual satisfaction increases, partly because you know you have beaten the odds. You enjoy sensual, playful, erotic, and intercourse touch. You need each other sexually in a way you didn't 20 years ago. Be intimate and erotic friends who turn toward each other whether the sexual encounter was wonderful or disappointing. Adopting GES and accepting the multiple roles, meanings, and outcomes of sexuality is freeing. Aging couples accept asynchronous sexual experiences. Mutual, synchronous sex is highly valued, but variety in sexual encounters is the norm. Most couples prefer partner interaction arousal, although with aging there is an increased use of self-enhancement arousal. A key to sexuality and aging is acceptance of a range of sexual experiences and the recognition of female-male sexual equity. You are freed from the constraints of rigid roles and gender restrictions. Enjoy the sexual experience for what it is. With a decrease in parenting responsibilities, you have greater freedom when to be sexual. Rather than late night sex, you can have sex in the morning, before or after a nap, before dinner (sex as an appetizer), or after dinner (sex as dessert). You need not be constrained by sex in the bedroom. With greater privacy enjoy sexuality in your living room, den, guest room, or on the secluded porch late at night. Be open to responsive sexual desire and touch rather than longing for spontaneous, dramatic, swept away sex. Sexuality belongs to you and is integrated into the reality of your lives. Freedom from myths and stereotypes allows you to enjoy self and partner acceptance.

Defining Sexuality as More than Intercourse

Whether age 25 or 75, most couples define sex as intercourse. Intercourse is highly valued, but recognize that sexuality is much more than intercourse. An empowering concept is that sexuality entails five dimensions (gears) of touching – affection, sensual, playful, erotic, and intercourse. This is crucial for sexuality and aging. Rather than counting number of intercourse encounters, accept that sensual, playful, and erotic experiences are integral to couple sexuality. Sensual and erotic scenarios have been a back-up if the experience did not flow to intercourse. Value sensual, playful, or erotic scenarios for themselves, not just if intercourse fails. This is a challenge for both men and women, although more easily accepted by women. Traditional men cling to "sex = intercourse". "Wise" men embrace awareness that sexuality is more than intercourse. The GES concept is that 85% of sexual encounters flow from comfort to pleasure to arousal to erotic flow to intercourse and orgasm. No matter what the reason that sexuality does not flow to intercourse, the optimal response is to enjoy sensual, playful, or erotic scenarios.

There is no need to apologize or panic (this is anti-erotic). Variable sexuality adds to your couple repertoire. Couples who embrace broad-based, flexible sexuality enjoy sex into your 60s, 70s, and 80s.

Be aware of psychological, medical, relational, and psychosexual skill factors which facilitate intercourse. Psychologically, the key is to view intercourse as a natural continuation of the pleasuring/eroticism process, not a pass-fail test. Medically, if you use resources such as a pro-erection medication, penile injections, medications to promote desire, or vaginal lubricants, you need to integrate this into your couple sexual style rather than expect it to be a stand-alone intervention (Althof, 2006). Relationally, you are sexual allies who share pleasure and eroticism which flow to intercourse. Psychosexually, the most important skill is not to transition to intercourse as soon as you can, but transition at high levels of erotic flow. A major cause of failed intercourse is rushing to intromission because you fear losing your erection. Negative motivation interferes with sexual pleasure and arousal. One strategy is that the woman decides when to transition to intercourse and guides intromission. This allows you to give and receive multiple stimulation before and during intercourse rather than be distracted by performance anxiety. This includes giving manual clitoral stimulation, oral breast stimulation, and buttock or anal stimulation, and receiving testicle stimulation, buttock stimulation, and kissing. The most common form of multiple stimulation is private erotic fantasies which serve as a bridge to erotic flow and orgasm.

In younger days, intercourse involved just thrusting. An advantage of sexuality and aging is increased involvement and simulation. Almost 15% of older men struggle with ejaculatory inhibition (delayed ejaculation). Thrusting is not enough stimulation to facilitate erotic flow. Women are also more likely to benefit from multiple stimulation before and during intercourse. A significant number of women find it easier to reach orgasm with manual, oral, or rubbing stimulation than during intercourse.

Perhaps the most valuable strategy for both men and women is not to transition to intercourse until you are into an erotic flow (subjective arousal is an 8 or at least a 7). The major cause of failure with pro-erection medications is rushing to intercourse as soon as you get an erection (subjective arousal 4 or 5). Rushing disrupts the sexual experience. The strategy is to experience intercourse as a natural extension of the pleasuring/eroticism process and engage in multiple stimulation during intercourse. This reinforces intercourse as a pleasurable, erotic, and satisfying experience.

Being Sexual When Intercourse Is Not Possible

Intercourse (insertive sex) has been an integral part of your sexual experience. If insertive sex is not possible due to ED or female sexual pain, does that end couple sex? Absolutely not. Although intercourse is highly valued, it is not the essence of couple sexuality. Manual, oral, rubbing, and vibrator stimulation are ways to share pleasure and eroticism. Although you mourn the absence of intercourse, it opens opportunities to share sensual, playful, and especially erotic sexuality. For many couples, arousal and orgasm is easier with erotic sexuality. This is especially true for women, but men find erotic sexually to orgasm satisfying. Couples feel emotionally connected with sensual scenarios. Others find that playful scenarios are a great addition to your sexual life and wish you had added this in your 30s instead of waiting until your 70s.

Ideally, couples value broad-based, flexible sexuality in addition to intercourse. It is the reality of stopping intercourse that challenges you to value sensual, playful, and erotic sexuality.

The Value and Traps of Asynchronous Couple Sexuality

An empowering insight is that asynchronous sexuality – whether involving intercourse or erotic scenarios – is normal and healthy. The sexual experience being better for one partner than the other is the norm. If all sex had to be mutual and synchronous, you would have a low sex relationship or give up sex altogether.

Accepting asynchronous sexuality is easier for the woman. Intercourse typically was better for the man. With aging, you spend more time and focus on sensual, playful, and erotic stimulation. Broad-based flexible sexual expression is healthy for men and women.

Are there potential traps with asynchronous scenarios? The core guideline is that asynchronous sexuality is healthy as long as it is not at the expense of the partner or relationship. On a ten-point scale of subjective arousal, one partner experiences a 10, while the other's experience might be a 6, 4, or even 1. This is acceptable. It is not acceptable if the partner experiences a -2 or -7. Another trap is pressure that the person must perform a specific scenario or technique to prove love or sexual openness. Sexual demands are harmful to your intimate relationship.

A common trap with asynchronous sexuality is that the partner settles for routine or mediocre sex. "Going along for the ride" becomes the norm. When this occurs, the partner gives up her "sexual voice" and no longer enjoys desire/ pleasure/eroticism/satisfaction. Asynchronous sexuality reinforces the positive functions of sex. Each partner's sexual pleasure and responsivity is acknowledged. Sexuality is a shared pleasure, with you accepting different levels of pleasure.

Exercise – Enhancing Sex and Aging

An important adage is that you can learn from the past, but cannot change the past. In this exercise, as in your lives, the power for change is in the present and future. What are your attitudes regarding sexuality and aging? Do you affirm the value of desire/pleasure/eroticism/satisfaction? What do you value about affectionate, sensual, playful, erotic, and intercourse touch? Is your partner your intimate and erotic friend?

The most important question is whether you are motivated to remain sexual as you age. Hopefully, your answer is yes. List at least two and up to five specific advantages of sexuality and aging. What are you willing to explore to keep sexuality vital and satisfying?

Do you accept the variable, flexible GES model of sexuality? For many people, sex is dichotomous, if it doesn't involve intercourse, it's a bad experience. That is not healthy, especially not for couples over 60. Embracing the multiple roles, meanings, and outcomes of sexuality is the wise decision. You need more than socially desirable words. Attitudinally, behaviorally, and emotionally, do you turn toward your partner whether the sexual encounter was wonderful, good, okay, or dysfunctional? Can you celebrate mutual, synchronous sex as well as enjoy asynchronous sexuality?

Have an honest dialogue about incorporating GES. Even more importantly, consciously practice GES. Create two playful scenarios and implement them. Are they a good fit for you? Then do this with two sensual and two erotic scenarios. Find ways of sharing sexuality which is pleasure-oriented and satisfying.

Now, the hardest challenge. When touching does not lead to arousal for one or both partners and/or you are unable to have intercourse, how do you feel and what can you do? These experiences become more common with aging. The issue is whether you and your partner can accept that it is normal to not have intercourse. Do not panic or apologize. There is nothing more anti-erotic than apologizing for yourself. It has no value for you or your relationship.

When arousal, erection, and intercourse do not flow which strategy are you comfortable with: (1) transition to a mutual or one-way erotic scenario, (2) transition to a sensual scenario, or (3) take a "rain check" and try again in a couple of days when you are open and receptive? Ideally, you would be comfortable with all three scenarios. What is not acceptable is avoidance. Avoidance reinforces sexual anxiety. You lose your sexual voice. Reading and talking has great value, but the key to change is trying out the three scenarios to see whether it fits for you.

Typically, 5–15% of sexual encounters are dissatisfying or dysfunctional. With age, these percentages are likely to increase, especially regarding intercourse. Contrary to the advice "just do it", which is likely to cause problems because it treats intercourse as a pass-fail performance, you need a pleasure-oriented engagement strategy. Find pleasurable and erotic ways to be with each other.

When sex is a performance, you are always one experience away from feeling like a failure. Sexuality is about sharing pleasure with multiple ways to enjoy your partner. Expand your sexual repertoire so you celebrate intimacy, pleasuring, and eroticism.

The last component of this exercise involves use of your veto power. An advantage of aging is you feel free to say "no" to sex (this is true for men and women). Unless you have the power to say no, you don't have the freedom to embrace sexuality. To promote this concept, each partner vetoes one, two, or three sexual scenarios you no longer (or never) found appealing. The veto can involve a single technique (rubbing your penis between her buttocks, use of a body lotion, having sex while standing) or a major change in sexual scenarios (no longer having anal or oral sex, stopping erotic talk in the bedroom, no longer using man on top intercourse). Your veto is honored (not debated – you do not feel pressured to give in). In addition, you commit to stay connected, so intimacy, pleasuring, and eroticism are reinforced. When you avoid touching, sexual anxiety increases and sexual desire is lowered.

Maintaining Positive Motivation

The reason we advocate for the psychobiosocial model of assessment and treatment is the focus on motivation and desire. More than physical health, medical interventions, love, or erotic scenarios, the key to sexuality with aging is desire and motivation. "Beat the odds" – enjoy giving and receiving pleasure. Positive motivations include reinforce intimacy, touch as a refuge, a message of personal worth, challenge stereotypes, validate physical attachment, deal with illness or disability, a positive model for adult children and grandchildren, share erotic vitality, enjoy cuddling, grow and experiment, and fully live your life. In addition to psychological and relational benefits, there are medical and physical health benefits for sexuality with aging. Touching and sexuality are good for your physical body. Sexual activity is a plus for your heart, lungs, and limbs. It keeps you invested in quality of life – emotionally, physically, and relationally.

The Negative Consequences of Stopping Sex

Stopping sex is one of your worst life choices. You not only give up arousal, intercourse, and orgasm, but you give up desire, pleasure, playful touch, and intimacy.

The most common reason to stop sex is ED – you feel sexually frustrated and embarrassed. Barry says to clients, "You can be a traditional man who demands problem-free intercourse and eventually give-up sex because you no longer feel in control or you can be a wise man who embraces Good Enough Sex (GES) and enjoys sexuality in your 60s, 70s, and 80s". For quality of life, staying sexual is a better investment than putting $200,000 in your retirement fund. The insistence on traditional penis-vagina intercourse drives the choice to give up sex. Stubbornly clinging to a narrow definition of sex is very costly in terms of emotional and relational consequences. One client lamented, "More than anything, I miss the intimacy of afterplay". You sacrifice pleasure for performance. A great loss for the man, woman, and couple.

Evan and Ophelia

Seventy-six-year-old Evan is in a 24-year second marriage to 77-year-old Ophelia. Ophelia was divorced and Evan had been a widower for three years when they met. They take pride in creating a satisfying, secure, and sexual marriage. Their adult children had not been in favor of the marriage, but Ophelia and Evan celebrated beating the odds and persevering. Their grandchildren are very fond of them as a couple.

Evan suspects that the majority of male friends and relatives have stopped being sexual. Sex and aging was a taboo topic in his peer group. He didn't brag to anyone, but was proud that he and Ophelia had a genuine sexual relationship. Evan was grateful that Ophelia was his "cheerleader" in embracing GES. They had fond memories of sex in their 50s – there was plenty of pleasuring, eroticism, and intercourse. Sexuality energized their bond as well as served as a "port in the storm" when dealing with conflicts, especially extended family problems. Ophelia appreciated Evan being an involved, giving lover. Although she enjoyed intercourse, arousal and orgasm was easier with manual stimulation. She would usually orgasm before intercourse and sometimes during intercourse (which Evan particularly valued).

Ophelia embraced her sexual voice and did not compare her sexual response to anyone else. She appreciated that he accepted the variability and complexity of her sexuality and did not pressure her to respond the way he did. Ophelia had a variable sexual response pattern. Sometimes, she would be multi-orgasmic, sometimes non-orgasmic, and other times have one orgasm. She enjoyed being the giving partner in asynchronous scenarios – especially mixing manual and oral simulation as she pleasured Evan to orgasm. Ophelia understood that Evan preferred intercourse. She enjoyed intercourse, although orgasm during intercourse was not a valued scenario for her.

Evan was aware that Ophelia's approach to desire/pleasure/eroticism/satisfaction was a better fit for them in their 70s than the traditional intercourse scenario. However, he felt particularly satisfied when both were orgasmic during intercourse.

In their 70s, each was dealing with health and medical concerns. The biggest issue for Ophelia was arthritis. She uses hearing aids (she takes them off when being sexual). Evan took medications for blood pressure, cholesterol, and gout. His biggest concern was adult onset diabetes and keeping his blood sugar in control. The illnesses and medications had a negative impact on erectile function. Evan took a daily low dose Cialis which was helpful, but erections were slower, less firm, and less predictable. The most important psychosexual skills were using multiple stimulation before intercourse, enjoying private erotic fantasies, piggy-backing his arousal on Ophelia's, and she guiding intromission. He didn't need a firm erection for intercourse. They continued multiple stimulation during intercourse.

At this point, about 50% of sexual encounters flowed to intercourse. If sexuality did not flow, it was counter-productive to try forcing intercourse. Their strategy was to seamlessly transition to a sensual or erotic scenario. Typically, Evan opted for a mutual sensual scenario which he found calming and pleasurable. Typically, Ophelia opted for a mutual erotic scenario, but enjoyed an asynchronous erotic scenario whether she was the receiving or giving partner. Unless Evan felt really turned on, he preferred being the giving partner and enjoyed her erotic responsiveness. This was a new scenario for them (adopted in the last four years). Evan was pleased that asynchronous scenarios added to vital sexuality. Ophelia feeling sexually satisfied was satisfying for Evan.

They were pleased that the number of dissatisfying sexual experiences was low, about once a month. If Evan apologized, Ophelia would tickle him until he stopped apologizing. Ophelia was accepting of the range of sexual experiences and outcomes – she embraced GES.

Ophelia and Evan hoped to enjoy sexuality into their 80s, including after 85. The key was to reinforce his, hers, and our bridges to sexual desire and accept sexual experiences with a range of roles, meanings, and outcomes. Ophelia particularly valued playful and erotic sexuality which could be synchronous or asynchronous. Evan enjoyed a range of sensual and sexual encounters.

Summary

Sexuality and aging is genuine and human. All the good things about couple sexuality come to fruition with aging, especially sharing pleasure. Embrace GES rather than view intercourse and orgasm as an individual pass-fail performance.

When the man gives up intercourse, the couple usually stop sensual, playful, and erotic sexuality. The variable, flexible approach to sexuality and aging affirms erection, intercourse, and orgasm as well as emphasizes a range of sexual scenarios. Enjoy pleasuring and eroticism with or without intercourse. The essence of couple sexuality is giving and receiving pleasure-oriented touching. GES recognizes the multiple roles, meanings, and outcomes of male, female, and couple sexuality.

14

DEALING WITH SEXUAL PROBLEMS

PE, ED, HSDD, and Ejaculatory Inhibition

Male sex dysfunction is more common than either men or women recognize. Ideally, sex dysfunction is dealt with as a couple issue. The woman did not cause the problem, but as your sexual ally she has an integral role in helping you regain sexual comfort, function, and confidence. Typically, men are embarrassed about sex dysfunction, minimizing or denying the problem. The most destructive reaction is to blame the woman for your sex dysfunction. Be honest with yourself and take responsibility for resolving the problem. Turn toward your partner as your sexual friend.

You hope that a pill (or other medical intervention) will guarantee perfect performance. You are disappointed and frustrated that a stand-alone medical intervention won't resolve sex dysfunction. Like most in our culture, you have been misled by the ads and overpromises of the drug industry. You need to use all your psychological, medical, behavioral, and relational resources to facilitate sexual change. This includes confronting the myth of perfect sex performance. Replace this with positive, realistic expectations based on a new model of male sexuality and adopt the Good Enough Sex (GES) model (Metz & McCarthy, 2012) with positive, realistic sexual expectations.

The Four Most Common Male Sex Dysfunctions

There are four common male sex dysfunctions. These affect approximately 40% of men. By order of frequency, they are:

1   Premature Ejaculation (PE)
2   Erectile Dysfunction (ED)
3   Hypoactive Sexual Desire Disorder (HSSD)
4   Ejaculatory Inhibition (Delayed Ejaculation)

Sex dysfunction is categorized as primary (life-long) or secondary (acquired). With the exception of PE, most male sex dysfunction is secondary. Over the course of your life, the majority of men experience sexual dysfunction which lasts a month or longer. Sex problems need not be stigmatized or a shameful secret. Approximately 40% of men experience chronic sexual dysfunction which is lower than for women, but a significant number.

The most important message is that your sexuality need not be defined by the sex dysfunction. You and your sexual relationship are much more than the sex problem. Sexual self-esteem is not contingent on perfect performance.

Most sex dysfunction is resolvable or at least modifiable. The key is motivation and persistence. Do you turn toward your partner as your sexual friend in addressing the problem and building a new couple sexual style? You can change the sexual problem and enhance desire/pleasure/eroticism/satisfaction. Create a couple sexuality that is special, not just functional. A key is that your partner is your intimate and erotic ally. Her sexuality is as important as yours. You win or lose as a sexual team.

The sex problem robs both partners of sexual pleasure. The best time to address a sexual problem is when it's acute, but most male sex dysfunction is chronic. Embarrassment has caused you to minimize and avoid. A legacy of the old model of masculinity is unrealistic performance demands and avoidance of dealing with sex problems. The new model of male sexuality urges you to accept your sexual strengths and vulnerabilities. Accept responsibility for sexuality, but do not feel pressure to change on your own. You are not a "rock and an island". You are a sexual man who turns toward your partner. As an intimate team, you build sexual comfort, skill, and confidence.

Success is more likely if you consult a couple sex therapist (Appendix A provides resources for choosing a therapist). Therapy provides a structure and helps you deal with the inevitable frustrations inherent in the change process. Therapy helps you stay focused on building pleasure-oriented sexuality.

Premature Ejaculation

The most common male sex dysfunction is premature (rapid) ejaculation (PE). The majority of young men begin their sex lives as premature ejaculators. With practice and continuity, men learn ejaculatory control and enjoy intercourse. Twenty to thirty percent of men experience PE as a chronic problem. Most PE is primary, but can be secondary.

Contrary to braggadocio, claims on the internet, and bar talk, the average length of intercourse is three to nine minutes. Few couples engage in intercourse longer than 12 minutes no matter what you hear. There are many definitions of PE (intercourse lasting less than one minute, less than 20 strokes, ejaculation before female orgasm). These rigid criteria are not helpful. Ejaculation before the woman is orgasmic is particularly self-defeating since one in three women never or almost never experience orgasm during intercourse.

Learning ejaculatory control is not about performance; it is about sharing pleasure and enjoying intercourse. Our definition of PE is intercourse lasting less than two minutes where you are not in control of when you ejaculate. You learn ejaculatory control not to prove anything to yourself or your partner, not to reach a 12-minute performance goal, not to "give her an orgasm", but to increase enjoyment of intercourse and couple sexuality (Althof, 2020).

There are many causes of PE, including a hyperresponsive physiological system, side-effects of medications, a goal-oriented masturbation pattern, and anxiety (Metz & McCarthy, 2003). Sometimes, additional therapeutic or bio-medical resources are necessary, but in the majority of cases, a cognitive-behavioral ejaculatory control program is effective. There are two core psychosexual skills. First, identify the point of ejaculatory inevitability. There is an orgasmic difference between men and women. Women can stop mid-orgasm (for example, a child crying or coming in which interrupts lovemaking). However, once you pass the point of ejaculatory inevitability, orgasm is no longer under voluntary control. You could be totally turned off, but still ejaculate. Orgasm and ejaculation are different physiological processes, but most men experience them as the same. Learn to identify the point of ejaculatory inevitability. On a scale of arousal with 0 neutral, beginning arousal 5, erotic flow 8, and orgasm 10, be aware of sensations and feelings between 6 and 8. Don't "test the limits" and reach 9.5. When masturbating, most men find it relatively easy to identify the point of ejaculatory inevitability. This is the beginning of orgasm and in one to three seconds, you begin to ejaculate.

The second step is to practice ejaculatory control with either masturbation or partner manual stimulation. Focus on stimulation lasting three to nine minutes before letting go and enjoying orgasm. When you reach the 6–8 arousal level stop stimulation. Then resume stimulation. Enjoy sensations of moderate arousal without moving toward orgasm. Some men use the "squeeze" technique as a clear differentiation, but most prefer the "stop-start" technique. If you use the squeeze, you or your partner squeezes the top of your penis with two fingers and thumb and hold for three to five seconds until the urge to ejaculate dissipates. With "stop-start", you stop stimulation for 30–60 seconds.

Learning ejaculatory control is a gradual step-by-step process which is practiced over weeks. It is not a fun exercise. You increase awareness, understanding your body's sexual response, and build sexual comfort and confidence.

The next step is the most challenging – ejaculatory control during intercourse. This requires working as a sexual team. Most couples find that it takes three to six months to develop ejaculatory control during intercourse. Key changes involve intercourse positions and movements. It is difficult to gain ejaculatory control using the man-on-top position with fast, short thrusting. Use the woman-on-top, side-by-side, or woman sitting-man kneeling positions. Experiment with slower, longer thrusting or circular thrusting. Typically, the learning process is "2 steps forward, 1 step back" as you engage in new ways of sharing pleasure-oriented intercourse.

Your goal is not perfect ejaculatory control. It is to enjoy the entire sexual experience, including intercourse. The GES model emphasizes that 85% of the time you feel control of when you ejaculate and intercourse is an enjoyable experience. Occasionally, when you rapidly ejaculate, enjoy your orgasm; do not panic or apologize. Embrace the variability and flexibility of intercourse and couple sexuality.

Sex does not end when you ejaculate. Whether it was a highly enjoyable intercourse, a good intercourse, a so-so intercourse, or a PE intercourse, turn toward your partner. Afterplay is an integral component of couple sexuality. Afterplay is not just for the woman, it is for you and your bond. Afterplay has a crucial role in promoting sexual satisfaction. This is especially true when intercourse involves PE. You could offer to pleasure her to orgasm, be sexually playful, or cuddle and enjoy intimacy.

Some men use a medication to promote ejaculatory control (a low-dose anti-depressant taken daily or two to four hours before sex). Other couples focus on the woman being orgasmic before intercourse. Still others focus on afterplay. PE is a changeable problem, especially if you focus on intercourse as sharing pleasure rather than an individual performance.

Erectile Dysfunction (ED)

When the public thinks about male sex problems, the focus is on ED. The great majority of ED is secondary. The demand for spontaneous and totally predictable erection is self-defeating and sets you up for ED. Your penis is human, not a perfectly functioning machine.

Rather than approaching ED as a bio-medical problem and turning to a stand-alone medical intervention (Viagra or Cialis, penile injections, or testosterone enhancement), adopt the comprehensive psychobiosocial approach which involves using all your resources, especially your partner as your sexual friend, and practicing erection psychosexual skill exercises (Kalogeropoulos & Larouche, 2020).

ED can have a number of causes:

1   psychological – anticipatory and performance anxiety, unrealistic expectations, sexual secrets, history of sexual trauma, depression
2   bio-medical – side-effects of medications, illness (especially poorly controlled diabetes and cardiac problems), vascular or neurological disease, extremely low testosterone, alcohol or drug abuse, poor sleeping and eating patterns
3   social/relational – angry or alienated relationship, resentment toward partner, afraid to make sexual requests, intimidated by partner's sexuality, poor psychosexual skills, routine and boring sex.

ED is multi-causal and multi-dimensional. Treatment usually requires psychological, bio-medical, and relational changes. As in other types of sex dysfunction, our suggestion is to consult a couple sex therapist. In conjunction, schedule a medical assessment with your internist or a sexual medicine specialist. The sexual tipping point model (Perelman, 2009) describes the range of factors that can cause ED and the need to address them in a comprehensive manner. Learn to maintain erectile comfort and confidence.

The comprehensive GES model is of great value. It provides the man and couple with a scientifically validated approach to ED (Metz & McCarthy, 2004). Women are supportive of integrating GES in treating ED. Her enthusiasm for GES is crucial for the man who insists on a medical intervention to return you to totally predictable erection and intercourse. This is an unrealistic, self-defeating goal. It ensures that you will stay in the cycle of anticipatory anxiety, tense performance-oriented intercourse, frustration, embarrassment, and eventually sexual avoidance. Replace this with the cycle of positive sexual anticipation, pleasure-oriented touching, enhancing subjective and objective arousal, transitioning to intercourse at high levels of erotic flow (8 or at least 7), and multiple stimulation before and during intercourse. A positive, realistic expectation is that 85% of sexual encounters will transition to intercourse. When sexuality does not flow, transition to an erotic or sensual scenario without panicking or apologizing. You don't need an erection or intercourse in order to feel good about a sexual encounter. The core message is that sexuality is a couple experience of sharing pleasure, not an individual performance test. The second core message is that subjective arousal (feeling turned on) is as important as objective arousal (erection). Neither you nor your partner needs a firm erection to enjoy sexuality, including orgasm.

The most important psychosexual skill exercise is "waxing and waning of erection". Almost all men prefer to transition to intercourse on their first erection and reach orgasm during intercourse. This is fine as a preference, but poisonous as a performance demand. The wax and wane exercise directly confronts this performance myth. When you obtain an erection, stop stimulation – your erection will naturally wane. If you remain comfortable and receptive to sensual and playful touch, your erection will wax again. Stop stimulation and your erection will wane a second time. As long as you remain mindful of sensual and playful touch, your erection will return. Then proceed to intercourse and orgasm. Few men (or women) enjoy this exercise, but you learn a crucial lesson – erections wax and wane. You need not panic if you lose your erection. The major reason men fail with Viagra or Cialis is that as soon as you become erect (subjective arousal 4–5), you rush to intercourse because you fear losing your erection. Negative motivation subverts sexuality. Do not transition to intercourse until you are into an erotic flow. This is promoted by giving and receiving multiple stimulation before and during intercourse.

A key concept when you utilize a bio-medical intervention is to integrate it into your couple style of intimacy, pleasure, and eroticism as opposed to treating it as a "magic pill". The more invasive the medical intervention (for example, penile injections), the more effective in obtaining an erection. The challenge is to integrate the medical intervention into couple sexuality. Your partner being actively involved in the pleasuring/eroticism process is crucial.

The good news is that dealing with ED as a couple and adopting GES set the stage for sexuality in your 60s, 70s, and 80s. You didn't want to experience ED, but you can use ED to learn a new respect for your penis and pleasure-oriented sexuality.

Hypoactive Sexual Desire Disorder (HSDD)

Male sexual desire was explored in detail in Chapter 9. The great majority of HSDD is secondary, but primary HSDD occurs with 10% of men. Total lack of desire for anyone or anything is very rare, less than 1%. In this case, a man's sexual orientation is asexual. This is not changeable – it is who he is.

Both primary and secondary desire issues are changeable. This is good news. However, you are so embarrassed by HSDD that you do not disclose it to anyone, especially your partner. When couples stop being sexual, especially after age 50, it is almost always the man's choice – made unilaterally and conveyed non-verbally (Lindau et al., 2007).

In primary HSDD, the issue is a sexual secret that you are too embarrassed or ashamed to share with your partner. This can involve a variant arousal pattern (fetish, cross-dressing, or bondage and discipline), preference for masturbation because you experience anxiety and discomfort with couple sex, a history of sexual trauma which has not been processed, a sexual orientation issue, or sexual shame.

The most common cause of secondary HSDD is ED. There are a number of other causes, including side-effects of medications, anger, partner alienation, boredom with routine sex, de-eroticizing your partner and relationship, an affair, alcohol or drug abuse, illness, depression, and belief that older people should not be sexual. Desire problems need professional intervention, specifically couple sex therapy.

Identify and address factors which inhibit desire. Some are resolvable, most modifiable, and others need to be worked around. You cannot return to the romantic love/passionate sex/idealization (limerence) phase. You can develop a new couple sexual style which integrates intimacy and eroticism, the basis for strong, resilient sexual desire. A key is openness to "responsive sexual desire" rather than hoping for a return to easy desire driven by spontaneous erections. Enjoy giving and receiving sensual and playful touch which reinforces responsive sexual desire. Pleasurable and orgasmic sexuality promotes desire.

The core of desire is positive anticipation, sense of deserving pleasure, freedom and choice, and erotic scenarios which are inviting and unpredictable. Use all your resources to facilitate sexual desire, especially turning toward your partner as your intimate and erotic ally.

Ejaculatory Inhibition (Delayed Ejaculation)

This is the least known and discussed male sex dysfunction, but has a negative impact on male and couple sexuality. Primary ejaculatory inhibition is rare (less than 2%). This means that you have never ejaculated intravaginally. Most are orgasmic with masturbation as well as partner manual or oral stimulation, but not intercourse. Typically, male peers and female partners view you as a "stud" – you have a strong erection and last forever. Men with PE are envious. However, they are missing a crucial point – you are performing for the woman rather than enjoying sexuality. The reason you don't ejaculate is that your subjective arousal is low – you are not into an erotic flow. Intercourse is for the woman, masturbation for you. This is not healthy for you or your relationship, but can continue for years. The impetus to address ejaculatory inhibition is fertility issues – your wife cannot become pregnant because you do not ejaculate intravaginally. That's sad because ejaculatory inhibition is a changeable problem (Perelman, 2020).

Intermittent secondary ejaculatory inhibition is more common, effecting as many as 15% of men after age 50. If not addressed, it becomes chronic and severe. Like other sex dysfunctions, ejaculatory inhibition is multi-causal and multi-dimensional. Causes include side-effect of medications and alcohol abuse, but by far the most common cause is following the same sexual routine you used for 20–30 years. For sex to remain functional with aging, you need new inputs and energy. Routine sex – predictable foreplay and intercourse with man on top focused on thrusting – is boring rather than vital. There are three strategies to change ejaculatory inhibition:

1 Do not transition to intercourse until you are into erotic flow (subjective arousal of 8)
2 Utilize multiple stimulation before and during intercourse
3 Consciously employ "orgasm triggers".

These strategies enhance your sexual repertoire. Spend time and be creative with pleasuring and erotic techniques so you are subjectively aroused before beginning intercourse. Utilize multiple stimulation before and during intercourse. Give clitoral, buttock, and breast stimulation and receive testicle, buttock, and kissing stimulation. The most common type of multiple stimulation is private erotic fantasies. Identify orgasm triggers by recognizing what you think about and do to transition from 9 to 10 during masturbation. Give yourself permission to use orgasm triggers – speed of movement, pressure of movement, type of movement, self-talk ("I'm going to come"), or using fantasies to reach orgasm.

Overcoming ejaculatory inhibition is not only good for you; it enhances the experience for your partner and makes couple sex fun and involving. Reinforce the desire/pleasure/eroticism/satisfaction mantra.

Exercise – Confronting and Changing Male Sex Dysfunction

Do this exercise on your own and then share with your partner. Examine each dimension of sexual function:

1   Sexual desire vs. HSDD
2   Arousal vs. ED
3   Enjoying orgasm vs. PE
4   Erotic flow to orgasm vs. ejaculatory inhibition

Are all four dimensions of sexual function positive or is there a problem? Be honest; don't fall into the traditional male trap of exaggerating sexual prowess and denying problems. Male sexual function is not about perfection; it is about sharing pleasure and enjoying your experience. Don't be embarrassed about sex dysfunction. Most men begin as premature ejaculators. By age 40, most men have an experience of not maintaining an erection sufficient for intercourse. By age 50, many men have the experience of not reaching orgasm during intercourse. Although you won't admit it, the majority of men have experienced low or no desire whether caused by fatigue, alcohol, anxiety, depression, or distraction. Occasional sex problems are normal. This is part of male sexuality. Variable sexual function is normal, very different than chronic sex dysfunction.

Discuss your perspective on sex problems of PE, ED, HSDD, and ejaculatory inhibition. Does your partner agree with your assessment or does she have a different perspective? Discuss her approach to couple sexuality. Is this new to you?

Half of couples experience sexual dysfunction or dissatisfaction. What is the best way to address these problems? Our recommendation is couple sex therapy. How do you (and your partner) want to address sexual problems? Do you deserve sex to have a 15–20% role in your life and relationship? Create a change plan and check-in with your partner in six months to see whether your sexual relationship has improved.

Is Good Enough Sex Acceptable?

What men dislike about GES is that it sounds like you're "settling" because you can't have perfect sex. GES motivates and empowers you to accept yourself, your partner, and the complexity of couple sexuality. GES encourages you to play to your sexual strengths while being aware of your sexual vulnerabilities. It allows you to celebrate outstanding sexuality, accept good sex, and not over-react to problematic sex. Adopt a variable, flexible sexuality rather than sex as a pass-fail intercourse test. Broaden sexuality to include sensual, playful, and erotic scenarios. Most importantly, sexuality is an intimate team experience of sharing pleasure rather than a pressured individual performance. GES allows you to enlist your partner as your intimate and erotic ally rather than someone to perform for and fear her judgment. GES promotes acceptance of the complex humanity of sexuality. It allows for the multiple roles, meanings, and outcomes of couple sexuality. Not only is this not settling, GES promotes understanding what it means to be a sexual man and accepts healthy masculinity.

Case: Geoff and Seraphina

When 34-year-old Geoff married 31-year-old Seraphina, he did so with great anxiety. His first marriage ended in a bitter divorce three years ago. His ex-wife demonized him because he was unwilling to have a baby with her. As well, she bitterly complained about his PE.

Geoff viewed Seraphina as totally different – empathic, kind, and committed to a satisfying, secure, and sexual marriage with two planned, wanted children. Family and friends were supportive (they viewed Seraphina as the opposite of the judgmental, self-centered ex-wife).

Geoff's major concern was sexual. He feared that PE would cause her to be so disappointed that like his first wife she would leave. Seraphina reassured Geoff numerous times that she loves sex with him, he is a sophisticated lover, he celebrates her orgasmic pattern with manual and oral sexuality, and she enjoys their short, intense intercourse. He was not convinced. He obtained a prescription for a fast-acting anti-depressant and took two pills before inter-course to ensure ejaculatory control. Trying so hard not to ejaculate caused a decrease in involvement and arousal leading to erectile anxiety and ED. Seraphina urged him to not overreact. Although well-intended, it had the effect of making him even more self-conscious and accelerated fears that she would give up on him.

Geoff scheduled an appointment at a men's sexual health clinic where they gave him testosterone enhancement pills, porn, and taught him to do penile injections. Bio-medically, the injections worked fine, but Geoff and Seraphina found it very awkward. His reaction to testosterone was heightened agitation and irritability. She reacted negatively to the porn – feeling intimidated by the type of erotic sexuality portrayed. She feared this was what he wanted sexually. Their sexual lives were a mess. This dramatically impacted their emotional relationship. His worst-case scenario was in danger of becoming the reality. It is amazing how sexual problems can undermine the man, woman, and relationship.

Seraphina consulted her minister who blamed the problem on Geoff's use of porn (not a good understanding), but did something very valuable – he referred them to a couple therapist with a specialty in sexual desire problems. At the first session, the therapist met a very demoralized couple. Seraphina felt confused. Geoff was in a full-blown panic, apologizing for himself sexually, and desperately afraid that Seraphina would leave. The clinician was empathic and respectful, but gave a clear message to Geoff – stop catastrophizing thinking, stop penile injections, stop testosterone pills, and stop watching porn. The second message was that desire is best addressed as a couple issue – they could rebuild sexual comfort and confidence as an intimate team. The clinician scheduled an individual session with each spouse. In his session, Geoff talked about his fragile sexual self-esteem and how hopeless he felt. He feared his sexual failures had destroyed his kind, loving wife. The clinician noted that Geoff's lack of sexual self-acceptance made it impossible to accept Seraphina and her sexuality. The therapist's message to Geoff was that he had dug himself into a hole. The first thing to do was stop digging. He needed to accept his wife as his intimate and erotic friend and begin developing a new couple sexual style focused on comfort and pleasure, not performance. The therapist assured Geoff that the marriage had a solid foundation, they had an excellent prognosis, that time was on his side, and to listen to Seraphina and her sexual feelings and requests. He needed to banish male performance myths and his ex-wife from his life. Geoff cried – which the therapist assured him was normal. Geoff had put tremendous pressure on his penis. He needed to let go of the self-defeating performance demands and embrace desire/pleasure/eroticism/satisfaction. Geoff could schedule an individual session if needed, but couple therapy was the primary approach.

When the therapist saw Seraphina three days later, it was clear that this would be an easy couple to work with. Geoff went home after his session and initiated a sexual date. Seraphina was open and responsive, including enjoying orgasm. When she pleasured him, he was responsive and they had intercourse. She enjoyed his rapid, intense orgasm. Seraphina liked the idea of creating a new couple sexual style. She accepted the therapist's assurance that she had not caused Geoff's sexual melt-down.

At the couple feedback session, the therapist suggested a six-session contract beginning weekly and switching to bi-weekly. They liked the idea of focused, time-limited therapy. It reflected the clinician's optimism about their capacity

DEALING WITH SEXUAL PROBLEMS

for change. The therapist said that past sexual experiences need not control them. They practiced resiliency skills, which was particularly important for Geoff's sexual self-confidence. Geoff and Seraphina were conscientious clients, engaging in psychosexual skill exercises between sessions. Psychologically, relationally, and sexually, Geoff had a lot going for him – he needed to heed Seraphina's feedback. She saw no need to engage in the ejaculatory control exercises. Seraphina enjoyed her arousal/orgasm pattern using erotic sexuality. Just as important she enjoyed Geoff's rapid, intense intercourse. The message is don't compare yourself with a rigid performance model – find your unique couple sexual style.

Summary

Male sex dysfunction is a hidden, stigmatized problem which is very common and is changeable. Each dysfunction – PE, ED, HSDD, and ejaculatory inhibition – has a different set of causes and different interventions. Success is more likely when treated as a couple issue. Confront the self-defeating traditional male performance model, adopt the GES approach, establish positive, realistic expectations, and use all your psychological, relational, and sexual resources to maintain healthy male and couple sexuality.

In dealing with sexual problems, do not deny or minimize. Establish a desire/ pleasure/eroticism/satisfaction pattern rather than stay stuck in dissatisfying or dysfunctional sex. You deserve sexuality to have a 15–20% role in your life and relationship.

15

VARIANT AROUSAL
What Fits Your Relationship

Women assume that all men want sex. Like most assumptions, "all men" is wrong. Over 90% of men value intercourse and intimate, interactive couple sexuality. However, approximately 4% of men have a variant arousal pattern. Less than 1% have a deviant arousal pattern. He almost never shares this information with his partner.

Variant arousal refers to a sexual pattern that is powerful, narrow, and very different from intimate, interactive couple sexuality. The most common type is a fetish arousal. Variant arousal also includes cross-dressing and bondage and discipline (BDSM) scenarios.

There is major scientific and clinical controversy about the meaning and treatment of variant arousal. There are three major approaches: Acceptance, Compartmentalization, and Necessary Loss. Be aware of what you want as well as what fits your partner's feelings and values.

Development of Variant Arousal

Learning that her partner has a secret sexual life is a major shock for the woman. She blames herself or feels that she's a fool. In fact, for the great majority of men, the variant arousal developed in childhood or adolescence, before you met your partner. The poisonous cycle involves high secrecy, high eroticism, and high shame. This is a powerful, destructive combination which controls your sexual desire. Variant arousal has been reinforced by thousands of masturbatory experiences.

For men in a new relationship, the romantic love/passionate sex/idealization (limerence) phase can override the variant arousal pattern for weeks or months, and in some cases, years. You naively hope that this will continue, so don't share the reality of the variant arousal with her. In the majority of cases, variant arousal returns to dominate your sexual desire and response. Variant arousal controls your relationship leading to avoidance of couple sex. Embarrassment takes over and variant arousal remains a shameful secret. She did not cause the variant arousal and had no reason to believe that this was the factor causing your low or no sex relationship.

When consulting a couple therapist, you typically blame the problem on relationship issues or on your partner. This distracts you from the core issue. The therapist is emphatic and respectful, but confronts the issue of your secret sexual life. Being truthful will not solve the problem, but pretending that there is not a major sexual secret is unfair and makes the problem worse (Scorolli et al., 2007).

The woman's reaction to the disclosure varies from shock, dismay, or anger to relief at finally understanding the core problem. You fear her response: that she will shame and abandon you. Although this does happen, in a majority of cases the woman is surprised and hurt, but does not want to destroy you or the relationship. The ideal situation is that she commits to being your intimate and erotic ally in choosing a strategy to deal with the variant arousal. It can't remain a secret. Sexual issues need to be addressed with a strategy both partners are committed to.

Strategies for Addressing Variant Arousal

There are three strategies to address the issue of variant arousal:

1   Acceptance
2   Compartmentalization
3   Necessary Loss.

These are not compatible strategies; you need to decide what is the right fit for your relationship. There is a tendency to give the socially desirable answer, but not mean it or be able to implement it. We promote the guideline suggested for parents when speaking with children about sensitive issues – no "sins of commission". Do not lie to your partner. Do not say things which are not true or you don't mean. This is disrespectful and destructive for you, your partner, and your relationship. A secret sexual world focused on variant arousal is a serious issue. The trap for the woman is to assume responsibility for the variant arousal and feel that it is her job to resolve the problem. The trap for you is to minimize the erotic intensity of the variant arousal and pretend that it's not a major problem. Variant arousal is a major sexual and relationship issue. Lying to yourself and your partner makes it worse.

Acceptance

The new trend is to advocate for the Acceptance strategy. The premise is that variant arousal is your "authentic sexual self". Asking you to deny your variant arousal is like asking a gay man to not have sex with men. Variant arousal is a challenge for the woman not just to accept, but to embrace. Acceptance is not at her expense nor does it compromise her sexuality. She doesn't lose anything and hopefully gains a special sexual experience.

Many women and some men reject the Acceptance strategy as not genuine. Playing out a fetish scenario, being sexual when you are cross-dressed, or assuming the dominant role in a BDSM scenario can be a turn-off and alienating for her. Seeing you erotically charged by something which is anti-erotic for her is unhealthy. Rather than sex bringing you together, it serves to separate or even alienate you. As one woman said, "I tried to please him, but bad sex is bad sex". A key to the Acceptance strategy is that you enjoy the erotic charge without feeling guilty. The key for the woman is to accept good sexual feelings and that it is okay for the scenario to be asynchronous (better for you). If the variant arousal scenario is at her expense or is destructive for the relationship, the Acceptance strategy will backfire. Usually, you advocate for the Acceptance strategy.

Compartmentalization

Compartmentalization is the traditional and most common strategy. It sounds like the sensible compromise. You use variant arousal fantasies during partner sex to facilitate erotic response. In addition, you act out the variant arousal whether weekly, monthly, or quarterly. You can do this on-line, with a different partner, or by utilizing paid sex.

The crucial question is whether this strategy is acceptable for the man, woman, and couple. Too often you are dysfunctional or dissatisfied with couple sex and avoid or are sexual to placate your partner. The woman does not feel desire or desirable. She develops low desire and resents partner sex. Does the Compartmentalization strategy have a positive role in energizing your bond? Does each partner feel desire and desirable? Or does it have a negative, draining role? If so, you need to adopt a different strategy.

Necessary Loss

The Necessary Loss strategy is utilized when the variant arousal cannot be successfully integrated into your couple sexual style. This is the most challenging strategy. It asks you to give up the powerful erotic charge of variant arousal and adopt a new couple sexual style which integrates intimacy and eroticism. It is the strategy most advocated by the woman. Erotic intensity in the new couple sexual style provides an erotic charge of 85 for you rather than 100. The payoff is that couple sexuality has a positive rather than conflictual role in your life and relationship. The challenge for the woman is to embrace the new sexual style and not feel guilty that your erotic response is less intense. Her enthusiasm for intimacy, pleasuring, and eroticism is motivating for you. Accepting the Necessary Loss strategy requires courage and is a symbol of genuinely valuing your relationship.

The danger with the Necessary Loss approach is when it's not genuine. You agree to eliminate the variant arousal, but you're not being honest with yourself or your partner. Eliminating variant arousal is a challenge. You need to use all your resources to succeed, including her emotional and sexual support. Unfortunately, you feel guilty and embarrassed and stop the sexual dialogue. You regress to a secret sex life where masturbation is much preferred to couple sex because during masturbation you use fetish materials and fantasies. During couple sex, you wall her off by using fetish fantasies to produce an erotic charge which allows you to have intercourse and reach orgasm. Couple sex is unsatisfactory for her because you are not there emotionally. You focus on stimulating her rather than sharing erotic feelings. For you, sex is a chore which becomes less frequent. You resume acting out the variant arousal whether in-person or on-line. This illustrates the failed strategy of Necessary Loss. For Necessary Loss to be successful, both partners value their new couple sexual style and share desire/pleasure/eroticism/satisfaction.

Choosing the Best Strategy for the Man, Woman, and Couple

There is not one "right" strategy for all couples. Relational and sexual success requires a genuine commitment to a shared strategy. This involves a good faith effort to implement the strategy whether Acceptance, Compartmentalization, or Necessary Loss. Of course, there are no guarantees, but is likely to succeed if you are an intimate team. Keep your agreement of "no sins of commission". What each says at home and in therapy will be honest, no emotional or sexual lies. Trust what your partner says. For example, she agreed on the Acceptance strategy, but it's not working because she experiences your variant arousal as an erotic turn-off. Don't pretend she's enjoying sex if it's not true. Or you find that acting out the fetish is not erotically satisfying (it is barely sexual). Don't pretend you're satisfied. Each partner needs to be honest. A different example is that you agree to the Necessary Loss strategy and the Complementary couple sexual style. This is good for her, but you are unable to reach orgasm because there is no erotic charge. Pretending you had an orgasm is counterproductive. A different example is that you enjoy the new couple sexual style and feel desire/pleasure/eroticism/satisfaction, but your erotic charge is 75. Accept this. It is a healthy "sin of omission". It will not help to argue about erotic intensity. Disclosure and processing is valuable when trying to change a problem. It is not valuable if the agenda is complaining, manipulation, or punishing the partner.

Case – Margaret and Steven

When 28-year-old Margaret met 32-year-old Steven, she felt her prayers had been answered. Steven was a good person who loved her and wanted marriage and a family. They began as a romantic love/passionate sex/idealized couple. Margaret was especially pleased that Steven was a caring and skilled lover who accepted Margaret's orgasmic pattern with erotic sexuality. She was concerned that since she was orgasmic before intercourse that he didn't feel sexually fulfilled. Steven assured her that wasn't true – he was a sophisticated man who accepted that she came first (Kerner, 2005). She didn't need to change anything for him.

After the birth of their first child, Margaret was pleased that Steven was an involved father and they were an affectionate, cuddly couple. However, they had not resumed erotic play or intercourse. After several gentle hints, Steven still did not initiate, so Margaret got up her courage. She made sure that their eight-month son was asleep and initiated sex. Steven was willing to stimulate her to orgasm, but when it came to intercourse, he was more than hesitant. He was not aroused and had no interest in intercourse. Margaret felt that she was on an emotional roller coaster. She loved being stimulated to orgasm, but felt bewildered by Steven's lack of sexual interest and arousal.

Steven minimized the problem, saying that he didn't want to physically hurt her. Margaret was reassured, but still concerned. This concern turned to agitation when the pattern continued for the next few months. When Margaret initiated, Steven was responsive to her sexual needs, enjoying giving manual and oral stimulation. He was pleased by her orgasmic response, but did not want intercourse. Margaret offered to pleasure him to orgasm, but he declined.

Margaret was very worried – they had not had intercourse in over a year. Steven responded that most new mothers would be pleased rather than hassle their husbands. Steven said that she had no basis to complain. He began a pattern of initiating erotic stimulation once a week. Afterward, he let her nap as he took the child for a walk.

When Margaret asked if there was anything wrong, Steven was reassuring that in every way he felt their marriage and three-person family were doing very well. He had no complaints.

Four months later, Margaret glanced at their credit card bill (Steven was an excellent financial manager who paid all their bills) and was stunned by a charge of over $500. When she asked Steven about this, he was flustered and irritated stating that it must be a mistake and he would take care of it. Next month, Margaret checked the bill and found a charge of $300. In querying Steven, he turned it around and asked whether she wanted to do the bills because she feared he wasn't competent. Margaret was on the defensive, saying that she admired his handling of finances. With that Steven walked away. Margaret felt confused and agitated. She knew something was wrong, but had no idea what it was or what to do about it.

This state of affairs continued as weeks turned to months. Steven still initiated erotic sex weekly, but Margaret was less enthusiastic. One-way sex had become stale. Routine and predictability inhibit desire.

Their son was almost two. Margaret told Steven that she had always hoped to have two children, ideally a son and a daughter. To Margaret's surprise and joy, Steven was enthusiastic about a second child. He promised they'd have intercourse three times during the high probability week. The resumption of intercourse was easier than Margaret expected. Steven had a firm erection and intercourse was pleasurable. Steven seemed to be enjoying himself, and joked that they should do this more often. However, during the rest of the month, they continued the pattern of Steven stimulating Margaret to orgasm, but not interested in anything for himself. By the third month of trying to become pregnant, sexual enthusiasm waned as did his erections. As soon as he became erect, he rushed to intercourse so he could ejaculate before losing his erection. Margaret had enjoyed intercourse, but rushed sex was not fun. Both persevered because they wanted a child. To their relief, Margaret became pregnant during the fifth month. Once they achieved pregnancy, sex totally stopped. They avoided sexual touch, although Steven was affectionate and solicitous of Margaret's feelings in all other areas.

After the first trimester, Margaret was feeling healthy and missed sexual contact. She asked Steven to pleasure her to orgasm. However, Margaret found it hard to feel turned on. Steven was a distant, reluctant lover. Eventually, she achieved orgasm, but it was hard work – like swimming against the tide. The next day, she asked Steven what was wrong – this time he responded with a harsh put-down. He noted how hard it had been to become pregnant. Steven didn't want to do anything to endanger the pregnancy. Margaret felt attacked for being sexually selfish. On the next visit to the obstetrician, Margaret asked her opinion about sex during pregnancy. The doctor reassured Margaret that it was perfectly safe. When conveying this information, Steven's response was "You can never be too safe when it comes to a baby". His message was clear "I don't want sex with you". At this point, Margaret had no interest in sex with Steven – she felt humiliated.

They were fortunate to have a healthy baby girl and Steven was active in parenting. However, by this point, it was clear to Margaret that something was happening sexually that needed to be addressed. She carefully examined the credit card bills for the previous three months and found unexplained charges from three different companies totally more than $700 per month. When she called the number on these accounts, she found that all three sold leather boots. Neither she, Steven, nor the children wore these types of boots.

After the children were asleep, Margaret confronted Steven with these facts. He tried to distract and blame, but this time Margaret was having none of it.

She was very surprised when Steven broke down in tears and begged her not to abandon him, saying they have a wonderful family. Margaret wanted the marriage and family, but needed to know what was happening sexually. Were the boots tied to sex? Once she said that and saw the look of shock and humiliation on Steven's face, she realized that he had a hidden sexual life involving boots. This was a pivotal moment. Margaret could have shamed and punished Steven. Although hurt and confused, she wisely chose to turn toward him and say "I love you. We can deal with this together".

It was Steven who called for an appointment with a couple sex therapist and asked Margaret to join him. In the first session, Steven said that he was committed to Margaret and their four-person family. He felt very badly about the sexual problem and didn't know what to do. Margaret was confused, but valued Steven's commitment to their marriage and family. She wanted to be his emotional and sexual ally, not his critic or judge. The therapist said he'd encountered this problem several times and was optimistic that their concern for each other and their family would make it easier to address these sexual issues. Margaret was surprised when the therapist asked whether she had consulted a divorce attorney and saw the relief on Steven's face when her answer was no.

The next step in the therapeutic process was individual histories. The therapist began the session by saying "I want to understand your psychological, relational, and sexual strengths and vulnerabilities, both before you met your spouse and since. I appreciate you being honest and forthcoming. At the end, you can red-flag sensitive or secret information. I will not share it without your permission, but I need to know as much as possible in order to help you deal with these difficult issues". If the clinician conducts the history with the spouse present, there will be a "sanitized" version, not the genuine narrative (Metz & Epstein, 2002).

The complexity of Steven's variant arousal became apparent in his individual interview. The clinician was empathic and respectful, but clear that Steven needed to be honest about his sexual history and the boot fetish. Steven was caught in the cycle of high secrecy, high eroticism, and high shame. He'd never spoke with anyone about the fetish. The variant arousal existed from childhood (which is a common pattern). He hoped that once married, the fetish would lose its controlling power (a typical self-defeating wish). Steven was afraid to share his variant arousal history with Margaret, but with the therapist's urging realized that there was no reason to keep it secret. The fetish history was processed in a therapeutic manner at the couple feedback session.

The couple session was a turning point. The clinician carefully reviewed each person's strengths and vulnerabilities, especially sexually. The key to understanding Steven was his shame regarding the boot fetish. Negative motivation, especially shame, subverts the change process. The therapist outlined three strategies (Acceptance, Compartmentalization, Necessary Loss) to deal with the boot fetish. The clinician emphasized that Steven and Margaret needed to make and implement a decision based on what would make a difference in their lives. Margaret agreed wholeheartedly.

Steven was orgasmic 25–35 times a month by himself, always using fetish materials or fantasies. Over the years, he had purchased hundreds of pairs of boots – he would fondle the boots during masturbation, sometimes rubbing his penis on the boots. During couple sex, he would fantasize about the boots with the hope that he would become aroused enough for intercourse.

It was Margaret who suggested trying the Acceptance approach. She was willing to wear boots during sex. At first, Steven was very excited, but by the third time admitted to Margaret and the therapist that it did not have an erotic charge. For Steven, secrecy and enacting the fetish in a ritualistic manner was the key for erotic response. Paradoxically, Margaret's openness and willingness de-eroticized the boot experience for him. They realized that the Acceptance strategy was not viable. Was Margaret willing to accept the Compartmentalization strategy where Steven would masturbate using the boot fetish and later would pleasure Margaret to orgasm?

Margaret said that perhaps now that she understood Steven's variant arousal, she could live with the Compartmentalization strategy. She wanted to feel intimate and share sexuality. The therapist asked Steven about the Compartmentalization strategy. Steven didn't believe that it would fit their needs for intimacy or eroticism.

The therapist asked if they were willing to commit to a six-month good faith effort to adopt the Necessary Loss strategy and create a new couple sexual style. The therapist's belief that there was a good possibility of success was motivating – a couple sexual style was what Margaret really wanted. This would be a major challenge for Steven – giving up the boot fetish and being open to intimate, interactive sexuality with Margaret as his sexual ally. Steven viewed couple sex as for Margaret, not a shared pleasure that involved his sexual feelings and needs. The therapist was clear that Necessary Loss required each partner being genuine. It was not a punishment for Steven's sexuality or a politically correct exercise. Steven agreed to not use fetish fantasies or materials. He brought all the boots (four large bags) to the therapist's office as a safe haven. Steven agreed to not visit internet boot sites. They set up a weekly five-minute check-in to ensure that Steven did not regress to a secret fetish world.

In terms of a couple sexual style, they read material, took a self-assessment questionnaire, and discussed which sexual style was the best fit for them. At the same time, they began the sexual desire psychosexual skill exercises of comfort, attraction, trust, and playing out each person's preferred sexual scenario (McCarthy & McCarthy, 2012).

The process of sex therapy is challenging. Changing sexual attitudes, behavior, and emotions is seldom easy and straightforward. The role of the therapist is to keep the couple focused and motivated and to process difficult issues.

Margaret's sexual responsiveness was crucial to the change process. She allowed herself to enjoy intimate, interactive sexuality rather than second-guessing Steven's sexual feelings. The therapist was empathic and respectful of Steven's struggles, encouraging him to meet these sexual challenges. At first, Steven found it hard to be sexually responsive to non-fetish fantasies. He was genuinely pleased (and surprised) that he was able to masturbate to orgasm without the fetish (it took five attempts). The erotic charge was less powerful, but masturbation was enjoyable. This learning was transferable to couple sexuality.

In the second month, Steven had his first orgasm during intercourse without using fetish fantasies. With that breakthrough, couple sex became genuine and satisfying, although less erotically intense. Key strategies and techniques included multiple stimulation throughout the pleasuring/eroticism process (including non-fetish erotic fantasies), Steven piggy-backing his arousal on Margaret's, using self-stimulation during partner sex, waiting until he felt erotic flow before transitioning to intercourse, and use of multiple stimulation during intercourse. Margaret provided testicle stimulation, while Steven used erotic fantasies and orgasm triggers to facilitate letting go. If Steven was not orgasmic during intercourse, they transitioned to her manual stimulation or his self-stimulation to orgasm. Steven and Margaret found that the Complementary couple sexual style was the right fit. The most important factor was that Steven valued couple sexuality which integrated intimacy, pleasuring, and eroticism. He felt desire and desirable. Sex was intimate and genuine, although less erotically charged.

Margaret and Steven continued six-month couple check-in sessions for two years after the termination of therapy. At the yearly follow-up session, Steven gave the therapist permission to donate the four bags of boots. This was a symbolic gift to Margaret (as well as a substantial tax write-off). Steven fully accepted the Necessary Loss strategy.

Therapy vs. a Self-Help Approach

This is one of the few chapters that does not contain a psychosexual skill exercise. The reason is that the secrecy/shame around variant arousal requires professional intervention. If the man and couple try to do this on their own, a likely outcome is an anti-therapeutic power struggle. The woman accuses you of lying and betrayal, and you counterattack saying that she is controlling, neurotic, or it's her fault. Approach this sensitive/secret issue in a respectful, non-shaming manner using the help of a therapist. Variant arousal subverts couple sexuality. It needs to be addressed as an intimate team. Engage in emotional problem-solving. Trying to address sexual issues as a self-help project is likely to increase alienation and blaming which is demoralizing and makes sexuality more difficult.

Deviant Arousal

Less than 1% of men have a deviant arousal pattern. Deviant arousal involves illegal sexual behaviors that harm others. This includes exhibitionism, voyeurism, frotterism, obscene phone calls, child sexual abuse, and pedophilia. Deviant sexual behavior needs to be confronted and stopped. This requires professional intervention (with the support of your partner). Deviant sexual behavior involves a powerful compulsive sexual life controlled by secrecy and shame.

Confronting you is necessary; shaming you is self-defeating and inadvertently reinforces deviant behavior. The more shameful you feel, the more likely you are to be controlled by the impulsive, compulsive sexual pattern.

You cannot moderate deviant behavior; it needs to be stopped because it harms others. Use all necessary resources, including individual therapy, couple therapy, medication, a self-help group, religious/spiritual support, and sexuality education. The woman has a crucial role in the change process, but cannot do it for you. Contrary to popular belief, treatment has a high probability of success with a low relapse rate as long as there is a clear, specific relapse prevention plan and couple accountability (McCarthy, 2015).

Summary

One of the most difficult sexual issues for women to understand is the man's secret world of variant arousal – whether a fetish, cross-dressing, or bondage-discipline scenarios. Approximately 4% of men have a secret sexual life centered on variant arousal. For most men, this remains a sexual secret, although some men unfairly blame the partner. This causes confusion, hurt, anger, and demoralization. She wonders if it's her fault, your fault, or a symptom of a loveless marriage.

Variant arousal typically begins in childhood or adolescence. You hope that a loving relationship will cure the problem. Although couple sex is functional in the short term, it does not resolve the variant arousal pattern. Variant arousal is driven by high secrecy, high eroticism, and high shame – a poisonous combination. You need professional intervention to deal with variant arousal. Decide whether to adopt the Acceptance, Compartmentalization, or Necessary Loss strategy. The woman did not cause the problem and cannot change the problem. What she can do is be your intimate ally in understanding and dealing with the variant arousal. Deviant arousal must be confronted and stopped.

16

GAY MEN ARE FIRST CLASS
Validating Sexual Diversity

Sexual orientation involves an emotional and erotic commitment to someone of the same sex (homosexual) or someone of the opposite sex (heterosexual). Traditionally, the culture has viewed homosexuality as pathological and unacceptable. There has been a dramatic change in the past 50 years, especially the last 10 years. The scientific and clinical evidence is clear; homosexuality is a normal sexual variation. Approximately 3–4% of males are gay. For the great majority of men, sexual orientation is "hard-wired"; it is not changeable (Janni, Blanchard, Camperio-Clanis, & Bancroft, 2010).

Your spouse "did not make you gay" nor can she make you straight. Accept yourself and feel loved as a gay man. For most couples, when there is a difference in sexual orientation, the wise decision is a "good divorce". In the traditional American divorce, the ex-spouses argue for years whose fault it was that the marriage failed. The primary emotion is anger. In the good divorce, the primary emotion is sadness. You wish each other well and agree to not be involved with the ex-spouse's psychological, relational, and sexual decisions. Acceptance of the divorce allows you to be respectful, cooperative co-parents.

In the past, a large self-help group was gay married men. You married with the hope that marriage would "cure" homosexuality or that the marriage and family would shield you from discrimination and stigma. You had a hidden sexual life. A "double life" is unhealthy for the man, woman, and family. The wife felt misused and betrayed. You felt caught in a dilemma. You were in a marriage where you did not have a genuine erotic bond. Your secret sex life often had a compulsive component. This is a very hard way to live.

The Core of Being a Gay Man

The culture (including mental health professionals) believed that sexual orientation was determined by who you fantasized about and who you had sex with. Simple, but wrong. There are two core components of sexual orientation. First, who you genuinely emotionally bond with. Second, who you genuinely share eroticism with (Ramirez & Brown, 2010). It takes many men years to accept your sexual orientation, but the truth is there for most gay people by age 16. A man who experiences a limerence phase with a woman is not lying to her. The problem is that over time the strength of your sexual orientation overwhelms the emotional attachment to the woman. Barry has sat with couples where the woman said, "I felt you loved me and we had good sex, was it all a lie?" It wasn't a lie; it was an unrealistic hope that because you loved her and she was pro-sexual that it would "cure" being gay. You don't cure sexual orientation. Sexual orientation involves accepting your genuine erotic charge and emotional attachment. The challenge is to embrace your authentic sexual self.

An important effect of accepting being gay as normal is that fewer gay men are entering heterosexual marriages. The gay married men self-help groups are much smaller. Acceptance that sexual orientation is about who you love and who you want to have sex with is a major step forward for both gay and straight people. Being gay is not the most important part of being a man but is integral to who you are and your psychological, relational, and sexual well-being. Being gay is not just normal but is your authentic sexual self and optimal for you.

Are There Other Sexual Orientations?

In addition to homosexual and heterosexual, there are at least two other sexual orientations – asexual and bisexual +.

Asexual is very rare (less than 1% of men), but is real. The asexual man does not value sexual touch. Asexual men have no attraction to sexual stimuli or being sexual with another person. Some asexual men are interested in marriage and parenting, but cannot create a genuine sexual relationship. Our strong recommendation is that you tell the woman about your asexual orientation early in the relationship. This allows her to make an informed decision about whether to commit to a marriage or life partnership with you. Asexuality also occurs with women, although the number is small (less than 2%). Respect individual differences and the complexity of people and relationships. Most asexual people decide against marriage. In dealing with asexuality, we encourage consulting a sexual health professional to process feelings and make wise life decisions.

Bisexuality + (also called pansexuality) has many definitions. The core is openness to being sexual regardless of your partner's gender. A significant number of bisexual + men advocate consensual non-monogamy relationships whether open, swinging, or polyamorous. Some value marriage and children, but a significant number do not value a traditional pair-bonded relationship. Do not assume that bisexual + orientation means the same thing to every man. Be clear about your self-definition regarding sexual attitudes, behaviors, emotions, and values. We urge you to disclose your orientation and what that means to your partner(s), whether female or male. Be aware that more women are bisexual + than men and that more women identify as bisexual + than lesbian.

Bisexual + men experience a genuine emotional and erotic bond with both a male and a female partner. It does not mean exact 50-50, but there is a desire to be emotionally and sexually involved with both genders. Unfortunately, gay men belittle bisexual + as you not having the courage to admit you are gay. Others believe that bisexual + people are controlled by ambivalence and indecisiveness. This is not respectful of the man who has genuine emotional and erotic feelings with both genders. In deciding how to successfully implement bisexual +, our recommendation is individual and/or couple therapy to help decide what is the right fit for you and people in your life.

The Most Common Situation – Acceptance of Being Gay

Acceptance is the key for healthy individual and couple sexuality. Identifying your authentic sexual self is crucial. Gay men have more resources and greater cultural acceptance than at any time in the U.S. culture. You cannot expect others to accept you unless you accept yourself. Be a first-class gay man psychologically, relationally, and sexually. A challenge is that unlike your heterosexual friends, you don't have a "socially desirable" path to follow. That can be an advantage because you don't have to confront the traditional traps of the old, repressive approach to masculinity. Commit to psychological, physical, sexual, and relational health. Affirm that being gay is optimal for you. You deserve sexuality to have a positive role in your life and to make wise personal and relational decisions.

In the past, the message to gay men centered on negative consequences – being harassed or harmed, acquiring HIV, alcohol and drug abuse, depression, suicide, losing a job, being rejected or shunned by family. These issues are real and need to be dealt with, but this is not where to start. Start with a commitment to live a healthy life as a gay man. A good life doesn't mean perfect. Unlike past generations, homosexuality is now accepted. Homosexuality has existed in almost all cultures and over thousands of years. Attempts to wipe out or punish homosexuality have failed because it is inherent in the person, not a lifestyle choice. Treating sexual orientation as a deviant behavior makes no scientific sense. Being gay is integral to who you are. It is much more than sexual behavior. You have a right to love who you love. Sex is important, but is not the essence of being gay. Use your resources and opportunities to be a fully functioning gay man.

Heterosexually Married Gay Men

Traditionally, gay men married as part of the denial process. It makes no sense to blame or demonize a gay man for marrying. Often, you married with the hope that this would resolve the sexual orientation issue which it never does. You hoped that being married and having a family would make you "normal". Gay men are normal; you don't need a woman to feel normal. Being gay is optimal for you.

It takes courage to disclose to your partner that you are gay (or bisexual +). It is hard to predict her response. Often, it is relief that the real issue is now clear. Other times, it is a shock – she had no idea. Sometimes, it is self-blame; she let you down and you had to turn to men for sex. Often, it is anger driven by feelings of rejection. You cannot control your partner's reaction, but be clear about yourself and what you feel. Start with an affirmative recognition that emotionally, relationally, and sexually, your attachment is to men not women. Your partner didn't make you gay nor did you mean to hurt her. Ideally, you would have acknowledged your sexual orientation before marrying, but you can't change the past. If you have children, you want to continue being their father, and ideally co-parent.

It is important to carefully consider individual and reality factors. For example, some married for practical reasons, but that's not true for most gay men. Most want to have a positive role with their children, but not all gay men. Most women eventually accept that their ex-spouse is gay, have a good divorce, and co-parent, but certainly not all. Be honest with yourself and deal with reality; do not expect a best-case scenario. Most of the time, the couple divorce because of a difference in sexual orientation. Yet, other gay men stay married and believe that this was the right decision.

The crucial issue is being true to your authentic sexual self. Accept being gay as optimal. It is healthy for you and your wife to process why you did not disclose this before marriage. Apologizing for the hurt and confusion caused facilitates the healing process. Be clear what you are asking. She probably won't give you everything you ask for, but you have a right to your requests.

Be open to her feelings, reactions, and requests. What you cannot allow is being blamed or shamed. Do not apologize for being gay – it is your authentic sexual self. In dealing with your partner, realize you have had time to process your feelings and values. She needs time to process her attitudes, emotions, and values. We encourage use of competent, non-judgmental therapeutic resources (guidelines in Appendix A) to help in this process. She can benefit from a supportive, gay-affirmative therapist. The woman has a right to establish her own agenda. As well, both of you need to address the feelings and needs of your children.

Each partner has the power to make a wise decision. A wise decision makes sense emotionally and practically and works in the short and long terms So much of "common sense" is simplistic and judgmental. It encourages dramatic emotional choices which sound easy, but are often self-defeating. The first issue is whether both spouses can accept the reality that you are gay. Being gay was not caused by the woman and she cannot change your sexual orientation. A crucial issue is whether to continue the marriage. This is not a simple decision that fits all people. Barry knows gay men, personally and professionally, with healthy marriages and families.

The wise decision for the majority is the "good divorce". The emotion is sadness, not anger. You genuinely wish each other well and agree to not be involved in the ex-spouse's psychological, relational, or sexual decisions. Be respectful, cooperative co-parents. Children want and deserve cooperative parents. Is this too idealistic? Sometimes, it does not work, but is successful in a number of families to the benefit of both the adults and children.

These guidelines are relevant if it is the wife who ends the marriage because she determines that her genuine sexual self is lesbian or bisexual +. Accepting this reality is healthy for her, you, and your children.

Marriages survive when there is a difference in sexual orientation, including being polyamorous. Some couples maintain an emotional, although not sexual bond. Most couples decide to divorce. Being lesbian was not caused by you, but the realization that her genuine emotional bond and erotic charge is with a woman needs to be accepted. Some couples find it is easier to accept a sexual orientation difference as the reason to end the marriage. Acceptance facilitates moving on with your lives.

Relational Decisions

For a gay man, a major decision is whether to share your life with a partner or choose sexual friendships. If the latter, we suggest not trying to integrate new men with your ex-spouse and children because there is too much change. When you establish a life partnership or gay marriage, the challenge is establishing a positive role for your partner. The usual recommendation is to create a cordial relationship with the ex-spouse and a "favorite uncle" relationship with the children. We have seen relationships where on one extreme the partner is like a second parent and on the other extreme is stuck in the role of the "bad guy". What is the right fit for your real situation?

The overarching theme is to reorganize your life as a first-class gay man. Ideally, this is supported by friends (both gay and straight) as well as family members. Some people are accepting, others maintain distance, and some are rejecting. Don't give power to the rejecting people whether family, friends, or neighbors. A particularly important resource is a religious community. Many religions are now accepting of gay men. Others are affirmatively pro-gay, including gay-majority congregations. Use all your resources to enhance your life and relationship.

Specific Issues of Sexual Behavior

The old view of gay sex was high frequency, multiple partners, focus on eroticism, downplay intimacy, and never say no to sex. The sexual theme was anything goes. A negative message was the dangers of gay sexuality, especially HIV but also STIs, manipulative and destructive relationships, rejection of older gay men and men with disabilities, and stigma about high-risk, anonymous sex. In this view, gay sex was for the young, beautiful, adventurous, experimental, and foolish. Another negative stereotype is that the passive partner in anal intercourse was a second-class man. What an unscientific, simplistic, and prejudiced view of gay sexuality. It negates what it means to be a healthy gay man relationally and sexually.

In most ways, gay sexuality is similar to straight sexuality. Healthy gay sexuality is integrative, not driven by eroticism. Gay relationships can vary from a traditional monogamous commitment to anonymous sex. Gay sexuality can be healthy and satisfying or it can be high risk and destructive. Gay sexuality involves a variety of scenarios, not a simple stereotype. Although anal intercourse is valued by many gay couples, a significant number prefer manual, oral, and/ or rubbing stimulation. Many gay men and couples value intimacy, pleasuring, and eroticism, but certainly not all. Contrary to cultural myths (including among gay men), you can be sexual in your 60s, 70s, and 80s. In the shame-based relationships of the past, older gay men formed "sugar daddy" connections where younger men were manipulative in return for sex. In the new model of gay sexuality, unhealthy relationships are not tolerated. The ex-wife urges her former husband to create a healthy gay relationship. The core issue is accepting being gay as optimal. You deserve sex to have a 15–20% role in your life and relationship.

What are the core sexual differences for gay men? Other than loving and being sexual with another man, there are few core differences. There are individual differences in preferences, patterns, and feelings. Be aware these differences are not true for all gay men or all gay relationships.

A common pattern is having more partners over a lifetime than straight men. Another difference is lower levels of marriage (life partnership) and higher levels of sexual friendships and casual sexual experiences. In addition, various types of consensual non-monogamy are accepted, including "monogamish" on one extreme and "fuck buddies" on the other. Gay men typically emphasize eroticism and downplay nondemand pleasuring. In oral and anal sex, a significant number take either the active or passive role, while others pride themselves in being versatile. Masturbation and use of porn are accepted. There is evidence of higher rates of impulsive/compulsive sexual behavior in the gay community (Braun-Harvey & Vigorito, 2020).

Gay men and straight men are not a different species. On most dimensions, there are more similarities than differences. Contrary to cultural myths, this includes sex problems. There are lower rates of PE, but higher rates of ED (especially with anal intercourse), HSDD, and ejaculatory inhibition. Sadly, there are higher rates of mental health problems, including drug and alcohol abuse, depression, intimate partner violence, and stress caused by prejudice and harassment. As a culture, we have come a long way, but have a long way to go to promote the psychological, relational, and sexual well-being of gay men. A major issue is not feeling deserving of love and acceptance. There are few positive models of gay men, healthy relationships, and gay families.

Nathaniel, Katharine, and Kris

Nathaniel is a 29-year-old married man who is in the process of divorcing Katharine, his 28-year-old wife. They had been a couple for almost ten years (four of them married) and have a two-year-old son. Nathaniel met Katharine when he was a sophomore in college and she a freshman. They enrolled in a class on literature and gender. They were attracted to each other's progressive ideas, united against traditional gender values, and opposed to the double standard. They did not become a sexual couple until the next year, but Katharine was aware of a strong attraction. When they began as a couple, Nathaniel felt swept away by her sexual enthusiasm. He was aware of conflicting sexual feelings.

When he masturbated, beginning at age 13, he had a range of erotic fantasies about boys, girls, and group sex. This pattern continued throughout college, although the predominant fantasy was giving oral sex to young men. His first partner experience to orgasm was at age 16 – a girl stimulated him through his pants while they were watching a movie. Each time he had a sexual experience with a girl, he felt encouraged, but his sexual ambivalence continued. The first time Nathaniel fellated a man to orgasm was age 17. It provided a powerful erotic charge.

Katharine was a vibrant and erotic woman. Nathaniel knew she loved him and felt love in return. He particularly valued giving and receiving oral sex. He was functional during intercourse, but sensations and feelings were less intense. About once a month, especially when drinking, he would have oral sex with a man, experiencing powerful feelings. When Nathaniel was a senior and making plans to apply to medical school, Katharine encouraged him to attend in the city they lived. Nathaniel received a generous financial package and decided to stay. Medical school and residency were stressful. Nathaniel valued Katharine's support and the continuity of their relationship. After graduation, she enrolled in a two-year medical administration program where she excelled. Their life was progressing and Katharine felt ready for marriage. Nathaniel loved her and was enthusiastic, but did not bring up his sexual ambivalence or concerns.

Their social/political stance was progressive and pro-gay, but they did not have a discussion about his sexual orientation conflicts. They attended a ten-session marriage preparation program which focused on communication and problem-solving, but ignored sexual issues. Theirs was a celebratory wedding and a year after became pregnant.

The first sexual crisis occurred during the pregnancy. Nathaniel was enjoying his residency and felt that there was much good in his life, but was sleep deprived. One night, he was in the break room at the hospital with an older gay nurse who Nathaniel fellated to orgasm. The next day, the nurse accused Nathaniel of sexual harassment. Nathaniel felt panicked and thought he should tell Katharine rather than her hearing it through gossip. Unfortunately, he felt shamed and could not disclose his sexual ambivalence. Katharine was very assertive with the nurse who dropped the accusation. Katharine felt great and Nathaniel felt terrible. He was living a lie – Nathaniel had a contingent sexual self-esteem. He was afraid of sharing his sexual struggles with Katharine. Sexual harassment was a bogus issue, but his sexual attraction to men, especially giving fellatio, was very real. Nathaniel obtained a referral to an individual therapist who was empathic, but not trained in sexual therapy and certainly not sexual orientation assessment. The therapist believed that fellating men was a symptom of an obsessive-compulsive disorder. Nathaniel attended individual therapy for five months, terminating just before their son was born. Nathaniel knew that the therapist was trying to help, but was not able to address his conflict over sexual orientation. This remained a "shameful secret". He loved his wife and was excited about the birth of their son, but felt like a sexual charlatan.

Two months after the birth, balancing medical practice and sleep deprivation, Nathaniel initiated a fellatio encounter with an intern. This man was proud of being gay and wanted to pursue a sexual friendship with Nathaniel. He urged Nathaniel to confine in him as a supportive friend. As a proud gay man, the intern made it clear that there was nothing shameful about being gay. He suggested that Nathaniel attend a meeting of the gay married men self-help group and offered to accompany him. This was a breakthrough in terms of self-acceptance.

Unfortunately, Nathaniel did not have the courage to disclose his growing awareness to Katharine. He was involved with the baby, but stopped being sexual with Katharine unless she insisted. He functioned sexually, especially in the giving role, but his heart was not in it. Three months later, Nathaniel met Kris, a 27-year-old gay man. Nathaniel fell in love. Kris strongly encouraged Nathaniel to disclose his sexual orientation to Katharine rather than her hearing it from others.

When he finally told Katharine, she was shocked. She asked how could he be gay since their sex had been so good before the pregnancy and he was a father. Katharine insisted that they consult a couple sex therapist. Nathaniel was ambivalent but agreed. The therapist employed a four-session assessment model beginning with a joint session, then seeing each person for an individual psychological/relational/sexual history. The therapist saw Nathaniel for a second individual session to ensure that this was his genuine sexual narrative. As well, the clinician had a second session with Katharine to assess her ability to deal with Nathaniel being gay. At the 90-minute couple feedback session, the therapist was empathic and respectful but clear in affirming that Nathaniel was gay. The therapeutic challenge was accepting this reality and making a wise decision of how to proceed. Nathaniel felt that a 500-pound weight was lifted from him. When Katharine cried, they held each other without blaming or shaming.

Therapy gave them the time and space to process their new reality. They decided to proceed with a good divorce. Katharine's concern was that Kris not replace her as a parent. They scheduled one session where Kris was invited to discuss his role as a "favorite uncle". Katharine and Kris established an emotionally distant but cordial relationship.

Nathaniel embraced his new life, including creating a first-class relationship with Kris with the hope that this would lead to a satisfying, secure, and sexual marriage. Nathaniel, with Kris's support, expanded his sexual repertoire to include manual and anal stimulation. He also expanded his medical practice as a gay-friendly physician. Nathaniel's life was a busy, multi-dimensional one as a first-class gay man.

Accepting Being Gay Is Necessary, But Not Sufficient

In the early years of the gay liberation movement, the naïve belief was that when the man accepts being gay, everything else would easily follow. Psychologically, medically, and relationally, you need to attend to the issues and problems in your life to ensure that you maintain a genuine sense of well-being. All men, gay, straight, bisexual +, or non-binary, have strengths and vulnerabilities. In assessing vulnerabilities and problematic areas, you need to determine which are resolvable, which modifiable, and which have to be accepted and worked around. You deserve to experience life as a healthy gay man. Don't blame your problems on other's prejudices (it is true that anti-gay people and institutions are a source of stress). An example is attending to physical and mental health. Alcohol and drug abuse is higher in the gay community and gay men (even more than straight men) are reluctant to consult a primary care physician. You owe it to yourself and those who care about you to take care of your health. Alcohol and drugs are misused as self-medication, especially for trauma. Don't hide or avoid; deal with difficult issues. An important decision is whether to organize your life around a pair-bonded relationship, a consensual non-monogamy relationship, sexual friendships, or casual sexual connections. What is the right fit for you emotionally and sexually? An important issue is work and finances. Many gay men have flexibility since they are less likely to have children or a mortgage. Organize your life so it's functional and fits your values. Barry had a gay client whose boss took advantage of his life flexibility to give night and week-end assignments. Some gay men are underpaid because they have fewer financial obligations. Gay men complain that their extended families take their flexibility for granted compared to siblings who have a conventional life organization.

Be aware of health, personal, career, and life organization issues that are challenges to being a first-class gay man.

Exercise – Assessing Strengths and Vulnerabilities

Be honest with yourself and share your relational and sexual issues with a trusted partner, friend, counselor, minister, or family member.

The first issue is acceptance as a gay man. Do you deserve a quality life? What aspects of your life are you proud of? How do you organize your relational life – gay marriage (life partnership), lover, sexual friendship, hook-up sex, anonymous sex? Do you attend sex parties, go to hook-up bars, engage in triadic or group sex? Do you practice safe sex or take the PreP medication? Are there high-risk people or situations in your life? In what ways do you feel most accepted as a gay man? Are these situations where you feel stressed or rejected?

If you were married and/or had children, have you processed sexual orientation issues with your wife or ex-wife? Depending on their age and maturity, have you discussed sexual orientation issues with your children? Are you actively involved as a father?

Set goals for the next year. Don't accept stereotypes or give socially desirable responses. What are your personal goals? Set at least one and up to three change goals. Examples include introducing nondemand pleasuring with your lover, writing a letter to your brother that acknowledges he can't affirm you being gay but he's family and you want to feel comfortable at family events, changing jobs to a gay-friendly employer, introducing an erotic oral sex scenario, reassuring your parents they did nothing wrong – being gay is optimal for you, planning a trip with your child, having a consultation with a gay-friendly minister, joining a therapy group for gay men, creating a retirement savings account.

Ask your partner, friend, or counselor for their perspectives. Remember, it's your life, you are not asking for approval. Seek inputs and perspectives that would add to your understanding and quality of life.

Summary

A book about men and sexuality needs to address the issue of homosexuality, other sexual orientations, and gender expression. The old belief was that homosexuality was a deviant behavior that had to be changed. Scientific findings reveal that this is a myth. For the great majority of gay men, sexual orientation is "hardwired". Being gay is optimal for you. Lead your life in a first-class manner. Traditionally, gay men married with the hope that marriage and family would change sexual orientation. For most couples, a "good divorce" is the wise decision. However, respect individual differences. You have a range of emotional and sexual options to deal with a mixed sexual orientation marriage. Be aware of your attitudes and values as well as your spouse's. Find the right fit for you, preferably with the help of an individual and/or couple therapist.

Accept that your authentic sexual self is gay. This allows you to organize your psychological, relational, and sexual life so that sexuality has a 15–20% positive role. A major decision is whether to organize your life around a gay marriage (life partnership). Another decision is whether you value monogamy or you choose consensual non-monogamy.

Our culture has made major changes in the past 50 years, especially the past 10 years. Accept homosexuality, bisexual +, and alternative sexualities. Be aware of challenges and stresses and make wise decisions. Use all your resources to establish a first-class life as a gay man.

17

MONOGAMY VS. CONSENSUAL NON-MONOGAMY

Developing a Genuine Commitment

Traditionally, couples assumed monogamy. Unfortunately, few couples have a clear, specific discussion about the role and meaning of monogamy. In reality, infidelity is common, especially among men. The most common type of affair is a male High Opportunity-Low Involvement affair. When discovered, the couple fall into a gender power struggle where the woman feels hurt and betrayed and you counterattack saying that this is normal male sexual behavior and she is overreacting. Usually, the affair did not involve an emotional connection. The affair might involve oral sex, intercourse, an on-line sexual experience, a one-night stand, or going to a massage parlor and paying extra for a "happy ending". She feels you broke the trust bond. You counterattack saying that this was a "sexual fling" that all men have, and she is being neurotic and causing a crisis. No one wins power struggles. It is about not being the "loser".

As a culture, our understanding of affairs and monogamy is sadly lacking. Affairs are treated in a simplistic, black-and-white manner. Treatment is simplistic – the "perpetrator" has to apologize and compensate the "victim". The affair ends the marriage because trust is destroyed. The assumption was that the cause of the affair was either a relational or sexual problem. The affair controls your lives and relationship. You are blamed for the affair and for the divorce.

Like so much in the sexuality field, the traditional approach to monogamy is not scientifically supported. The traditional approach harms men, women, couples, and the culture.

Affairs are multi-causal, multi-dimensional, with large individual, couple, cultural, and value differences. Although well-intentioned, concepts about affairs are iatrogenic (the attempt to help makes the problem worse and causes greater damage). In truth, there are many causes of affairs, many dimensions, many meanings, and many outcomes. Although the science regarding affairs is weak because of lack of research and value conflicts, there is clinically relevant scientific information which can facilitate understanding and help you make a "wise decision" (makes sense emotionally and practically, short and long term). A valuable guideline is never end a marriage because of an affair. This gives the affair more power than it deserves. The best assessment and treatment program (Snyder, Baucom, & Gordon, 2007) urges individuals and couples to not make impulsive choices. Do not "listen to your gut" when you discover an affair. Instead, engage in "self-care". Do not assume that you know the meaning of the affair or that the affair was caused by something you did or did not do. Do not listen to the advice to kick the spouse out of the house, call a lawyer, or tell her mother and friends what a terrible person you are. Self-care means engaging in healthy coping using exercise, sleep, prayer, or meditation. Don't drink, demand to know all the affair details, post on Facebook, or hire an aggressive divorce attorney. Slow down the process and take care of yourself. Don't do anything harmful to you or your family. This is especially true if you learn about your wife's affair.

A crucial strategy is to make genuine meaning of the affair. Create a narrative that makes sense to the "injured partner" and the "involved partner". Be sure you understand the meaning of the affair for your marriage and sexual relationship. We strongly recommend a marital or sex therapist who approaches affairs as a couple issue rather than a simplistic, adversarial approach. Like intimacy and sexuality, affairs are best understood and treated as a couple.

In understanding the affair, was it the most common type of male affair, a High Opportunity-Low Involvement, Compartmentalized/Ongoing, or Comparison affair? What is the meaning of the affair from the perspective of the involved partner, injured partner, and your relationship?

A common conflict is over what constitutes an affair and whether this was really an affair. The involved partner says that it's not an affair because they did not have intercourse. The injured partner counters that it involved manual, oral, or paid sex so of course it was an affair. Or in a Comparison affair, the involved partner says that we never even kissed. Yet, the reason you avoid sex in the marriage is that you'd be betraying the affair partner who you are in love with. Affairs have different emotional and sexual meanings and are different for the involved and injured partners. This is an example of the multi-dimensional role of affairs, especially in terms of your marital bond. The traditional belief is that an affair is always a symptom of a relationship problem. It is very important to assess that, but don't assume it because it's usually not true. The majority of affairs occur with the involved partner feeling fine about the marriage and sex in the marriage.

It is crucial to understand gender, cultural, and value dimensions when exploring the role and meaning of an affair. The traditional gender assumption is that male affairs are "normal" as long as it didn't threaten the marriage or family. This difference in meaning is particularly significant in young marriages and when there is a female Comparison affair. The gender split in behavior and meaning exists across generations and cultures. Traditionally, male affairs are treated with less judgment.

A common fight after the discovery of an affair is whether or not the couple had an agreement about monogamy. The injured partner insists that they have a clear understanding and the affair is a major betrayal. The involved partner says that they did not have a specific agreement and she is "making a mountain out of a mole hill". No one wins this argument; it is a charge-counter charge fight which generates much heat but little light. It's about whose fault it is, not about understanding the role and meaning of the affair and how to move forward. There is more bad advice in the media about affairs than almost any other area of sexuality. A dramatic, extreme reaction to an affair is destructive for you, your relationship, and your family.

The issue of monogamy is very important. It requires thought, awareness, dialogue, and making a wise decision, not a simplistic, cookie-cutter approach. Sexually, one size does not fit all. This illustrates the need for a wise decision rather than an emotional choice based on simplistic gender assumptions.

The Importance of Having a Clear Agreement

Monogamy is something to dialogue about and decide on, not assume. A prime question is whether both partners are committed to a satisfying, secure, and sexual marriage (life partnership). Do not assume; have an honest, personal, and clear discussion. For you, how important is sexuality and how important is monogamy? Be honest; don't give the socially desirable answer. Explore your family, cultural, and religious beliefs and values. A crucial issue is whether there are gender differences or are the values the same for both genders. Tradition-ally, affairs were "normal" for men, but not for women. People are surprised to discover that personal assumptions and values are different than traditional gender assumptions.

Affairs are an example of sexuality being multi-causal, multi-dimensional with large individual and value differences. Is an affair always a threat to the marriage? Does an affair have to involve intercourse? Do you believe that high opportunity is the major cause of affairs, especially for men? What constitutes an affair – is it intercourse, use of porn, paid sex, betrayal, lying, kissing and touching, trading sex pictures or erotic stories, acting out a secret arousal pat-tern, sharing sexual texts or stories, oral or anal sex, fantasies about another person? Do you have an explicit agreement covering these dimensions? Or do you prefer the "don't ask, don't tell" approach? It is dangerous to have very dif-ferent understandings and values. This sets you up for hurt, betrayal, and crisis.

Types of Affairs

The possible types of affairs are endless. We focus on three major types. First, the High Opportunity-Low Involvement affair, the most common type for men.

It could involve one affair partner or a hundred partners. The important characteristic is that it is primarily about sex with little to no emotional involvement. Women do engage in High Opportunity-Low Involvement affairs. The belief that a woman would not have this type of affair is an example of a false gender stereotype. This is the easiest affair for the involved partner to give up and for the injured partner to forgive.

Second, the Compartmentalized/Ongoing affair. This can be in-person or on-line, choice or paid, someone from work or the neighborhood, involve elaborate planning or impulsive encounters. The affair can last six weeks or six years. It begins as a sexually focused affair, but can take on emotional dimensions which were unplanned. An example is the classic movie "Same Time Next Year" that features a couple who meet for a sexual weekend each year for 25 years. The affair took a meaning very different than originally intended. Compartmentalized/Ongoing affairs are easier to get into than get out of.

Third, the Comparison affair which meets emotional and sexual needs more than your primary relationship. Because of the mixture of emotional and sexual dimensions, the Comparison affair is the most challenging to deal with. Unlike other affairs, people do not plan to have a Comparison affair – you "fall in love". Comparison affairs are the most common female affair. Interestingly, women seldom marry the affair partner. Marrying the affair partner is a male pattern. These marriages have a high risk of a second divorce. What makes for an exciting affair is different than what makes for a healthy second marriage.

Men react very strongly to finding that your wife had an affair partly because it is a reversal of the double standard and partly because of the emotional complexity of the affair. It violates a common guideline "Don't fall in love with the affair partner". A Comparison affair has a major impact on the involved partner, injured partner, and affair partner.

Don't Give the Affair More Power than It Deserves

Affairs are an important issue, but when it is the defining issue for your relationship, you are giving the affair more power than it deserves. Your marriage is more than the affair. An important guideline is to not end a marriage because of an affair. Whether it was your partner's affair or your affair, the wise strategy is to take the time to make genuine meaning of the affair so you make the best decision moving forward. Sometimes, the message of the affair is that this is a fatally flawed marriage. More commonly, the message is that you ignored important psychological, relational, or sexual issues that need to be addressed. In other situations, the affair was a high opportunity that your partner or you stumbled into. Other possible meanings are that the affair is a product of loneliness, depression, a secret arousal pattern, to prove something sexually, or revenge. A common theme is the affair caused you to feel desire and desirable.

The affair was not about wanting to leave the marriage, but to feel better about yourself.

The affair has a message. Do not assume that you know the message. Explore its meaning for you, your partner, your relationship, and your sexuality. Engage in disclosure and discussion so that the message makes sense to the involved partner and the injured partner. This puts you in a position to make a healthy decision about your marriage. Don't go with your gut; make a wise decision. The decision to recommit to your marriage (partnership) or to end it isn't "right-wrong", but what is the right decision for the present and future. The reality of marriage is that it takes both to commit, and the reality of divorce is that it only takes one to leave. In the United States, different than other cultures, it is the woman who decides to divorce. The decision is based on the understanding that this is not a healthy marriage in the present and won't be in the future. It needs to be a thoughtful decision based on an exploration of attitudes, behaviors, emotions, and values – including sexuality. The decision to recommit is based on you revitalizing your relationship and developing a bond of respect, trust, and intimacy. You can learn from the past, but cannot change the past. You don't get a "do-over" for the affair. Your power for change is in the present and future. The decision should not be based on the fact that an affair occurred.

Affair Statistics

The science of affairs is quite weak. The best estimate is that some type of emotional or sexual incident, in-person or on-line, choice or paid, occurs in 35–45% of marriages. Contrary to popular belief, affairs are most likely to occur early in the marriage (the first five years). Married couples have lower rates of affairs than cohabiting or dating couples. The majority of couples survive affairs, especially the male High Opportunity-Low Involvement affair (Allen et al., 2005).

Most couples do not have a clear agreement about monogamy, and do not create an agreement even after an affair has been discovered. Contrary to popular belief, those in couple therapy do not repeat the affair pattern. The saying "Once a cheater always a cheater" is not empirically supported. The important issue is how the affair is processed and whether you create a clear agreement about monogamy in the future. Our theme whether discussing primary prevention or recovery from an affair is the importance of a clear, personally relevant agreement. The majority of couples commit to monogamy after an affair. The difference is that both partners are clear about personal and couple vulnerabilities and what to do in a high-risk (in terms of person, mood, or situation) environment (McCarthy & Wald, 2013). The monogamy commitment is not "holier than thou" or about being perfect, but based on genuinely valuing your partner and marriage.

Consensual Non-Monogamy (CNM)

Some couples reject monogamy, instead experiment with consensual non-monogamy (CNM). Couples (perhaps 5–12%) adopt CNM as their sexual value. A clear agreement regarding the boundaries of CNM is even more important. There are three dimensions to a CNM agreement. First, what you value about your marriage (partnership). Second, what type of CNM is right for you. Third, what are the red lines which would destabilize or destroy your relationship. There is probably a higher rate of affairs in CNM than in monogamous relationships. Be aware that CNM agreements are often revised or revoked.

With CNM, one or both partners value adventure, exploration, testing boundaries, making your own rules, and sexual flexibility.

There are all kinds of CNM, but we focus on three types – Open, Swinging, and Polyamorous. Open relationships involve one or both partners being sexual with others. This usually involves High Opportunity-Low Involvement or Compartmentalized/Ongoing affairs. Open relationships are the most common CNM pattern, especially for men. Seldom do partners share information about their affairs, although for others talking about the affair details enhances erotic response.

Swinging involves being sexual with other couples. It can be "open swinging" which means that your partner is present while you are sexual or "closed swinging" where you know your partner is sexual, but you are not present.

Polyamorous relationships are the most discussed, but least practiced, type of CNM. Polyamorous people have a range of emotional and sexual connections (often in the context of a Polyamorous community). These are complex relationships – an alternative lifestyle.

These brief descriptions point out the complexity of CNM. CNM has different roles and meanings for each partner and relationship. In many CNM agreements, the partner's roles are different rather than equitable.

Exercise – Your Couple Agreement about Monogamy or Consensual Non-Monogamy

We urge you to have an open dialogue and create a clear agreement about monogamy or CNM. Be honest with yourself. What is the right fit for you? Do not give the "socially desirable" response. You cannot expect your partner to be honest if you are not honest.

Most couples affirm the value of a satisfying, secure, and sexual marriage (life partnership). They decide on monogamy to promote intimacy and security. Monogamy is much more than good words or good intentions. Create a specific monogamy commitment which is personally meaningful. Be aware of the type of person, situation, or mood which would make you vulnerable to an affair. All people and all relationships have vulnerabilities. Honesty about vulnerabilities is a crucial step in preventing affairs and strengthening your monogamy commitment. It is very rare that both partners have the same vulnerability. For example, your partner might be vulnerable in a group setting where alcohol is flowing, while you might be vulnerable in a situation where you feel isolated and marginalized. Share vulnerabilities with your spouse. Rather than feeling badly about yourself or your vulnerability, turn toward your partner and discuss what an affair would mean for you and your relationship. Affairs thrive on secrecy and impulsivity. Treat affairs as you would any major life decision (having a third child, switching careers, buying a house). Dialogue about the impact of an affair on you, your spouse, and your relationship.

If there were an incident (in-person or on-line, intercourse or touching), make an emotional commitment to disclose it within 72 hours. Do not keep it secret. The cover-up adds to feelings of betrayal which is more impactful than the sex itself.

A monogamy commitment is not based on fear, being a sexual detective, or feeling you are better than others. The foundation is valuing the intimacy and security of your relationship. Monogamy is an emotional and sexual commitment based on a positive influence process.

If you and your partner decide on CNM, an agreement is even more important. You want sexuality to have a positive role in your life. Your CNM agreement has three components. First, be clear what you value, emotionally and sexually, about your marital (partnered) relationship. Be sure that CNM does not subvert this. Couples choose CNM to eroticize their lives, create their own sexual rules, add sexual drama, explore emotional and sexual boundaries, and reinforce sexual adventure and vitality.

Second, what type of CNM is the right fit for you – Open relationships, Swinging, Polyamory, or something else? For example, open and closed Swinging is very different, with different types of arousal and different sources of vulnerability. Think this through by yourself and with your partner. Be personal and specific, not abstract or vague. People are clear about what they don't want. Be clear about what would work for you. Don't let yourself be blindsided by emotional or sexual factors you did not consider.

Third, deal with difficult issues – "red flags". What factors and boundary violations would destroy your CNM relationship? Examples include falling in love with the affair partner, becoming pregnant, contracting an STI, being manipulative, feeling set up, realizing you can't accept your partner being sexual in public, or pressure to incorporate the partner's variant arousal pattern. Rather than CNM having a positive role, it has a destabilizing or destructive role.

Do people "cheat" on their CNM agreement? Yes. Be sure your CNM agreement is clear, functional, and fits your emotional and sexual values.

This exercise is not a "politically correct" game. It involves a thoughtful dialogue to promote a wise decision. Create an emotional agreement which reinforces your sexuality and values.

A significant majority of couples commit to a monogamy agreement because they put high value on intimacy and security. Does this guarantee that neither partner will have an affair? No, affairs happen for a number of reasons, especially emotional factors and high opportunity. What a monogamy commitment does ensure are the traditional gender assumptions about affairs and the secrecy/betrayal pattern is confronted. As a client said to Barry "Two affairs over a 40-year marriage does not negate the value of monogamy or our marriage". A clear monogamy commitment reduces the frequency of affairs, especially High Opportunity-Low Involvement affairs. It confronts the traditional gender wars regarding affairs.

For couples who decide on a CNM agreement implement this so sexuality has a positive, rather than destabilizing role in your life. CNM needs a positive agenda, not just a rejection of monogamy. Like much in life, positive motivation is likely to result in a successful outcome. Couples who decide on CNM value individuality, emphasize eroticism, and encourage experimentation with boundaries and sexuality.

Fears Behind the Monogamy Dialogue

Change is a given in individual and relational life. We are in a 54-year marriage. Personally and relationally, we have experienced many changes, some planned others totally unexpected. The mantra of a satisfying, secure, and sexual marriage was not in vogue in 1966. Like most couples of our generation, we did not engage in a clear dialogue about marriage, sexuality, or monogamy. We, especially Barry, were aware of traditional sex roles and hypocrisy about monogamy. Barry ignored the destructive role of traditional gender conflicts until he began teaching a human sexuality class in 1970. Teaching causes you to confront hypocrisy. You don't want to teach one thing and practice another.

Conservatives fear that if you challenge one sexual boundary, you wind up challenging all sexual boundaries and eventually are caught in sexual chaos. Contrary to those fears is the challenge to develop an integrated view of sexuality which affirms that sex is a good thing in life, integral to you as a person, with sexuality having a 15–20% role in your relationship. This includes attitudes, behavior, emotions, and values. The decision about monogamy vs. CNM is a crucial personal and relational decision. Be sure sexuality has a positive role in your life.

Bethany and Alberto

Bethany and Alberto were a bi-cultural and bi-racial couple whose marriage was thrown into crisis over the issue of affairs. They had been a romantic love/ passionate sex/idealized couple who were strongly supported by friends but in conflict with their families. They met as young professionals. Alberto was a Ph.D. economist from South America who worked for an international consulting firm. He was determined to have a better quality of life than his family. His parents were a conservative, traditional couple where mother managed the family and looked the other way at father's long-term Compartmentalized/ Ongoing affairs. Alberto's sexual learning was totally different than his sister's who married at 18 because of a pregnancy.

Bethany was raised by her African-American single mother and had little contact with her wealthy Caucasian father who had a traditional marriage and family that Bethany never met. One thing her parents agreed on was the importance of education. The major contact with her father involved academic decisions. He would not pay tuition at Howard University, a Black college where she had been accepted, instead insisted that she attend Georgetown University. Bethany had planned to major in sociology, but father insisted that she major in either business or pre-law. She became a lawyer with a specialty in civil rights enforcement which thrilled her mother. Bethany's mother was a proud Black woman who embraced activism and sexuality. Mother supported Bethany's marriage, but her father did not attend the wedding because he did not believe Alberto would value Bethany and their marriage, including monogamy. Bethany loved her father, but felt that he was a hypocrite.

It was easy for Bethany and Alberto to attack traditional norms and feel special as a couple. Unfortunately, they avoided a personally meaningful conversation about their marriage, including monogamy.

Two years into the marriage, their careers and reputation as a non-traditional couple were thriving, but intimacy and sexuality were problematic. When he was home, Alberto was monogamous, but on business travel, especially internationally, he had High Opportunity-Low Involvement affairs. He made sure the woman used effective contraception and he always used condoms. He found paid affairs with women he met at a hotel bar particularly erotic.

Bethany's affair pattern was quite different. She valued being a sexually expressive woman and was attracted to lawyers and sociologists active in the civil rights movement. These were Compartmentalized/Ongoing affairs. She fell in love with a high-profile, charismatic lawyer who claimed to be separated and moving toward divorce. This was Bethany's Comparison affair. She was shocked to open an e-mail from the affair partner's wife informing Bethany that the affair was undermining their family and children and begging her to end it. Bethany felt betrayed. This was compounded when she learned that the wife had e-mailed Alberto – a painful way to learn of Bethany's affair.

Bethany and Alberto felt drained by the drama. They needed to address questions of what affairs meant for each spouse, their marriage, and their sexual relationship. They had seen friends engage in highly emotional, attack-counter-attack reactions to discovered affairs. They did not want to go that route.

They scheduled a session with a couple therapist whose sub-specialty was affairs. The therapist utilized a four-session assessment beginning with a couple session which reinforces that like intimacy and sexuality, affairs are a couple issue. The message of the first session was to slow down the process, not do anything to make it worse, and engage in self-care. They were advised not to compare each other's affairs nor use friends to complain about and demonize the spouse. Sessions 2 and 3 were individual psychological/relational/sexual history sessions to start the process of making meaning of their affairs as well as reaction to the spouse's affairs. Each was given the homework assignment to write a therapeutic letter to the spouse. Take responsibility for the affairs, discuss the themes (not the details) of the affairs, apologize for the hurt you caused, own your positive and negative learnings from the affairs, and say what you want going forward. The therapist's role is to ensure that the letter is genuine and comprehensive. Each letter is read aloud in the therapy session. The injured partner can ask questions and clarify information and perceptions. The involved partner apologizes for the pain caused. When the apology is accepted, you continue to process the meaning of the affair, but not use the affair as a weapon to punish the involved partner.

This process was helpful for Bethany and Alberto. You can learn from the past, but cannot change the past. A core issue was whether to rebond their marriage. This would involve creating a new couple sexual style and a new trust bond, including discussion about monogamy vs. CNM.

There was much that Bethany and Alberto respected and loved about each other. Although they were sexually functional, sex did not energize their bond. The drama of the affairs interfered with intimacy and marital sexuality. Neither Alberto nor Bethany had a good marital or sexual model. Their affair pattern served to keep them from developing a healthy marital bond and couple sexual style.

Bethany and Alberto committed to a satisfying, secure, and sexual marriage, including having two children. Would a monogamy commitment or a CNM agreement facilitate those goals? Bethany was clear about wanting a marriage where sexuality was vital and energizing. She valued a monogamy commitment for herself as a first-class woman in a satisfying and secure marriage. Alberto would have to give up the male privilege to have affairs, but the rewards of a genuine bond made this worthwhile. They agreed to a relapse prevention plan and consulted the therapist once a year to stay accountable to their commitment. If a problem or conflict occurred, they would call for a "booster session".

Summary

The issue of monogamy is very important – it needs to be carefully explored, not assumed. Deal directly with monogamy issues. Couples (married or partnered) routinely endorse monogamy, but do not make a clear commitment. Treating monogamy with benign neglect is a major cause of affairs and feelings of betrayal. If you commit to monogamy, be sure it is a clear, specific, and personally relevant commitment. This includes being honest about personal, relational, and sexual vulnerabilities. Your agreement identifies high-risk situations, moods, and people.

For couples who choose CNM, it is even more important to have a clear, specific agreement. Implement CNM so that sexuality has a positive role in your life and does not subvert your relationship.

The commitment to monogamy or to CNM is a core relational decision. Make it thoughtfully and wisely. Implement your agreement so that it promotes sexual desire and satisfaction.

18

CREATING AND MAINTAINING A SATISFYING, SECURE, AND SEXUAL BOND

A valued goal is to create and maintain a satisfying, secure, and sexual marriage (life partnership). Marriage meets needs for intimacy and security better than any other relationship. A healthy couple bond is very different than a perfect relationship. You feel loved and respected for who you really are with your strengths and vulnerabilities. You feel secure in your relationship with its difficulties and challenges rather than pretending you have an ideal relationship.

A healthy relationship is based on a positive influence process. This brings out the best in you. You value a respectful, trusting, and intimate commitment. Sexuality has a 15–20% role in energizing your bond and reinforcing feelings of desire and desirability (McCarthy & McCarthy, 2019b).

Sexuality has a paradoxical role in your life and relationship. Sex is a small, integral factor in sharing pleasure, reinforcing your intimate bond, and serving as a tension reducer to help cope with the stresses of life, including sharing your lives. The paradox is that dysfunctional, conflictual, or avoidant sexuality has an inordinately powerful negative impact, demoralizing you and threatening relational stability. Bad sex can kill a good relationship, but good sex cannot save a bad relationship.

This chapter is especially important. Traditionally, men were supposed to be loyal to the marriage and support the family, but it was women who valued intimacy and the relationship, not men. For you, sex was the payoff for marriage. This gender split is scientifically untrue and destructive for the man, woman, couple, and culture. It is true that women enjoy and celebrate healthy marriages and families more than men, but you need a healthy marriage more. One factor which is different in the United States compared to other countries is that it is women (especially college-educated) who leave marriages (Amato, 2010). The most common reason is that she is disappointed in the man and relationship. Divorce is hard on you and your role with your children.

You benefit from a healthy relationship. Creating a respectful, trusting, emotionally committed marriage is one of your best life decisions. Even more important, and more challenging, is to maintain a healthy bond, including sexually. Traditionally, men valued sex, but not intimacy, nondemand pleasuring, or emotional bonding. Rigid stereotypes about men and masculinity are oppressive. You are discouraged from being a fully functioning human being. Valuing your strengths is important but denying or minimizing vulnerabilities is destructive. Many men have a contingent self-esteem and/or a contingent relationship. You fear that if people, especially your partner, knew your history or anxieties, they would not accept or love you. That is a very hard way to live.

The old model of masculinity based on the double standard was unhealthy for the man, couple, and culture. We present a humanistic, accepting model of being a man and a cooperative, pleasure-oriented approach to masculinity and sexuality. The core sexual issue is a broad-based couple approach rather than sex as a pass-fail individual performance. Good Enough Sex (GES) empowers you to accept a range of sexual roles, meanings, and outcomes rather than a narrow, rigid approach to masculinity. The mantra of desire/pleasure/eroticism/satisfaction is motivating. Perhaps the most important concept is to value the woman as your intimate and erotic ally rather than the traditional split of men valuing eroticism and women valuing intimacy. Female-male sexual equity reinforces the integration of intimacy, pleasuring, and eroticism.

The new approach to masculinity generally, and sexuality specifically, is challenging yet worthwhile. The model of the strong man who is always in control with no questions or doubts was simple and seductive, but wrong. Likewise, the traditional model of totally predictable performance with the demand that a real man be able to have sex with any woman, anytime, and any situation was oppressive. Men are complex and male sexuality is complex. Sexually, one size never fits all. Focusing on giving and receiving pleasure is the essence of the new model of male and couple sexuality. Share desire/pleasure/eroticism/satisfaction. You do not need to perform for the woman or impress male peers.

Satisfying Is a Crucial Dimension

Traditional men undervalue their intimate relationship. Valuing a satisfying relationship is crucial. A satisfying relationship includes sexuality as an integral component, but not the most important. A satisfying relationship involves accepting your strengths and vulnerabilities, your partner's strengths and vulnerabilities, and strengths and vulnerabilities of your relationship. A satisfying relationship is anti-perfectionistic, the opposite of the idealized limerence phase. Your relationship is based on a positive influence process. You are a better person because you are in this relationship. The relationship brings out healthy parts of you. You feel respected and loved for who you really are – with your flaws as well as positives.

Satisfying involves positive, realistic goals for change. Healthy marriages change; they do not stagnate. A key to the change process is the realization that only 30% of relationship problems are resolvable. It is very important to address and change those. The majority of relationship problems are modifiable.

It is worth your time and effort to make realistic changes even though the problem is not totally resolved. The hardest issue is that even for the most loving, well-intentioned couples, 10–20% of problems are not changeable or modifiable. Satisfied couples accept this and work around problems so they do not subvert your marriage (Gottman & Silver, 2015).

Positive, realistic goals are especially important in terms of sexual issues. "Pop sex" would have you believe that with enough love, communication, eroticism, and willingness sex can be wonderful every time. This sets you up for sexual dissatisfaction if not alienation. Play to your strengths as a sexual man and couple, but don't expect all sex to be wonderful, powerful, and swept away.

The best sex is mutual and synchronous. Both partners experience desire/pleasure/eroticism/satisfaction. Most sexual experiences are asynchronous, positive but better for one partner than the other. Even among loving, sexually aware couples, 5–15% of sexual encounters are dissatisfying or dysfunctional. Maintaining positive, realistic expectations is key to sexual satisfaction. Satisfied couples accept a range of meanings and outcomes rather than demanding that all sex be mutual and wonderful.

Secure vs. Stable Marriage

In many cultures, the key to marriage is stability and children, not emotional or sexual satisfaction. The underpinnings of a stable marriage were community norms, family, religion, finances, and the stigma of divorce. A secure marriage is much more than stability. In a secure marriage, you value your spouse and celebrate your relationship which meets needs for intimacy and security. Yes, family, community norms, and religion are important resources but genuinely valuing your relationship and feeling loved and accepted is the foundation for a secure bond. For men and couples, secure is much healthier than stable. A secure bond speaks to a high-quality relationship, while stable accepts a marginal or even destructive relationship. In Barry's clinical practice, he was saddened to see how lonely and disconnected men feel in an unsatisfying, but stable marriage. Don't settle for a marginal marriage.

Stability does not promote sexual desire or satisfaction; security promotes vital and satisfying couple sexuality. A secure bond frees you to take risks and strive to eroticize your relationship. A secure bond facilitates sexual exploration which invites playful and erotic scenarios. A secure bond promotes male and couple sexuality.

The Paradoxical Role of Sex

One of the most interesting and controversial concepts is the paradox that healthy sexuality has a 15–20% role in the man's and couple's lives, while dysfunctional, conflictual, or avoidant sexuality has a powerful destructive role. Healthy sexuality energizes your bond and reinforces feelings of desire and desirability. Don't take sexuality for granted. Put time, energy, and creativity into couple sexuality.

The paradox is that sex problems destabilize you and your relationship. Sex cannot save a bad relationship, but sex problems, secrets, dysfunction, and avoidance can destroy a loving relationship. Rather than blaming your partner or denying problems, turn toward your partner as your intimate and erotic friend. Secrecy and shame subvert sexuality. Being an intimate sexual team promotes pleasure and bonding. Respecting and trusting your partner is critical, but not enough. Sharing intimacy, pleasuring, and eroticism ensures that sexuality remains vital.

Eric and Vivian

No couple is perfect, but Eric and Vivian were a model of a satisfying, secure, and sexual marriage. Eric took great pride in his life and relationship. Sadly, his family and cultural history did not promote healthy relationships. Eric was proud he'd beaten the odds and their marriage promoted psychological, relational, and sexual well-being.

Eric's parents were deceased. He does not blame them nor is he ashamed of his background. Eric's mother was murdered when he was 13 – it was a case of being in the wrong place at the wrong time. She was a bystander in a fight involving male gangs and was killed by a wayward bullet. Eric's father quickly remarried because he was unable to care for the older sister, Eric, and younger sister. That tumultuous marriage lasted less than five years. Eric's father became an angry man who hated anyone different than himself. It was the sister, not the father, who encouraged Eric to complete high school before joining the Navy.

The structure of the military was a foundation for Eric's life. He learned a valuable skill set involving technology. Refining job skills elicited a love of learning and provided Eric opportunities for mastery and promotions. After he left the military, Eric used veteran's benefits to complete a college degree with a double major in technology and business. He was 27 when he met Vivian. They were a couple for three years before marrying. Both Eric and Vivian lacked a positive model for a healthy relationship, but were committed to creating a satisfying, secure, and sexual marriage. Eric told friends that developing a loving, secure bond with Vivian was the best decision that he ever made. The concept of "beating the odds" was highly motivating for Eric.

Vivian had taken advantage of Pell grants to finance her education, beginning at a community college and finishing at a state university. She majored in digital communication which she chose in part because it gave her flexibility of where and how to work. Having a career and income was crucial. Watching her mother struggling financially and without an independent identity motivated Vivian to organize her life with greater autonomy.

Early in their relationship, Vivian made clear that the double standard was not acceptable. She wanted more for herself and expected more from Eric. As an adult, Eric no longer accepted the rigid male role regarding relationships and sex. He looked back at adolescence and young adulthood relationships with regret. He was ready to meet the challenges of a healthy life and relationship. Eric was a "new man" and Vivian supported Eric's growth.

Eric and Vivian enjoyed the limerence phase. Most importantly, they discussed how to create a healthy bond. They had serious discussions on walks after a sexual encounter. Sex was energizing and set the stage for explorations about life, marriage, and family. Rather than splitting by traditional gender roles, Eric was committed to creating and maintaining a life he was proud of. They were honest about their family backgrounds. Eric was saddened by his mother's murder but did not feel shameful about this. He was frustrated that he knew so few details about his mother and her life. Vivian encouraged him to speak with an aunt who was outspoken in her antagonism toward Eric's father, but was willing to fill in important details about his mother's life. Eric tried to reestablish contact with his two sisters – he established a good relationship with the older sister, but the younger sister resented Eric's successes and they had a marginal relationship. Vivian made the helpful comment that perfect endings only happen in movies and novels.

The concept of "beating the odds" was empowering and motivating. Vivian emphasized couple friendships to provide support for their goals. A particularly hard realization was that one of Eric's best friends from the military was now a negative force in his life. The ex-friend's motto was "Never trust a woman". Vivian encouraged Eric to establish male and couple friends who supported his life values, especially female-male equity. Eric wanted people who were friends of the marriage, not those who negated women and marriage.

Most of their friends were childless or had one child (one and done). Vivian supported their decisions, but she wanted two or three children and for Eric to be an involved father. This was a difficult challenge since Eric was not experienced with babies or young children. Fortunately, a couple friend had two young children and Vivian volunteered them to watch the children for a three-day weekend, while the parents went on a canoeing trip. This "test of fire" opened Eric to enjoying parenting (not just surviving it).

The decision of whether to have children and how many is one of life's most important and one of the hardest to reverse. Vivian didn't want to coerce Eric. She wanted them to make a joint decision. Eric needed Vivian's assurance that he wouldn't be treated as a second-class parent. She was more experienced and skilled, but parenting is not a competition. Eric brought up the issue he was concerned about – would they stay a sexual couple while parenting or was being a mother more important than being an intimate and erotic woman? Vivian had talked about this with female friends – she wanted to be a good mother and a first-class sexual woman. If Eric shared in parenting – both routine and fun activities – this would allow Vivian the time and energy for pleasuring and sexuality. This was a new and empowering concept. What Eric remembered before her death is that mother did 95% of the parenting. When Vivian asked him whether they were a good sexual model, Eric said that he had no idea, but assumed that they had the traditional role of the man initiating sex and the woman saying no – then he laughed. Vivian was put off; this was not going to work for their marriage. Vivian was enthusiastic about sex. She wanted Eric to be open to her sexual scenarios. If something didn't fit, Eric could say no. Eric looked very uncomfortable and Vivian pushed him to be honest. Finally, Eric said that it wasn't a big deal, but he found her wearing cowboy boots a turn-off. Vivian laughed and couldn't stop. An old boyfriend had asked her to wear cowboy boots as an erotic charge and she assumed that was a common male turn-on. It was funny but demonstrated how important it is to be honest about sexual turn-ons and turn-offs. Remember, you are not clones of each other.

The advantage of having a good marital and sexual model is that it provides a pattern to follow. However, most of us don't have that advantage, especially about sexual issues. The challenge is to create a couple sexual style that allows you to be responsible for yourself sexually and be a sexual team who integrate intimacy and eroticism. This takes time, energy, dialogue, trying out scenarios, and feedback. You can get it right, but you can't get it perfect. Nor can you rest on your laurels. We have been married 54 years, and still put thought and energy into couple sexuality.

Maintaining a satisfying, secure, and sexual marriage is an ongoing challenge. Eric and Vivian developed a couple ritual. Every six months, they took a two-night trip to their favorite small town and reserved the same room at a boutique hotel. They had two favorite hikes, two favorite breakfast places, and one fancy restaurant for dinner and one funky place for their second dinner. One night, Eric initiated his favorite sexual scenario and the next night, Vivian initiated her erotic scenario with a prohibition on intercourse. The most important dimension of their weekend was sitting by the lake, reviewing the past six months and setting a goal for the next six months. This was particularly important for Vivian who saw too many couple friends coast until there was a crisis. For Eric, the important thing was to reinforce the quality of their lives and be sure that their marriage is a core focus rather than their lives controlled by work and parenting. He looked forward to the "couple again" phase. Eric and Vivian were committed to a satisfying, secure, and sexual marriage.

How Much Is Enough?

A theme throughout this book is that traditional male expectations for intimacy and satisfaction are too low, while expectations for sex performance are oppressive and dehumanizing. We advocate positive, realistic psychological, relational, and sexual expectations. The GES model is empowering for men whether 30, 50, or 70. So how much is enough?

Begin with acceptance of yourself as a sexual man. Accept yourself with psychological, relational, and sexual strengths and vulnerabilities. Healthy male sexuality is anti-individual sex performance. Confronting the double standard and the rigid male sex role is necessary, but not sufficient. Just saying you are a new man who affirms female-male sexual equity is not enough. Attitudinally, behaviorally, and emotionally implement these concepts.

When you have a dissatisfying or dysfunctional sexual experience, do you turn toward your partner without apologizing? Is she your intimate and erotic friend? Do you end the experience in a sensual or erotic manner? This confronts the myth of total predictability and performance. GES is an empowering concept, not compensating or settling. GES is important for male sexuality, especially after age 40 and is crucial after age 60. Embracing GES allows you to enjoy sexuality in your 60s, 70s, and 80s. GES promotes a satisfying sexual relationship which enhances the quality of your life, especially with aging. GES is about sexual acceptance and dropping oppressive, performance-oriented demands.

Exercise – Implementing a Satisfying, Secure, and Sexual Relationship

This couple exercise ensures that the new model of masculinity and sexuality is successfully implemented. It requires you to value satisfaction and security, not just sexuality. Satisfying is the key to a healthy relationship. What does satisfaction mean to you and your partner? Each person lists three relational components which enhance satisfaction. Don't be misled by idealization or perfectionism; focus on what allows you to feel good about yourself, your partner, and your relationship. Examples include feeling listened to in a conflict situation, supporting each person's career goals, feeling accepted as a desirable sexual partner, valuing a variety of touching experiences from affection to intercourse, feeling accepted for who you really are, being a healthier person because of your relationship.

Secure means feeling loved and valued, knowing that your partner has your back. Secure is much different than stable – secure means you are a valued person in a valued relationship. Although children, home, finances, joint experiences are important, it is your emotional bond which is the core of relational security. Security is about feeling respected and loved with your vulnerabilities as well as strengths. Secure is much more than stable.

Problems need to be addressed, but not be driven by fear. A secure bond promotes confidence that you can process feelings and emotionally problem solve. You trust that your partner will make a good faith commitment to deal with issues. If there are experiences which undermine relational security, process these and do what is necessary to rebuild a secure bond. You cannot treat your relationship as a done deal – you need to reinforce satisfaction and security.

Sexuality is integral to your bond. The energizing role of couple sexuality cannot be underestimated. Set aside time and energy for vital and satisfying sexuality. You cannot take sexuality for granted nor treat it with benign neglect. Strategies to reinforce healthy sexuality include every six months each partner initiates something new in terms of pleasure, eroticism, or intercourse; every two months have a sexual date with a prohibition on intercourse; each year schedule a couple weekend without children; when you have a disappointing or dysfunctional sexual experience, turn toward your partner rather than apologizing or avoiding; once a quarter, create an asynchronous sexual scenario; develop a new afterplay scenario; surprise your partner with a sexy outfit; be sexual somewhere other than your bedroom.

The goal is not an erotic performance, but to spice up your sexual life – sharing intimacy, pleasuring, and eroticism. A key is acceptance of the inherent flexibility and variability of couple sexuality, including a range of outcomes.

We suggest engaging in this exercise on a yearly basis. Maintaining a satisfying, secure, and sexual relationship is a challenge which requires awareness and commitment.

Summary

Writing this book has been a joy, especially this chapter. Establishing realistic goals for an intimate relationship is especially important for men. A traditional male trap is to take the relationship for granted and have low expectations of the marriage, including marital sex. Adopt the female-male equity model; embrace desire/pleasure/eroticism/satisfaction; integrate intimacy, pleasuring, and eroticism; accept GES; and view the woman as your sexual ally.

Sexuality facilitates a respectful, trusting, intimate relationship. Sex does not dominate you or your relationship, but has a positive, integral role in energizing your bond and feeling proud as a sexual man. Unlike the double standard or the individual pass-fail performance approach, this model centers on acceptance, sharing pleasure, female-male equity, and GES expectations and experiences. You are responsible for yourself sexually while recognizing that the essence of sexuality is sharing intimacy, pleasuring, and eroticism. Being a proud sexual man involves owning your vulnerabilities as well as strengths. Unlike the past where men had a contingent sexual self-esteem or a contingent relationship, male sexuality is based on acceptance.

A satisfying, secure, and sexual relationship brings out the best in you as a man. This is true psychologically, relationally, and sexually. Good luck in your journey to healthy male and couple sexuality.

Appendix A

CHOOSING A SEX, COUPLE, OR INDIVIDUAL THERAPIST

This is a self-help book, but not a do-it-yourself therapy book. Many individuals and couples are reluctant to consult a therapist, feeling that to do so is a sign of weakness, a confession of inadequacy, or an admission that your life and relationship are in dire straits. Unfortunately, this is even truer for men who are fearful that the therapist will blame them for individual, couple, and sex problems. In reality, seeking professional help means that you are a wise man who realizes that there is a problem. You have made a commitment to address the issues and promote individual, couple, and sexual growth.

The mental health field can be confusing. Sex therapy and couple therapy are clinical subspecialties. They are offered by several professionals: psychologists, marriage therapists, pastoral counselors, psychiatrists, social workers, and licensed professional counselors. The professional background of the clinician is less important than his competence in dealing with sexual, couple, and individual problems.

Many people have health insurance that provides coverage for mental health; thus, they can afford the services of a private practice therapist. Those who have neither the financial resources nor insurance can consider a university or medical school mental health clinic, a family services center, or a local mental health clinic. Most clinics have a sliding fee scale program.

When choosing a therapist, be direct in asking about credentials and areas of expertise. Ask the clinician about the focus of therapy, how long therapy is expected to last, and whether the emphasis is specifically on sexual problems or on individual, communication, or relationship issues. Be especially diligent in asking about university degrees and licensing. There are poorly qualified individuals – and some outright quacks – in any field.

One of the best ways to obtain a referral is to call or search on-line for a professional organization such as a state psychological association, marriage and family therapy association, or a mental health organization. You can obtain a referral from a family physician, minister, imam, rabbi, or a trusted friend. If you live by a university or medical school, call to find what specialized psychological or sexual health services are available.

For a sex therapy referral, contact the American Association of Sex Educators, Counselors, and Therapists (AASECT) at aasect.org. Another resource is the Society for Sex Therapy and Research (SSTAR) at sstarnet.org.

For a couple therapist, check the website for the American Association for Marriage and Family Therapy (AAMFT) at therapist locator.net.

If you want to see a psychologist who can provide individual or couple therapy for anxiety, depression, behavioral health, and other issues, we suggest the Registry of Health Service Providers in Psychology at findapsychologist.org.

Feel free to speak by phone with two or three therapists before deciding with whom to see. Be aware of your level of comfort and degree of rapport with the therapist as well as whether the therapist's assessment of the problem and approach to treatment seems right for you. Once you begin, give therapy a chance to be helpful. There are few miracle cures. Change requires commitment; it is a gradual and often difficult process. Although many people benefit from short-term therapy (fewer than 10 sessions), most find that the therapeutic process will require four months or longer. The role of the therapist is that of consultant rather than decision-maker. Therapy requires effort on your part, both during the session and between sessions. Therapy helps you change attitudes, behaviors, and feelings. It takes courage to seek professional therapy. Therapy can be a tremendous help in assessing and changing sexual, couple, and individual problems. Therapy allows you to be a healthier person, couple, and sexual man.

Appendix B

SUGGESTED READINGS

Readings on Male Sexuality

Bader, M. (2008). *Male sexuality.* Lanham, MD: Rowman & Littlefield.

McCarthy, B. & Metz, M. (2008). *Men's sexual health.* New York: Routledge.

Metz, M. & McCarthy, B. (2003). *Coping with premature ejaculation.* Oakland, CA: New Harbinger.

Metz, M. & McCarthy, B. (2004). *Coping with erectile dysfunction.* Oakland, CA: New Harbinger.

Murray, S. (2019). *Not always in the mood.* Lanham, MD: Rowman & Littlefield.

Zilbergeld, B. (1999). *The new male sexuality.* New York: Bantam.

Readings on Couple Sexuality

Kleinplatz, P. & Menard, A. (2020). *Magnificent sex.* New York: Routledge.

McCarthy, B. & McCarthy, E. (2009). *Discovering your couple sexual style.* New York: Routledge.

McCarthy, B. & McCarthy, E. (2012). *Sexual awareness* (5th ed.). New York: Routledge.

McCarthy, B. & McCarthy, E. (2019). *Enhancing couple sexuality.* New York: Routledge.

McCarthy, B. & McCarthy, E. (2020). *Rekindling desire* (3rd ed.). New York: Routledge.

Perel, E. (2006). *Mating in captivity.* New York: Harper-Collins.

Snyder, S. (2018). *Love worth making.* New York: St. Martin's.

Readings on Female Sexuality

Brotto, L. (2017). *Better sex through mindfulness.* New York: Greystone.

Foley, S., Kope, S., & Sugrue, D. (2012). *Sex matters for women* (2nd ed.). New York: Guilford.

McCarthy, B. & McCarthy, E. (2019). *Finding your sexual voice*. New York: Routledge.

Mintz, L. (2018). *Becoming cliterate*. New York: Harper.

Nagoski, E. (2015). *Come as you are*. New York: Simon & Schuster.

Readings on Relationship Satisfaction

Doherty, W. (2013). *Take back your marriage* (2nd ed.). New York: Guilford.

Finkel, E. (2017). *The all or nothing marriage*. New York: Dutton.

Gottman, J. & Silver, N. (2015). *The seven principles for making marriage work* (2nd ed.). New York: Harmony.

Johnson, S. (2008). *Hold me tight*. Boston, MA: Little, Brown.

Markman, H., Stanley, S., & Blumberg, S. (2010). *Fighting for your marriage* (3rd ed.). San Francisco, CA: Jossey-Bass.

McCarthy, B. & McCarthy, E. (2004). *Getting it right the first time*. New York: Routledge.

McCarthy, B. & McCarthy, E. (2006). *Getting it right this time*. New York: Routledge.

Other Sexuality Readings

Maltz, W. (2012). *The sexual healing journey* (3rd ed.). New York: William Morrow.

Snyder, D., Baucom, D., & Gordon, K. (2007). *Getting past the affair*. New York: Guilford.

REFERENCES

Allen, E., Atkins, D., Baucom, D., Snyder, D., Gordon, K., & Glass, S. (2005). In-trapersonal, interpersonal, and contextual factors in engaging in and response to extra-marital involvement. *Clinical Psychology: Science and Practice*, 12, 101–130.

Althof, S. (2006). Sex therapy in the age of pharmacotherapy. *Annual Review of Sex Research*, 17, 116–132.

Althof, S. (2020). Treatment of premature ejaculation. In K. Hall & Y. Binik (Eds.) *Principles and practice of sex therapy* (6th ed., pp. 134–154). New York: Guilford.

Althof, S. & Rosen, R. (2007). Combining medical and psychological interventions for the treatment of erectile dysfunction. In S. Leiblum (Ed.) *Principles and practice of sex therapy* (4th ed., pp. 157–186). New York: Guilford.

Amato, P. (2010). Research on divorce. *Journal of Marriage and Family*, 72, 650–666.

Baumeister, R. (2000). Gender differences in erotic plasticity: The female sexual drive as socially flexible and responsive. *Psychological Bulletin*, 126, 347–374.

Braun-Harvey, D. & Vigorito, M. (2020). Out of control sexual behavior. In K. Hall & Y. Binik (Eds.) *Principles and practice of sex therapy* (6th ed., pp. 269–293). New York: Guilford.

Byers, E. & McNeil, S. (2006). Further validation of the interpersonal exchange model of sexual satisfaction. *Journal of Sex and Marital Therapy*, 32, 53–69.

Chivers, M. (2017). Gender. In C. Pukall (Ed.) *Human sexuality* (2nd ed., pp. 232–259). New York: Guilford.

Daigle, L., Evier, B., & Cullen, F. (2008). The violation and sexual victimization of college women. *Journal of Interpersonal Violence*, 23, 1296–1313.

Doherty, W. (2013). *Take back your marriage* (2nd ed.). New York: Guilford.

Foley, S., Kope, S., & Sugrue, D. (2012). *Sex matters for women* (2nd ed.). New York: Guilford.

Frank, E., Anderson, C., & Rubinstein, D. (1978). Frequency of sexual dysfunction in "normal" couples. *New England Journal of Medicine*, 229, 111–115.

Gottman, J. & Silver, N. (2015). *The seven principles for making marriage work* (2nd ed.). New York: Harmony.

Heiman, J., Long, J., Smith, S., Fisher, W., Sand, M., & Rosen, R. (2011). Sexual satisfaction and relationship happiness in midlife and older couples in five countries. *Archives of Sexual Behavior*, 40, 741–753.

Hyde, J. (2005). The gender similarities hypothesis. *American Psychologist*, 60, 581–592.

Janni, E., Blanchard, R., Camperio-Clanis, A., & Bancroft, J. (2010). Male homosexuality: Nature or culture? *Journal of Sexual Medicine*, 7, 3245–3253.

Kalogeropoulos, D. & Larouche, J. (2020). An integrative biopsychosocial approach to the conceptualization and treatment of erectile disorder. In K. Hall & Y. Binik (Eds.) *Principles and practice of sex therapy* (6th ed., pp. 87–106). New York: Guilford.

Kerner, I. (2005). *She comes first*. New York: William Morrow.

Lindau, S., Schumm, L., Laumann, E., Levinson, W., O'Muircheartaigh, C., & Waite, L. (2007). A study of sexuality and health among older adults in the United States. *New England Journal of Medicine*, 357, 762–774.

Maltz, W. (2012). *The sexual healing journey* (3rd ed.). New York: William Morrow.

Master, W. & Johnson, V. (1970). *Human sexual inadequacy*. Boston, MA: Little-Brown.

McCarthy, B. (2015). *Sex made simple*. Eau Claire, WI: Pesi Publications.

McCarthy, B. & McCarthy, E. (2004). *Getting it right the first time*. New York: Routledge.

McCarthy, B. & McCarthy, E. (2009). *Discovering your couple sexual style*. New York: Routledge.

McCarthy, B. & McCarthy, E. (2012). *Sexual awareness* (5th ed.). New York: Routledge.

McCarthy, B. & McCarthy, E. (2019a). *Finding your sexual voice*. New York: Routledge.

McCarthy, B. & McCarthy, E. (2019b). *Enhancing couple sexuality*. New York: Routledge.

McCarthy, B. & McCarthy E. (2020). *Rekindling desire* (3rd ed.). New York: Routledge.

McCarthy, B. & Metz, M. (2008). *Men's sexual health*. New York: Routledge.

McCarthy, B. & Wald, L. (2013). New strategies in assessing, treating, and relapse prevention of extramarital affairs. *Journal of Sex and Marital Therapy*, 39, 493–509.

McKinlay, J. & Feldman, H. (1994). Age related variation in sexual activity and interest in normal men: Results from the Massachusetts male aging study. In A. Rossi (Ed.) *Sexuality across the Lifespan* (pp. 261–285). Chicago, IL: University of Chicago.

Metz, M. & Epstein, N. (2002). Assessing the role of relationship conflict in sexual dysfunction. *Journal of Sex and Marital Therapy*, 28, 139–164.

Metz, M., Epstein, N., & McCarthy, B. (2017). *Cognitive-behavioral therapy for sexual dysfunction*. New York: Routledge.

Metz, M. & McCarthy, B. (2003). *Coping with premature ejaculation*. Oakland, CA: New Harbinger.

Metz, M. & McCarthy, B. (2004). *Coping with erectile dysfunction*. Oakland, CA: New Harbinger.

Metz, M. & McCarthy, B. (2012). The Good Enough Sex (GES) model: Perspective and clinical application. In P. Kleinplatz (Ed.) *New directions in sex therapy* (2nd ed., pp. 213–230). New York: Routledge.

Mosher, D. (1980). Three psychological dimensions of depth involvement in human sexual response. *Journal of Sex Research*, 16, 1–42.

Nobre, P., Carvalho, J., & Mark, K. (2020). Low sexual desire in men. In K. Hall & Y. Binik (Eds.) *Principles and practice of sex therapy* (6th ed., pp. 63–86). New York: Guilford.

O'Sullivan, L., Cheng, M., Harris, K., & Brook-Gunn, J. (2007). I wanta hold your hand: The presentation of social, romantic, and sexual function in adolescent relationships. *Perspectives on Sexual and Reproductive Health*, 39, 100–107.

Perelman, M. (2009). The sexual tipping point: A mind/body model for sexual medicine. *Journal of Sexual Medicine*, 6, 629–632.

Perelman, M. (2020). Delayed ejaculation. In K. Hall & Y. Binik (Eds.) *Principles and practice of sex therapy* (6th ed., pp. 156–178). New York: Guilford.

Ramirez, O. & Brown, J. (2010). Attachment style, rules regarding, and couple satisfaction: A study of gay male couples. *Australian and New Zealand Journal of Family Therapy*, 31, 203–213.

Scorolli, C., Ghirlanra, S., Enquist, M., Zattoni, S., & Tannisi, E. (2007). Relative prevalence of different fetishes. *International Journal of Impotence Research*, 19, 432–437.

Snyder, D., Baucom, D., & Gordon, K. (2007). *Getting past the affair.* New York: Guilford.

Stanley, S., Rhoades, G., & Whitton, S. (2010). Commitment: Function, formation, and the securing of romantic attachment. *Journal of Family Theory and Review*, 2, 243–257.

Stosny, S. (2017). *Empowered love.* New York: IXIA.

Zilbergeld, B. (1999). *The new male sexuality* (Revised ed.). New York: Bantam.

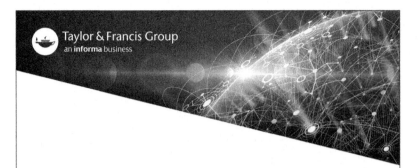

Printed in the United States
by Baker & Taylor Publisher Services